BROTHER L. JOSEPH

D1064354

COLLABORATION IN
SCHOOL GUIDANCE

BROTHER L. JOSEPH

COLLABORATION IN SCHOOL GUIDANCE

A Creative Approach to Pupil Personnel Work

by

MARY A. SARVIS

and

MARIANNE PENNEKAMP

LIBRARY
CHRISTIAN BROTHERS COLLEGE
650 E. PARKWAY S.
MEMPHIS, TENN. 38104

37065

BRUNNER/MAZEL *Publishers*

New York

Copyright © 1970 by Marianne Pennekamp
Published by
BRUNNER / MAZEL, INC.
80 East 11th Street
New York, N. Y. 10003

Library of Congress Catalog Card No. 71-91922

SBN87630-021-2

MANUFACTURED IN THE UNITED STATES OF AMERICA

1.4
523

To the students and staff of the
Oakland Public Schools

Contents

Introduction

IRVING N. BERLIN, M.D.*

Today's crisis in the schools reflects many crises in society. As a member of the Board of Directors of the Congressional Joint Commission on Child Mental Health, I have, because of my many years as a psychiatric consultant to the schools, served as Board liaison to special committees on education and conferences called with important educators from the Office of Education and teachers colleges to discuss the serious educational problems of the child in America and education's importance in the total problem-solving effort. The Joint Commission, on both its Board and Task Forces, had as members some outstanding experts in education, teacher training, and guidance services in the schools. From these many meetings will come substantive documents. However, one recurrent issue has been the critical need for educators and mental health personnel in the schools to learn how to work effectively as a team in serving the many disturbed, non-learning, disruptive, and seriously emotionally and motivationally disadvantaged children from both the ghettos and the suburbs.

In this light the Sarvis-Pennekamp book is both timely and important. It fills a gap in our literature because both its conceptual framework and the richness of detailed interaction are so important for the renewal process which is critical for all who work in the schools. By renewal I speak of the need for periodic fresh understanding and reordering of one's own ideas and efforts so they are more effective and thus more satisfying.

---

* Irving N. Berlin, M.D. is Professor of Psychiatry and Pediatrics, Head, Division of Child Psychiatry at the University of Washington School of Medicine, Seattle, Washington.

I knew Mary A. Sarvis, M.D., as a valued colleague for many years before her untimely death. It seems to me the philosophy and emphasis in this volume preserve and underscore a vital point of view in school guidance literature. The book is a dynamic monument to Dr. Sarvis. She and her colleague, Mrs. Pennekamp, long worked together in the Oakland schools, and I worked in a similar capacity on the other side of the Bay. I am particularly delighted with the thorough documentation of the methods, strategies, and the dynamic understanding of problems and related interventions used by Dr. Sarvis and Mrs. Pennekamp, which are now available to educators and guidance workers in this volume.

Only through such detailed documentation can one understand both the development of approaches and the rationale for the methods employed by these very talented workers. The written word inadequately conveys the obvious spirit of cooperation and mutual respect between the guidance workers, teachers, and administrators which has made the work reported so effective.

While I would have liked for others to know the particular vitality, honesty, and vigor as well as charm inherent in Mary Sarvis's contacts with other human beings, I suspect these do not come through with vividness to those who did not know her. Perhaps only a poet or novelist could reproduce these characteristics. An indication of the effectiveness of the joint efforts of Dr. Sarvis and Mrs. Pennekamp is that Mrs. Pennekamp has been able, especially in case vignettes, to give readers a full flavor of the kind of interaction that has taken place between mental health workers, school people, children, and parents.

Since, for a number of years, I have been similarly involved in consultation efforts with other nearby school systems, I would like to emphasize from my experience what makes this presentation particularly unique and why I feel its widespread reading is mandatory for both school personnel and guidance workers.

Mental health professionals, when they are tolerated or accepted in a school system, have often had attributed to them a kind of magic. As in most instances involving magic, the performer is a soloist who is expected to produce dramatic results to prove his use to the educational enterprise. We have in this volume very beautifully documented the fact that mental health professionals who function effectively in a school setting have no real magic and that they must indeed depend upon their professional training and the expertise they have developed, in close collaboration with the expertise of educators, to be of any help to the children they both hope to serve.

This book makes clear that much of what is done by both teacher and mental health professional needs to be task-oriented. Each professional person needs to use his particular area of knowledge, either of the educational process or of the inter- and intrapersonal dynamics of a child and family, to try to delineate together those tasks which might help a child feel more effective as a student, and parent and teacher more effective in their roles.

When the mental health worker as consultant or guidance person has also been effective, he feels validated in his professional knowledge of how to help children and teachers realize their potential more fully. As this book has so honestly shown, this process of learning how to work collaboratively with effectiveness is neither easy nor quick for the mental health professional.

The idea of task orientation is emphasized early in the book. Inherent in it is a rather critical problem of our present-day, impersonal world, with its often automated and unconcerned interactions between children and the important adults in their lives. The task-orientation and the heavy emphasis on working with the individual child and teacher are precisely the ways some of the depersonalization is dealt with and reduced. There can be no more convincing experience for a child, a parent, or a teacher than to have a mental health person spend the requisite time to help him become more effective in his own particular effort as student, parent, or teacher. Certainly the experience of teachers shows that their persistent efforts with troubled students, sometimes—as illustrated in this volume—with the help of mental health personnel, make a great deal of difference in how the student sees himself and the world around him.

Another educational opportunity is provided by this volume. It begins to define the variety of collaborative efforts possible within the spectrum of talents found in both mental health professionals and educators, and shows how these talents in their various combinations and permutations may be made useful to students and parents, as well as to educators.

I would also like to stress one other major value of this volume to me. It is one Mary Sarvis herself embodied—the problem-solving effort versus the blaming game common to some school guidance personnel. A troubled, non-learning child requires a characteristic kind of collaboration. Each collaborator, rather than looking for someone or something to blame, such as parent or environment, looks to his own background, skills, and knowledge to help formulate a tentative collaborative plan to help the child begin to learn. Similar efforts of task orientation rather than blame are required of the parent and are amply demonstrated in the Sarvis-Pennekamp book. It seems to me the problem-solving effort, so nicely documented here, is of critical importance to all of us who work in schools.

Perhaps of greatest satisfaction to me as a mental health consultant to schools is to find in this volume repeated emphasis on the need to help teachers, children, and parents over a long enough period of time for efforts really to begin to pay off. So often, solutions proposed in the literature appear so easy and simple that we know in our hearts they cannot actually be that effective. In fact, sometimes we know from our own practices that they may not work at all. Consequently, it is delightful to find this volume depicting the real world.

Devising a program flexible enough for guidance worker and teacher is another necessary aspect emphasized in this book. A flexible program permits an easy shift in focus to find a more effective approach with child or parent. Such flexibility is currently of critical importance, especially on the part of guidance personnel and teachers. Many school systems are locked into a rigidity of curriculum and methodology and require some living examples of how flexibility can be effective within the school system. I have observed that flexibility on the part of mental health and school personnel may be impetus for a change within the building or system itself.

I am certain that teachers, administrators, counselors, and other school guidance workers will find this book both a recurrent resource for ideas for their own work and a validation of the importance of collaboration between educators and guidance workers to help with the difficult problems of our time.

Foreword

by NEIL V. SULLIVAN, Ed.D.*

Mrs. Marianne Pennekamp, social worker of distinction, offers practitioners and students in the pupil personnel fields, school teachers and administrators the fruits of her collaboration with Dr. Mary A. Sarvis, beloved and renowned psychiatrist, who died at the height of her career.

"Collaboration in School Guidance" is a fitting memorial to Dr. Sarvis and a lasting tribute to Mrs. Pennekamp who carried their joint pioneering enterprise to completion.

Here is a creative approach to pupil personnel work stressing task-oriented guidance work. It shows how the specialists in social work, psychology and counseling must learn to pool their disciplines to meet the unique needs of children who are handicapped or retarded, and an increasing number who suffer difficult personal problems of adjustment. It puts its faith in the team which provides services to the classroom teacher far beyond the narrow confines of professional training. It stresses equally the requirements of the school and the learner and the continuous interaction between the institution and the student. It describes the ways in which the specialists can and do remove the roadblocks to learning.

The approach is comprehensive, total and experimental, providing the vital common framework for the professionals engaged in pupil personnel work. This framework must extend to all professionals who work with children. Indeed, the pupil personnel team is the complement of the teacher and an essential if auxiliary part of the larger teaching-learning encounter.

---

* Neil V. Sullivan is the former Superintendent of Schools, Berkeley, California, and presently Commissioner of Education, Commonwealth of Massachusetts Department of Education.

This book places history, theory and cases in perspective. It tells it like it is. It has to be an essential ingredient in the continuing educational revolution and partner of teaching and administration.

This pioneering work of Pennekamp and Sarvis is required reading for pupil personnel worker and student, for teacher and administrator who would be in the forefront of the human struggle for survival in world, community, and school.

Acknowledgments

This book is the outcome of many years' collaborative work and discussion between Dr. Mary Alice Sarvis, then consulting psychiatrist to the Oakland Public Schools, and a number of guidance consultants, both psychologists and social workers, employed by that school district's Department of Individual Guidance. The task of conceptualizing and illustrating the key ideas emerging from these discussions eventually fell to Dr. Sarvis and myself who collaboratively wrote the present book in the early 1960's.

Following Dr. Sarvis' untimely death in 1965, after the completion of an earlier version of the manuscript, publishing plans were disrupted.

It soon became apparent, however, that, far from becoming obsolete, Dr. Sarvis' insights and conceptualizations were becoming ever more timely as the problems of American education became more acute and more oriented to the psycho-social dimension in children's lives. The intensity and rapidity of change in education and the increasing volume of pertinent literature necessitated revisions in some of the chapters. I undertook this task with the support, most generously given, of a group of people who were thus paying tribute to Dr. Sarvis' intense commitment to advancing psycho-social knowledge relevant to the education and treatment of children. Funds set aside from a Mary Sarvis Memorial Lecture, arranged by a committee of the National Association of Social Workers, Golden Gate Chapter, were made available to me for expenses in connection with retyping the manuscript. Most valuable was the unstinting help of the following "Friends of the Manuscript": Lydia Rapoport, Professor of Social Welfare, University of California, Berkeley, who assisted in a major way with the editing and present revisions of the manuscript; Robert A. Wasser, Lecturer and Field Work Consultant, University of California, Berkeley, who tested the manuscript with his

xvi COLLABORATION IN SCHOOL GUIDANCE

students in the School of Social Welfare at the University of California and with significant individuals across the country; Mary Ann Freiberg, who wrote an insightful critique of the manuscript as part of her work as an advanced student in Social Welfare; and last but not least, Elizabeth D. Morrison, Guidance Consultant, Oakland Public Schools, whose unflagging support kept my morale up at low points in the history of this manuscript.

This book could never have come into being without the trusting collaboration of the many Oakland administrators, teachers, children and parents whose efforts formed the basis of our material, nor the patient and sympathetic support of all the members of my family. Case material has been disguised throughout to protect the privacy of staffs and families.

MARIANNE PENNEKAMP

Oakland, California
January, 1970

COLLABORATION IN
SCHOOL GUIDANCE

CHAPTER I

Task-Oriented Guidance and Its Structure

School guidance is an emerging profession, or rather a series of related professions, in a state of rapid growth, performed by workers with a variety of training backgrounds. Much prior writing has focussed on the differences between the guidance professions and has thus obscured the very real similarities in the tasks which school administrators, teachers and parents expect their guidance workers to perform.

In this period of intense demands on school systems across the nation, the time seems to have come to describe the job confronting guidance workers, no matter what their training backgrounds and titles.

A guidance worker, as we define it, is a professional person with at least two years of graduate training in social work, psychology, child development, counseling or special education, including at least one year of closely supervised internship in a school setting. Various school districts refer to their guidance workers as visiting teachers, school psychologists, school social workers, guidance consultants, home-school counselors and the like. We will refer, in this book, to "guidance workers" as a generic term for any of the above or similar titles.

Most guidance workers have entered the field from backgrounds in either psychology or social work. This means that their initial points of reference and training have tended to emphasize either individual psychosocial services to children and families who are in personal difficulties or psychological testing of children in the interests of educational planning (for gifted children, under-achieving children, non-conforming children, etc.). Neither of these backgrounds prepares the guidance worker to engage in an interaction with the public school as an institution or helps him in a productive collaboration with this institution, of which he is a member.

In the clinic or social agency, the institutional structure is organized specifically to facilitate the exercise of psychosocial skills. The goal of the institution and the technical skills of the worker are congruent.

In the public school setting, however, the *institution* is organized to promote and to implement *educational* goals. The guidance worker is employed primarily as a person who can help facilitate the educational process in situations where psychosocial skills might be useful in understanding or dealing with an upset child, teacher, child-teacher or school-community interaction. Thus a social institution, the public school, is being enriched by the utilization of knowledge provided by the psychosocial disciplines. The guidance worker is the professional person who has the responsibility for introducing this new dimension into education. In this context, he may need to be a generalist, when his prior training may have prepared him to be a specialist.

To this task he brings his psychosocial skills. These include observing child behavior via interviews, tests, informal classroom visitations, teacher conferences, etc., and drawing inferences from such observations. He will also possess skills in working with parents and with other significant adults in the child's life, either in his own home or in the community. He expects to use the services of public and private agencies concerned with the health and welfare of children and families. With this background to draw on, he informs himself of the history and idiosyncratic structure of his own public school department and of any particular school in which he is working at a given time. He adapts to and utilizes the developmental stage and the strengths of his own schools and school district, he becomes skilled in bypassing (and sometimes enduring) their weaknesses in the psychosocial area, recognizing how recently such insights have become available to the general public in usable form. He involves himself in the creative interaction which becomes possible when the psychosocial dimension is added to the other skills involved in the education of children.

This transactional or interactional way of working is called, in this book, task-oriented guidance. It represents a synthesis of two historical trends which will be described below.

In the United States, public school guidance work developed as an extension of and in close connection with the child guidance clinic movement on the one hand and the psychological testing movement on the other.[1] When the Commonwealth Foundation decided to underwrite the development of child guidance clinics, shortly after World War I, there was a major upsurge of organized interest in observing and treating children with emotional difficulties. A logical extension of clinic treatment was an effort to reach more emotionally disturbed children sooner by organizing treatment services within the public school. Some of these guidance services were integrated into the administrative structure of the public schools; others remained under the aegis of the child guidance clinic but all received their impetus and direction from the early child guidance movement.

Just as the early psychoanalysts were concerned with mapping the *terra incognita* of the unconscious before they turned to a study of ego psychology, so, in child guidance clinics and in public school guidance departments, the focus tended to be on direct service to the "patient." The schools served as a referring agency, but the child received treatment directed at his inner conflicts. This treatment tended to be isolated from the child's interaction in the ongoing educational process. Such a pattern fitted with the retrospectively utopian hopes of the time that laying open the inner man or working through inner conflicts could result in major improvements in society and the individual's functioning in society.

Educators soon became dissatisfied with the practical educational results of public school guidance departments which were oriented primarily to direct services to children on the child guidance clinic model. While the child went, week after week, to see his worker in an effort to get at the roots of his emotional difficulties, the teacher often saw little or no change in the child's classroom behavior and received little help with the problems of how to cope educationally with him. Educators were frustrated by their lack of understanding of, or effective communication with, what went on in the therapeutic process. Such frustrations heightened the ambivalence which is present in any guidance department/educator relationship. A swing occurred in many school departments toward a focus on direct services to teachers and school personnel instead of direct services to individual children. This opposite focus was aided and abetted by a concept not unlike Freud's early idea that all teachers should be analyzed, namely that helping one teacher to modify his attitudes would, in turn, influence the twenty, thirty or forty children in his educational care. In some guidance departments, in-service training of teachers, seminars, workshops and group discussions became the primary focus of work.

As an organizing *modus operandi* for guidance departments, each of these models proved to be inadequate. Several fallacies in conceptualization were involved.

1. The goal implied in both of these approaches was to effect deep-seated characterological changes in either child or teacher. It became clear that this expectation was unrealistic, particularly with the teacher-centered approach. In the child-centered approach, deep-seated characterological change might occur in some cases but not necessarily in those children who were the most disruptive or difficult from the point of view of the school.

2. Neither of these approaches put the realistic situation in a central position in determining the useful next step with a given child or teacher. (By the realistic situation we mean such things as socio-economic issues, psychological motivation, the realities in a given school situation, etc.). Conceptualization was concerned with severity of psychopathology and the ideal goal became mental health *per se*. Neither the child-centered nor the teacher-centered worker dealt adequately with problems of the ongoing educational process nor integrated his insights back into it. Approaches to either child alone or school personnel alone neglected the central fact that education is concerned with an *interaction* between child (parents, etc.) and teacher (principal, etc.) and that task-oriented guidance must focus on the concrete nature of this interaction.[2]

The psychological testing movement did not fare much better than the child guidance clinic movement in becoming an integral, interactional participant in the educational system. While testing became widely used in education as a device to sort out children eligible for special placement in programs for the gifted or the mentally retarded, psychologists often found themselves relegated to the role of "testers" whose reports were filed away and not used constructively on behalf of the improved education of children. What educators seemed to want was a score, a label, not a pattern for intervention. Psychologists have become understandably impatient with this limited technical role assigned to them and are searching for a new professional model or models.

There is similar ferment among counselors who are rebelling at being "programmers." This kind of soul searching and redefinition of function is of course a part of a general ferment in education. The common denominator in this unrest among guidance workers seems to be an awareness that the guidance worker's focus needs to be on any person, situation or interaction causing a roadblock in the educational venture, no matter what their specific point of access may be. Child and teacher impinge on each other, interact with each other, teach each other and change each other. Erikson, in talking of child rearing, says,

> We distort the situation if we abstract it in such a way that we consider the parent as "having" such and such a personality when the child is born and then, remaining static, impinging upon a poor little thing. For this weak and changing little being moves the whole family along. Babies control and bring up their families as much as they are controlled by them; in fact, we may say that the family brings up a baby by being brought up by him. Whatever reaction patterns are given biologically and whatever schedule is predetermined developmentally must be considered to be a series of *potentialities for changing patterns of mutual regulation*. (Italics his.)[3]

We view the interaction between the child and his teacher in the same way.

What is the guidance department structure which makes an interactional approach possible?

The structural organization of a guidance department will obviously influence process or the way in which its workers can operate. Recently there has been increasing interest in conceptualizing the interaction of structure and process. The most gifted teacher is limited or assisted by the size of his class. On the other hand, two teachers with classes of identical size might achieve different results. Structure represents the enabling and limiting framework within which process operates. For instance, a worker in a psychiatric clinic or social agency may be very interested in working promptly with an applicant around the issue of what caused the client to seek help at a given time and how the worker can assist him in getting his personal "show on the road." Yet, if the clinic or agency does not maintain an open intake and does have a waiting list, the worker will be unable to operate in this way.

In public school guidance departments, one clear example of the influence of structure on process is seen in the model in which the child guidance clinic was transplanted into the public school setting. The guidance worker who sees children in a central clinic with both structure and viewpoint oriented around the child's or the family's psychopathology, cannot work with the school in terms of the ongoing educational process, even though he may be able to give information to the school which they can use in educational planning for the child. The difference is that he will be giving information without knowing how it will be interpreted by teacher or principal, what the climate of the school is like, what use will be made of the information, what the other children in the class are like, what happened in this school the year before, whether the principal is concerned about his own promotion and hence, perhaps, anxious not to be too permissive with difficult children, what possibilities there are for groupings within the classroom, etc.

Obviously there are variations in structure among guidance departments. However, there are certain structural considerations which we feel are essential to task-oriented guidance work regardless of local variations, such as worker load.

1. At present, we feel that guidance departments should comprise workers from various backgrounds (social work, psychology, child development, etc.). It is not commonly recognized today that guidance work imposes a relatively unitary method of functioning on workers from these various disciplines, even though an individual worker has his own style and his own special technical skills which he brings to the task. It is advantageous to avoid the freezing of operations within the framework of any contributing discipline or the terminology of any contributing background, such as casework practice or clinical or school psychology.

The use of workers from multiple backgrounds makes the task in some ways more difficult. In public school guidance, where the pressures are so great, there is often an extreme temptation to simplify the task by over-structuralizing it, *e.g.* by limiting one's function to giving tests or interviewing students or working with faculties. Such structural oversimplifications lower anxiety temporarily by making things seem more clearcut but eventually raise anxiety and defeat themselves because they do not adequately meet the actual needs of the situation. Utilizing workers from various backgrounds helps to keep the worker's concept of the task as complex as the task actually is by introducing various skills and various points of view, by combatting compartmentalization, intellectualization and oversimplification or mechanistic manipulations. Guidance workers are supported in the development of broadly realistic, flexible and concrete attitudes toward the task involved.

2. The second structural concept is that the guidance department

should have a central base (like the administration building) even though workers are trying to become part of the educational process in their various schools and spend most of their time in the schools. A central guidance office is important so that guidance workers can consult informally with one another, overcome a sense of isolation, share their anxieties, exchange methods of approach to various situations, supplement one another's knowledge of community resources and maintain morale within the department.

The guidance department, as a whole, must meet for in-service training, psychiatric and other specialized consultation (if available to the total group) and clarification of departmental policy. A guidance department, for instance, must develop attitudes toward its school district's policies, such as the official criteria for disciplinary action or exclusion of students. The guidance department is expected by its school district to develop a semi-independent attitude toward such educational policies and to exert realistic, though responsible and task-oriented, pressures in the direction of including the psychosocial dimension in the educational process.

3. The third structural necessity for task-oriented guidance workers is that they make regularly scheduled visits to their schools. Workers who are only called upon in an emergency are often asked to help with a situation which is already beyond the point of no return. In such a situation, they necessarily become involved at the level of individual psychopathology of child or teacher rather than at the level of interaction in the ongoing educational process. Visiting a school regularly on schedule enables a guidance worker to become integrated into the faculty as a specialized contributor to the educational effort in that school and to define his role in those terms. In the early stages of his work with a new school, the regularity of his visits helps a guidance worker to show the school that he is willing and able to be helpful. After the guidance worker's relationship with the school has become continuing and durable, the guidance worker has more opportunity to become flexible. His schools will understand an emergency in another school which necessitates a change in the schedule. When the continuity of function is assured and the image of the guidance worker is clear, structural mechanics become less important.

4. The fourth essential for guidance departments concerns interpretation of guidance function to the school. The style and explicitness with

which this interpretation is done varies widely among workers. Yet guidance work is so ambiguously defined in the culture that educators have no way of knowing what to expect unless the guidance worker structures his role quite clearly. He must make it clear, for instance, that he will neither cure nor exempt every troubled or troublesome child. His distance from hiring/firing procedures must be made explicit. Yet again, guidance work must not be structured in an overly rigid or mechanistic way. Structuring is toward the concept of trouble-shooting, toward the guidance worker's operation as a skilled person who diagnoses and helps to work with situations which impede the educational process, rather than toward a list of things the guidance worker will or will not become involved with. He tries to make this image of the trouble-shooter sufficiently vivid and practical so that educators will understand it and will actively participate in a creative collaboration.

5. An example of flexibility within structure is the referral sheet or other descriptive comment on a child which most guidance departments ask schools to prepare. On such a sheet, the school people are asked to give identifying data about the child and family, information about the problem, test results, observations on social adjustment, results of health studies, etc.

In the early days of a guidance department's function or in the behavior of a new worker, such a referral sheet is apt to be routinely demanded before a child is seen. Then, as a guidance worker becomes better integrated in the schools, there is a tendency to neglect formal referral concepts altogether and to work in an extremely fluid way within the school setting. This second approach almost abandons intensive concern with individual children's problems and backgrounds in favor of working with the impediments to the educational process seen in classroom interactions, in problems between student and teacher, etc. Such an attitude has much to commend it. Certainly it is preferable to a refusal on the part of the guidance worker to look at a child unless the files are in shape or the school has been brought to the point of a formal referral. Guidance workers are often involved in observing children in the classroom and on the playground and in working with teachers on whatever kind of difficulty the latter may be having with a group of children or a certain kind of child. In school lunchrooms and in informal conferences, teachers raise issues and problems with which they have every reason to expect help from their guidance worker. Guidance intervention may be very helpful in some of these situations without the necessity of the more cumbersome referral sheet.

However, the formal referral sheet should not be abandoned. There are two major reasons for setting up a formal folder or case history. The first of these is an indication that the child will be a continuing case with the guidance department—a child in crisis whom the guidance worker will want to keep an eye on, or a child who will obviously have chronic, recurrent difficulties. Such situations suggest that all data pertinent to the child's personality, background and learning patterns should be assembled. The second indication for a formal referral is that administrative action of some kind is likely: limited day, retention, acceleration, etc. Many transitory and situational issues can be handled by the guidance worker without formal referral. A guidance department should allow its workers and the schools marked latitude for their individual styles; a formal referral is merely a tool, like psychological testing, which is an appropriate step at a given stage in the diagnostic and guidance process.

6. The sixth structural criterion which will determine function within a guidance department is the concept of open intake and of the guidance worker as basically a trouble-shooter, looking for and trying to deal with impediments to the educational process. An open intake policy does not imply that a guidance worker can be available for every conceivable situation; even one worker to a school would not insure this. At times, the guidance worker limits what he can do, saying, "If you want me to work with such-and-such, then so-and-so will not be possible this term." Yet this is a different concept from a school guidance clinic which says that no more cases can be accepted until further notice. The latter concept implies that the guidance worker selects a case load from the emotionally disturbed children in his schools and works with them as individuals until some resolution has been achieved. Task-oriented guidance means that the optimal needs of individual children are considered in terms also of the total school situation and that, at times, the guidance worker has to tell a child that he will not be seen frequently even though both child and guidance worker might wish that he could be.

In the next chapters we turn to a discussion of the process of task-oriented guidance work.

NOTES
(Chapter I)

1. George S. Stevenson, "Child Guidance and the National Committee for Mental Hygiene," in Lawson Lowry, ed., *Orthopsychiatry, 1923-1948,* (American Orthopsychiatric Association, 1948), pp. 50-82; and Mary A. White and Myron W. Harris, *The School Psychologist* (New York: Harper and Brothers, 1961), Ch. 1, p. 2.
2. Roy Grinker, Sr., *et al., Psychiatric Social Work: A Transactional Case Book* (New York: Basic Books, Inc., 1961), p. 7.
3. Erik H. Erikson, *Childhood and Society,* Rev. Ed. (New York: W. W. Norton and Co., Inc., 1963), p. 69.

ADDITIONAL READINGS
(Chapter I)

Arbuckle, D. S. *Pupil Personnel Services in the Modern School.* Boston: Allyn and Bacon, Inc., 1966.

Costin, Lela B. *An Analysis of the Tasks in School Social Work,* Project No. 6-8315, U.S. Department of Health, Education and Welfare, Office of Education, Bureau of Research, 1968.

Gray, Susan W., *The Psychologist in the Schools.* New York: Holt, Rinehart and Winston, Inc., 1963.

Grinker, Roy Sr., *et al., Psychiatric Social Work: A Transactional Case Book.* New York: Basic Books, Inc., 1961.

Johnson, Arlien. *School Social Work.* New York: National Association of Social Workers, 1962.

Katz, Fred C. "The School as a Complex Social Organization," *Harvard Educational Review,* Vol. 34, No. 3, Summer 1964, pp. 428-454.

Lee, Grace, ed. *Helping the Troubled School Child.* New York: National Association of Social Workers, 1959.

Magary, James F., ed. *School Psychological Services.* Englewood Cliffs, N.J.: Prentice Hall, Inc., 1967.

O'Shea, Charles and William Lee, "Twenty California School Superintendents' Opinions of Pupil Personnel Services," University of California, Berkeley, School of Social Welfare, 1964.

Orthopsychiatry and the School. New York: American Orthopsychiatric Association, 1958.

Shaw, Melville C., "Role Delineation among the Guidance Professions," (reprint) 1967.

Stanton, A. H., and M. S. Schwartz. *The Mental Hospital.* New York: Basic Books, 1954.

Stevenson, George S. "Child Guidance and the National Committee for Mental Hygiene," in Lowry, Lawson, ed., *Orthopsychiatry,* 1923-1948. American Orthopsychiatric Association, 1948, pp. 50-82.

CHAPTER II

The Guidance Process with Principals and Teachers

We have said that the sole task of public school guidance is to improve the educability of children or their educational opportunities. The guidance worker is a trouble-shooter whose job is to make a psychosocial diagnosis and plan useful next steps in any situation where there is an impediment to the educational interaction which impairs the teaching/learning process.* The guidance worker is concerned with attitudes on the part of children which impair their learning: evil self-image, mistrust, fearfulness about self, aggressiveness, alienation from the culture, etc. Similarly, the guidance worker is concerned with attitudes of educators—their anxiety about phobic, withdrawn or deprived children, their hostility toward aggressive or lower-class children, their impatience with underachievers—which might distort their accurate perception of a child, make it difficult for them to teach him, or make the child and his family feel alien, uncomfortable or depreciated. In yet a third category, the difficulty lies not so much in the intrapsychic problems of either child or teacher but in the interaction between them. No one teacher can recognize and meet every child's needs; no one child can feel in tune with every teacher. Often a relatively poor fit between child and teacher is simply part of growing up in a public school situation and learning to adapt to some differences in style and approach. Yet at other times a mismatch can be a serious problem, either because child or teacher is in a state of heightened vulnerability or because the mismatch itself is quantitatively too difficult. Here the guidance worker's task is to help match children and teachers so that the best use can be made of known assets in either case and so that known liabilities can be bypassed.

---

* This focus does not imply that guidance is restricted to crisis consultation. Many students will be followed over a long period of time.

Concepts of "absolute" adjustment or "absolute" unlimited teacher competence are so widely held that one seldom sees in print the arguments in favor of the obvious practical advantages of matching to promote optimal interaction. Teachers, like psychiatrists and social workers, often believe that they should be able to work with anyone. As long as this concept of ideal operation is believed, they tend to react with guilt to the undeniable experienced fact that they do better with some kinds of people and problems than with others. The matching concept is imperative in school guidance. We believe that matching is also done rather widely in psychiatric clinics and case work agencies, although agency structure and policies about assignment of cases, based on the concept that any worker should be able to work with any case, limit the explicit recognition and exploitation of the matching concept.

The guidance task does not lend itself to easy generalizations, as the guidance worker may use widely disparate steps to achieve identical ends. An over-simplified example might illustrate the concept:

Johnny is a rebellious, needling boy in the fourth grade. In School A, his principal is a rather authoritarian, discipline-oriented person who, if approached by Johnny's teacher for support, might take drastic action. Here the guidance worker might urge keeping Johnny in school while he and the teacher began studying the situation in an attempt to understand it better and work out a suitable plan.

The principal of School B, by contrast, tends to keep children in school and implicitly to condone misbehavior by habitual "patting on the back" of teacher and student to the extent that cases may not come to the guidance worker's attention until they have gone too far—when teachers are saying, *in extremis,* "Just get rid of him, get him out of our hair." The guidance worker in School B might work with the principal toward sending Johnny home for the balance of the day quite promptly when the child is tense, hyperactive, or misbehaving, thus gaining respite for the teacher and enlisting his cooperation for more basic, long term remedial steps.

Here, two diametrically opposed procedures would have been used to achieve the same functional result: setting the stage for psychosocial diagnosis of the difficulty and for the planning of a useful next step for a particular Johnny in troubled interaction with a particular school.

The example of Johnny has also begun to give a glimpse of a school child's social matrix beyond his interaction with his own teacher. Every agency has, as its starting point, a particular client interacting not only with his own internal problems but with his environment. Grinker *et al.*[1] have recently described their efforts to reintroduce explicitly into a psychiatric clinic the patient's family, class and cultural background, job and realistic life situation. They refer to this as the patient's "social matrix."

The child's own teacher, other teachers, the custodian, the nurse, the child's reputation, sometimes the reputations or achievements of the child's brothers, sisters and parents are forces in his social matrix. Impinging on this individual situation are the centrally-based specialists within the school system: curriculum supervisors, speech therapists, psychologists coming in to administer tests, guidance workers, etc. Outside the school, parents, relatives, friends are all involved in the child's interactions. The neighborhood: what it has been, what it is becoming, how static or chaotic it is, its individual ethnic composition and shared social history or customs, *as well as its relationship with the school,* comprise a vital part of the child's social matrix. The child and his problems cannot be understood without thinking of him in dynamic interaction with these people, reputations, histories and hopes.

Granting that this viewpoint might have theoretical value, is it relevant or helpful in the guidance process? Can school guidance make a unique contribution to the educational functioning of the many school children beset by a variety of psychosocial ills? Despite the fact that school and home problems often reinforce each other, we estimate that only a very small percentage of elementary school children referred to the guidance department at any given time are completely paralyzed in school functioning by the impact of out-of-school conflicts.* In almost all referred children, enough leverage exists within the school and guidance situation to produce some modifications of basic attitudes in the child, in his milieu or in the interaction which will improve the educational opportunities of the child.

One reason for this leverage in the school situation is the central role

---

* Any percentage figure is misleading except in terms of a total public school system. Individual schools may have larger (or smaller) figures at a given time because of "infectious" crises among children, difficulties among staff, rapid class/cultural transitions, demoralization, coincidence, etc. Even a total school department can be affected by demoralization due to administrative policy, rapid sociocultural change, etc.

of school in the life of the child. School is even more crucial for the child than work is for the adult because the child is a more rapidly developing organism and school is a more crucial culture carrier than work. School is usually the child's first organized experience away from home. It presents an opportunity for the child to test and to supplement the ways in which his previous experiences have prepared him for the world at large. Efforts to separate adjustment, personality integration or acculturation from academic learning are invalid. Learning, unless it in itself is defensive, e.g., a retreat from human intimacy, occurs in a context of involvement with and productive adaptation to the milieu. The concept of learning as an ego function needs further research attention but there is no doubt, on a pragmatic level, of its relevance and importance.

The way a child feels about himself and his relationships to teacher, classmates, and the acquisition of skills affects the way he performs as a student and as a member of his class. Failure as a student often establishes a vicious circle which leads to evil self-image and promotes failure as a person. Demoralized students become discipline problems, truants, drop-outs. The guidance worker is a person who may have the background to assist principals and teachers in clarifying the reasons for an individual pupil's lack of learning and the way in which the vicious circle might be attacked.

From the principal's and the teacher's point of view, the guidance worker usually comes into their school community and then leaves it; he works with the school but is not a daily member of the faculty. He is often the only representative of the centrally-based corps of specialists who visits the school on a regular basis. This gives the guidance worker the opportunity of being a sympathetic but more detached participant in the affairs of a school. The guidance worker, secondly, is usually the only person in the public schools with extensive information about individual development and psychodynamics; he can add the dimension of individual psychosocial diagnosis to the educational diagnosis of the school. Thirdly, from the point of view of the school, the way in which it can use its guidance worker depends on the particular attributes of the worker: his age, sex, personality, temperament, skills, interests, how long he has worked with the school in question, how much time he spends at the school, etc.

Even at the present time, however, ambivalence between educators and guidance workers is a major factor. The number of children in need of attention seems to be growing, particularly in large, urban school districts. On the one hand, educators sometimes expect to utilize guidance workers only in terms of severely divergent youngsters; on the other hand, the guidance worker is often assigned to so many schools that realistic attention to a broad range of psychosocial problems within the school is impossible. Many school people feel that, if only class size were reduced (and it certainly needs to be), all guidance problems could be handled in the classroom without psychosocial intervention. Experience has shown, on the contrary, that smaller classes will make children's problems more visible and will make additional guidance services not only more necessary but potentially more meaningful. Increased availability of guidance services will enable the principal to conceptualize more accurately the importance of psychosocial services to his school.

The principal is the key person with whom the guidance worker must collaborate. He and the guidance worker must plan together the ways in which, at a given time, the guidance worker can be useful to him and to his school. The principal is responsible for everything that goes on in his school; he must try to achieve harmonious interaction among the needs of children, teachers, specialists, parents; he must balance the often conflicting needs of the individual and the group; he must support and yet educate and lead his teaching staff. He has a rather lonely job, since he is at the head of his own school and often cannot talk over problems with his staff. The guidance worker is a person to whom the principal can turn, if he likes, for talking over the singular anxieties and perplexities of his job.

The guidance worker must come to know the personality, sophistication and style of the principal. (This does not imply personal value judgments but merely the way in which and the degree to which an educational collaborator will participate in the *psychosocial* task. Educators, likewise, appraise guidance workers in terms of the guidance worker's usefulness to them in the *educational* task.) These considerations influence the guidance worker in working with the principal himself and in getting cues about how far the principal will go or let the guidance worker go in working toward a psychologically sound, task-oriented educational program in his school. Let us turn to some examples of guidance work in different kinds of schools.

The guidance worker's first problem is to overcome the apathy of schools which have had no experience with task-oriented guidance. These schools are not necessarily discouraged and apathetic in general (although some may be). They may have high morale and skilled educational techniques but no acquaintance with the usefulness of guidance collaboration. Such schools are passive with respect to guidance services. When a guidance department is thoroughly integrated into a school system, passive schools still exist as relatively isolated "pockets" of resistance to active collaboration with guidance workers. Resistant classrooms also exist in many actively collaborative schools. These individual classrooms represent less of a problem to the guidance worker because they can usually be bypassed and constructive alternatives worked out for children in difficulty.

When a school has its first experience with a task-oriented guidance worker, children are usually referred to the guidance worker because of a crisis in discipline (or a symptom, such as not talking, which makes teachers anxious). The guidance worker is told to "work on Jimmy." The school may have no awareness of how it has contributed to the child's stress. The guidance worker often finds that the child has acted in desperation, from a complete sense of noncommunication with his milieu. Sometimes the crisis is due to specific mismanagement and covert hypocrisy or fear of a directly honest approach. In one case, an enigmatic child was moved from class to class, then retained in grade, then placed in a class for mentally retarded children on the basis of a test during which he had acted stubborn and dumb. On the basis of a retest, he was placed back in regular class. He was never given an explanation for the changes. School people may tell the child: "We are moving you to Miss M's class because her class is smaller," when the real reason is that Mrs. H., the former teacher, could not tolerate the child and felt that he was too stupid to learn. In our opinion, the child always senses the real, though hidden, attitude and tends to go into panic or to become belligerent when it is not explicitly dealt with. Obviously, the guidance worker finds it very difficult to move into such a situation in a neutral way which does not put the school or its teachers on the spot.

Again, in schools resistant to guidance, principals who are aware of children in difficulty may be reluctant to let the guidance worker work with them, feeling that "everything has been tried" (in the multiple transfers, retention, etc.). So it has, but without ever taking the student's own makeup, self-image or needs into consideration and without ever really talking over the problem and the useful next step honestly with the child. Guidance workers sometimes over-react to such a situation by hasty manipulation based on inadequate knowledge and implied criticism of the school. Usually, a more useful approach is to work with the child until his behavior begins to make sense to the worker and to the child himself, at which point it can be made sensible to the teacher and the principal. Once a guidance worker has worked with enough such children and achieved reasonably good improvement in their school functioning, it may be possible to broaden the scope of guidance activity within the school. In all schools, but particularly in apathetic ones, the guidance worker must adapt his style and skills to the kind of operation which the school sees as the useful next step for them. The guidance worker is likely to begin with individual children who are severe problems to the faculty and gradually to broaden the scope of his services.

It is quite possible for services which are useful and valuable in the abstract to boomerang if they are too much out of synchrony with the attitudes, values, anxieties and operational level of the school. A guidance worker in a low-morale school organized a club of five hyper-active, aggressive children. The children in this club prospered and improved enormously in their behavior and attitudes. Yet this very improvement put the school faculty on the spot by showing them too rapidly that the children were not incurable and, therefore, that their handling had been partly responsible for the bad behavior. The morale of the faculty slumped further and collaboration with guidance deteriorated. This intervention had been used *before* the faculty trusted the guidance worker. It was premature.

In schools oriented to collaboration with their guidance worker, the guidance worker must still find progressive points of access. One woman principal was a very direct, outspoken person who had come up the hard way herself, from a lower middle-class background. She had gone into education via recreation work. She talked about parents, children and teachers in very explicit, sometimes hostile, but generally very earthy terms. This principal's previous referrals to guidance had been either children in a crisis situation or hostile, odoriferous children who were sullen and apathetic rather than aggressive. The guidance worker responded to this principal at the same earthy level but ignored the hostile comments and stressed the students' and families' potentialities and their specific, concrete, demonstrable strengths. As a relationship of mutual respect and trust began to grow up between principal and guidance worker, referrals became increasingly positive.

The personality of this genial, outgoing principal was such that she understood aggressive youngsters well and handled them easily. The guidance worker needed to discover and work with young, shy, isolated children, the kind with whom the principal had difficulty empathizing and who, in turn, were scared off by her big voice and size. The guidance worker offered a supportive relationship to several of these children, formed a club with several more and, as her partnership with the principal grew, was able to function more and more effectively in a way that complemented that of the principal. Problems discussed between the principal and guidance worker became less stereotyped and larger in scope, *e.g.* issues of prevention.

We have said that this was a well-functioning school with high morale. The guidance worker's job was to overcome the principal's belief that psychological approaches were antithetical to her own direct, concrete earthiness. This kind of task is not accomplished in any school within the first year. The principal in this school, by the end of the guidance worker's fifth year at her school, asked her guidance worker to think of ways to help the school do a better job with a group of Spanish-American families who were reluctant to send their children to school, not out of negligence but because of their fearful isolation. We feel that the guidance worker usually does not reach his maximal level of functioning within a school until he has worked there for some such period of time. Naturally, too, the guidance worker's level and quality of involvement is subject to the vicissitudes of life in a public school. Changes in personnel, school stress, etc. offer new problems and opportunities for the guidance worker.

In another school, the former principal had run interference for the teachers with parents, keeping parent and teacher apart. This over-protective attitude was unconscious but, because of it, teachers were unsure and clumsy in their approach to parents. The guidance worker had to help the teachers and the new principal in how to approach family problems in a task-oriented way rather than being evasive, autocratic, or flattering.

The following, rather typical example illustrates this and also underlines the importance of paying attention to the observations of non-academic personnel. The school faculty had been talking about their problem with a fourth-grade girl, who was the only child of older, very anxious, over-protective parents. The girl had an accident away from school, in which she fell and hit her head. The medical report was negative but the mother became very anxious, kept the child out of school for a long period and then began coming to school every day and hovered over her girl at recess and lunchtime. This created a very embarrassing situation for the child and disrupted the school routine. The principal and teacher were reluctant to talk to the mother for fear of upsetting her even more. The nurse had tried to insist on further medical evaluation without success. The school secretary was very much concerned that the situation might become serious since she remembered something neither the principal nor the guidance worker knew (both of them were newer to the school than she). She told them that this same problem had been present when the child was in kindergarten and had persisted into the first grade. The mother then, too, had come to school very frequently to check on her daughter's health, to eat lunch with her and to harass the teachers through her anxious, placating, endless need for reassurance. The child's absorption into routine school life was seriously interfered with and the secretary feared that the current situation would develop into a similar chronic disruption.

The guidance worker arranged for the child to report to the nurse where the guidance worker could meet and get acquainted with her in a context which followed logically from the nature of her complaints. The principal accidentally happened to be present and was able to observe the guidance worker's informal, commonsense discussion of the problem with the child. The principal saw that the child was less fragile than he had thought and recognized the advantage of using the school secretary as a woman who had known the family for a long time and who could consciously encourage a direct, non-threatening relationship with the girl and her mother. Thus, school staffs often learn more about their guidance workers by seeing them in action. This counteracts "magical" expectations and ambivalent feelings, and facilitates collaboration.

Experiences such as these create a strong collaborative bond between the guidance worker and school staff. Once the principal has become an active collaborator, he will help the guidance worker find progressive points of access to teachers (and children). In working with teachers, the guidance worker usually tries to give very concrete help with a given child or given situation. In so doing, he focuses on neither child alone nor on teacher alone but on the interaction, the interpenetration of the child's problem and the teacher's situation.

Classroom observation is often useful in helping the guidance worker to evaluate the concrete steps which might be of assistance to the teacher in some educational impasse. The guidance worker can, in this way, get a general impression of the classroom atmosphere, of the general style and special interests of the teacher, of how well the children mesh with each other and with the teacher and, where one or more disturbed children are involved, of how they tend to neutralize or to aggravate each other's problems.

The teacher's need for very concrete help rises out of the fact that he has much less distance than the principal from the children in his classroom and will soon become anxious or defensive if there are difficulties in educating them. Teachers who are having a hard time with their children or who have unusually troublesome children in their classes are not assisted by psychological generalities. They become understandably furious by general (often false) statements, like "Don't worry, you're doing just fine" or unhelpful advice, such as "You know Johnny has a terrible home situation, just be patient with him."

We have found that teachers are wonderfully accurate observers—often against their own biases—but frequently lack a frame of reference within which the observations could be made meaningful and often impose value judgments which cancel out the leverage their accurate concrete observations could give. The task of the guidance worker is (1) to serve as an informant, who is skilled in understanding and drawing inferences from the child's developmental, psychodynamic and social predicaments as they are revealed in these teacher observations. The guidance worker has an opportunity to see parents and other significant figures in the child's environment and usually is able to see the child's problem in a broader context than the teacher. (2) The guidance worker must be able to translate his information and inferences to teachers at many levels of teacher awareness and sophistication so that the teacher can perceive the concrete problem and can start, with the guidance worker, in planning the useful next step. The issue of how teachers and guidance workers can collaborate and experiment together in developing individualized teaching strategies and a classroom climate conducive to maximum student involvement in their own learning needs continued attention.

The guidance worker rarely addresses himself to the personal problems of teachers except in the indirect sense of bypassing certain classrooms where the personal problems of certain children would almost certainly be aggravated. On the other hand, the guidance worker does take the personalities of teachers into account in planning for a given child or for a group of children. We have said that good matches between child and teacher comprise an important area of guidance work. Good matching between teacher and guidance worker is equally important and does not necessarily follow automatically from the fact that each is a competent professional person. Good matching implies that personalities are compatible and styles mutually agreeable. The personal style of the teacher also plays an important role in the direct relationship between guidance worker and teacher. One young, inexperienced teacher may be helped by a good deal of direct reassurance or support. Another teacher at the same level of experience may want to be left alone until he has found his own sea legs; another may not want to refer children because he fears it would reflect on his competence. The guidance worker must take these factors into account in his *modus operandi* with a given teacher.

A group of primary teachers, who were fairly young and inexperienced, had spent a difficult year struggling with a sizeable number of hyperactive children. They had supported one another in projecting their own anxiety and frustration (due to their inexperience) onto the children; they did not want the guidance worker to intervene. The next year, with less pressure on them and with more self-confidence, they requested a series of in-service training meetings on guidance. The guidance worker arranged for these to be conducted as informal, roundtable discussions and included the curriculum supervisor so that the guidance and educational approaches would remain integrated.

A beginning teacher was very interested in, but new to, a neighborhood of lower-class Negro children. She was having trouble in establishing her authority because she took too much time with each child before planning adequately for the whole group. The guidance worker helped her to establish priorities, to orient herself to the group she was teaching, to prepare for parent conferences. In the case of two boys whom she had known before, the guidance worker had brief interviews in an effort to improve their attitude in the classroom. Through these concrete actions, the guidance worker helped the teacher to avoid wasteful trial and error and to establish a more effective classroom climate.

It should be emphasized that the guidance worker is by no means always the pacesetter. Many a guidance worker is broken in by a principal who is knowledgeable and skilled in the ways and customs of a neighborhood or subculture new to the guidance worker. Sensitive, interested, experienced teachers often demonstrate to a guidance worker new skills and imaginative methods for reaching children. With many skilled teachers and principals, the guidance worker can develop an extremely satisfying peer relationship to the mutual enrichment of all concerned. These master teachers and principals also give the guidance worker an added tool in that the guidance worker can transmit information about educational approaches and methods which might be useful to teachers or principals in other situations.

Nevertheless, educators tend to have certain differences in training and attitude of which the guidance worker should be aware. Teacher training, while stressing the importance of meeting the needs of individual children, is seriously lacking in helping teachers to approach children in difficulties in a frank way in the evaluation of problems. Teachers are seldom helped to recognize and overcome covertly hypocritical attitudes. They are led to believe that no good teacher could be racially prejudiced, that teachers do not object to dirty or ungrammatical students, that euphemisms are only tactful in breaking bad news to students. Teachers also often share community stereotypes, diagnosing a student with problems as immature, lazy, spoiled, etc. Often the use of these stereotypes signifies, in reality, a breakdown in communication between teacher and student, a deadlocked situation which needs further concrete diagnosis and planning by the guidance worker so that collaboration between child and teacher can once again proceed.

School personnel, by and large, have not had the relevant experiences in their training to enable them to handle problems that are primarily human and only secondarily educational. Often, educators will try to cope with an essentially personal problem by educational maneuvers. Thus, a passive, nonresponsive child, whose daily work is deficient, might be retained to "wake him up" even though his achievement tests show him to be at grade level. This may not be punitiveness but a misguided feeling on the part of the school that they need to "get through" to the child from an educational point of view.

Possibly the weakest weapon in the educator's arsenal is his lack of awareness that children could frequently tell him how they see their problem and plan with him on how to tackle it. This difficulty is related to the educator's lack of background and training in interviewing techniques. Educators may feel that everything has been tried, although this everything has been on a manipulative level: no one has established a personal contact with the child on an honest interactional basis, namely a mutual attempt to diagnose the problem and plan how to meet it. The guidance worker is in a position to demonstrate the fruitfulness of skilled interviewing as opposed to the stereotyping which is apt to arise from poor interviewing techniques. School people need to see their guidance workers in action as much as possible so that they can appreciate the specific skills in guidance work, learn to adapt relevant guidance skills to their own functioning, and broaden the guidance base in school management and educational practice.

A direct approach to or attack on a teacher's values, though sometimes tempting to the guidance worker, is almost never useful and almost certain to create alienation, antagonism or lessened cooperation in the psychosocial task with children. A teacher, for instance, may have attitudes which are quite repugnant to guidance workers—the belief, for instance, that all families on any form of public assistance are lazy and worthless. The guidance worker can modify this attitude most effectively by work with specific children and discussion with the teacher of their concrete problems, motivations and possibilities rather than by an attack on the ideological issue *per se*. Teachers' attitudes and values do change, over a period of time, just as the guidance worker's stereotypes about education are modified. These changes are effected more through concrete experience and broadened identification than through exhortation and argument.

Most of our ideas about work with teachers will be shown in the case examples; they are very difficult to discuss in the abstract because they are so concretely related to a given teacher, a given classroom, a given situation. Teachers vary so widely in self-concept, in concept of role with respect to special services and in frame of reference that few generalizations are possible except the generalization that the guidance worker's focus should be very concrete and problem-oriented.

Some teachers have no experience with collaborative work and refer children so that they can be cured by magic, so to speak. Others think of referral only in terms of severely deviant children. Most teachers, however, have, or can be educated to have, a concept that collaborative work with the guidance worker will support their own effectiveness. These teachers, given proper clarification of the guidance role and appropriate support, make a wide range of uses of their guidance worker. The guidance worker's task will vary from classroom, individual or group observation, to casual discussion of classroom groupings, to informal help in formulating an approach to a number of children in the class, to working formally in an intensive, extensive or intermittent way with one or two children in the class who have been formally referred and to whom the guidance worker has a long-term commitment which involves parent contact, consideration of further steps with the child, added resources, etc.

The guidance worker who expects a high degree of privacy, who will say nothing about a case until a full psychosocial history has been obtained and who applies concepts of confidentiality defensively, is departing so far from the realities of public school operation and from a helpful interaction in terms of the teacher's task that the school will seldom, if ever, find him useful. A guidance worker respects confidentiality in operational terms, considering the relevance of information to the educational process with the child and evaluating the interpretation that the educator might put on information given to him. However, teachers rightfully resent the attitude of arbitrary secrecy which hampers their educational efforts. Most of these misguided concepts of confidentiality have to do with content issues which are often irrelevant; the information which needs to be transmitted has to do with approaches or handling which might be useful in the educational setting.

A guidance department cannot dichotomize its work with children from its efforts to be useful to school people. Merely giving the teacher or principal information about the child's progress does not constitute such integration. Educators must have free and easy access to the guidance worker. They need to be able to request informal classroom or playground observations. There should be encouragement of the two-minute conference in the hall or at lunchtime. Such informal exchanges cannot, as a rule, completely handle a problem but they can get work started and help to keep mutual planning and cooperation in force while the guidance worker continues with his diagnosis and ideas for further steps. Sometimes a teacher with a highly disturbed child or situation needs to be seen weekly for these two to five minute contacts. Such interchanges between guidance worker and school staff not only enable information to be transmitted promptly, suggestions to be made flexibly and positive relationships to develop but also emphasize the commonplace, non-threatening, reality-oriented character of the teacher-guidance worker interaction. They help to keep guidance work within the routine framework of school procedure and out of an ambiguous esoteric climate. The guidance worker has to be as pragmatic, concretely knowledgeable about the school and neighborhood, ingenious and flexible as he wishes teachers to be.

An expanded role for teacher-guidance worker collaboration is emerging within the context of the changes and challenges occurring within the core city school systems. As teachers themselves, spurred on by their own classroom problems, begin to grapple with values, strategies and the use of power, they may find the guidance worker a useful resource person in assisting with staff discussions, staff-community discussions and student-staff discussions and action programs. More of this in Chapter VII.

ADDITIONAL READINGS
(Chapter II)

Bruner, Jerome S. *The Process of Education.* Harvard University Press, 1962.

Combs, Arthur W., Chairman, Yearbook 1962 ASCD, "Perceiving, Behaving, Becoming."

Flair, Merrel D., "The School Administrator and Pupil Personnel Services," *Psychology in the Schools*, 2 (October 1965), 369-372.

Hymes, James L. *Behavior and Misbehavior.* New York: Prentice-Hall, Inc., 1956.

Newman, Ruth G., Fritz Redl and Howard L. Kitchener. *Technical Assistance in a Public School System.* Washington, D.C.: Washington School of Psychiatry, 1962.

Newman, Ruth G. *Psychological Consultation in the Schools—A Catalyst for Learning.* New York: Basic Books, Inc., 1967.

Redl, Fritz and Wattenberg, William W. *Mental Hygiene in Teaching.* New York: Harcourt, Brace and Co., Inc., 1951.

CHAPTER III

The Guidance Process with Parents and Children

Now we turn to the interaction between the guidance worker and children and their parents. In actual practice, work with school people and work with families are as interrelated as the warp and woof of a piece of material. Our examples will demonstrate this but, for the sake of descriptive clarity, we have turned the spotlight first on one aspect of this interaction, then on the other.

How does the guidance worker go about his task of approaching children and their parents and working with them? Traditional concepts of motivation and treatability do not apply. Operation within a public school guidance department is based on the assumption that one is seeking to discover the useful next step in a given case and that implementation of this useful next step in itself is the most powerful agent to create motivation for further collaborative work among parents, child, teachers, etc. The issue for guidance workers is not: "Does this child or family meet our criteria of motivation or readiness to be helped?" but rather, "What is the useful next step with this child or family? How can we gain access into the problem? How can constructive collaboration be begun?" The burden is not on the family to prove that they meet certain criteria for being helped; the burden is on the guidance worker to find a useful way into an impasse. This point of view is sharply emphasized for guidance workers by the fact that compulsory school laws mean that families of every level of accessibility will be in contact with the school and the guidance worker.

The guidance worker tries, at the outset of a case, to assess two things. (1) He looks for the point of access in a given situation, whatever it may be—how to intervene in an impasse so that diagnostic and remedial work can get started. This direction of access implies the useful next step that is closest to the awareness of the crucial person involved (parent, child, teacher, etc.). (2) He looks for the available psychosocial resources which would be relevant at this time to "get the show on the road" in an adaptive or supportive direction while the dynamics of the impasse are being explored. These resources include teachers, peers, relatives, activities and community resources. He encourages or works for minimal stability in the environment: if a family is moving every three months, the guidance worker's role may be to say, "Why don't you stay put long enough for us to get going with your child's reading troubles?" As the psychosocial problem, dilemma, or impasse becomes more comprehensible, further psychosocial resources can be called upon with more and more specificity; more sharply relevant planning can be done to improve the adaptive function of the child and family.

How do parents react to such an approach? Since the 1930's and early 1940's, the period when most big city school districts developed their guidance departments, the professional point of view as well as the climate in the community stressed the theory that emotionally disturbed children came from emotionally disturbed homes. The category of "emotionally disturbed" was used so loosely that any child who did not follow the "expected" pattern of child development and school learning was—at least by implication, if not by referral to the guidance worker—included in the "disturbed" school population. This same point of view resulted in the school's turning to the parent to "straighten out the problem" which they were seen as having caused.

As a result of this widespread attitude, parents would often respond to a call from the guidance worker (or a threat by the school that their child was about to be referred to such a specialist) with intense anxiety, guilt and either denial of the problem or overcompliance with "the experts." Guidance workers had to learn to break down these negative expectations, both for the parent and for the school, before they could intervene positively in any given situation.

However, the total context of working with parents is undergoing marked changes. Spearheaded by two segments of the parent population, parents are "talking back" to the schools and their guidance "experts" and are no longer willing to take the whole blame for their children's failure in school.

The first group of parents to do so were the parents of neurologically handicapped and/or emotionally disturbed children—a group of children sometimes labelled earlier as autistic, schizophrenic or atypical. These parents have mounted vigorous campaigns to pass legislation guaranteeing their children an education, be it in special classes or in special part-day programs using techniques designed to help their children take arms against their sea of educational and behavioral troubles. In the process of working with other parents in similar circumstances, these parents have found new strength, a sense of their own power and an ability to work constructively. An initial by-product of this new-found strength is frequently an anti-psychiatric, anti-guidance bias. These parents tend to look on psychiatry as "the god that failed." However, as they encounter individuals within the educational, guidance, pediatric and psychiatric professions who are willing to work with them in a task-oriented, collaborative manner, these parents can often become exceedingly competent co-workers in overcoming not only educational but also emotional obstacles to their children's school functioning. Parents who might have become "intellectualizing" or "defensive" when they felt blamed, are now able to help in a developmental approach when the steps are worked out jointly by educators, guidance workers, parents and, more and more frequently, the child's doctor. The guidance worker may be the "anchor man" in such a collaborative effort, the person who is responsible for keeping the channels of communication open, to deal with hurt feelings, misinformation, resistances and the myriad of mechanical complications characterizing any collaborative effort, as well as to bring relevant steps into focus at the appropriate time. His role is therefore dependent not only on his ability to be a good coordinator, but also on his diagnostic skills and sense of timing, his ability to clarify current issues and encourage "significant others"—the teacher, the parent, the doctor—to review what they are doing and work out new steps to cope with newly emerging issues. Such steps might involve changing the dosage of medication on the part of the doctor, increasing the level of expectation in a particular subject area on the part of the teacher, setting limits on a specific piece of behavior on the part of the parent, etc. Within a collaborative framework, each individual's perceptions and efforts become more highly relevant and rewarding.

The second group of parents who are no longer willing to "bear the blame" are the parents of poor and culturally isolated children. They, too, are saying to the schools: "You have a responsibility to educate our children. Ghettos, poverty, absent fathers are the result of the community's neglect and indifference. Now is the time to break the vicious circle and what better place than with our youngsters!" These parents often initially resent the implication that something is "wrong" with their child and may react with a great deal of hostility. Once the wall of distrust is broken down, however, collaborative efforts can proceed and will be further discussed in Chapter X.

The change in the position of parents vis-à-vis the school and its guidance worker emphasizes the crucial role of a parent's attitudes toward his child and his child's education. In a paper entitled "Etiological Variables in Autism" the senior author states: "In evaluating a given family, an effort must be made to separate reactive from original etiological variables. This separation is important because it may bear on prognosis, even though it is recognized that once a vicious circle is set up, reactive attitudes become etiological agents, too."[1] Implied in this article is the belief that, when parents' own difficulties are a major cause of a youngster's difficulties, then these parents and their child are best served by addressing the parents' problem directly. Many more parents, however, are merely reacting with discouragement to their child's lack of success and can be helped by becoming actively involved in solving their child's problem collaboratively. Other parents, if carefully listened to, are actually able to set the pace for the professionals in habilitating their child: they know what is wrong, but need collaborators in order to "fix" it. In such cases, the parent himself can become the "anchor man" as described above.

Now let us turn to the children whose learning and adjustment difficulties are the reason for all that has been stated so far.

In the past, much effort has gone into labelling these children using such descriptive terms as "acting out" or "withdrawn" or psychiatric terms such as children suffering from primary behavior disorders, from neuroses or from psychotic disturbances. While these labels were frequently accurate within a framework using psychiatric reference points, they were far from useful in determining what intervention would be helpful in the school context. Gradually, such labels are being replaced by dynamically oriented, observation-based statements which pinpoint a child's present status in terms related to his learning process, his interaction with the teacher, his interaction with peers and his apparent self-concept. In other words, the labels are being replaced with statements concerning the child's observable ego functioning as they are relevant to teacher, parent, guidance worker, and, last but not least, the child himself. For it is the child having the problem who is often in a crucial position to tell us how he sees his own situation. With the help of a trained adult, a child can be encouraged to explore and describe—often vividly—his personal situation, to "perceive" it more clearly, to "behave" differently as a result of this "looking at what is," and to "become"[2] in the process, a person functioning with a wider array of resources. The case material in this book will amply illustrate how children can become involved in the resolution of their own problems. Techniques will have to be modified to suit the age, self-image and verbal facility of a given youngster but the common denominator remains one where the problem is honestly shared with the youngster in operational, concrete, non-value laden terms which offer a common meeting ground to the child and his potential helper.

Again, one needs to take care that one does not disdain past knowledge of psychiatric childhood disorders in one's eagerness to make the educational arena central to the diagnosis of a child's difficulties. Rather, one needs to see the interaction between a child's learning—or lack of it— and his personality development—or lack of it, as if they were two sides of one coin.

The following examples will illustrate work with parents and children.

PROMPT INTERVENTION IN A CHILD'S CRISIS

Late in September, Miss Yee, a young but experienced teacher of Hawaiian-Chinese ancestry, called me with some urgency. One of her first grade pupils, who had seemed to have gotten off to a good start in the early weeks of first grade, was suddenly more and more reluctant to come to school. Miss Yee added that today Mrs. Lum, the mother, had attempted to bring Marilyn to school an hour late but Marilyn had "carried on" so that her mother had finally taken her home. Miss Yee said that she had been reluctant to intervene but was now concerned lest the little girl's parents blame her for the difficulty; the child's year in kindergarten had been a happy one. Could I please get in touch with the parents and help get the situation straightened out?

Miss Yee, in answer to my question, could think of no specific reason for Marilyn's sudden panic but referred to the general conditions in the school. Because of nearby highway construction, the school was being soundproofed while classes were in session. The resultant noise and confusion had been particularly bad during the past few days. Perhaps this had upset Marilyn, a usually quiet and cooperative youngster.

Armed with these facts, I phoned Marilyn's home. Both parents were puzzled and protective. Marilyn had never acted this way before, she had been used to walking to school with her two older sisters. She had loved kindergarten. Now she was crying and finding excuses to stay home. They had tried punishing her and forcing her but this did not seem to them to be the answer. Besides, it hadn't worked. We made an appointment for me to stop by their home that afternoon.

When I arrived, only Marilyn's father was home, her mother having been detained at the beauty parlor. Marilyn, a very dainty little girl, seemed friendly and talkative in a shy way. Mr. Lum, the father, seemed very alert and very much involved in his children's education and upbringing. He conveyed the impression that, of his four children (the two older girls, Marilyn and a very lively pre-school boy), Marilyn came closest to her mother in temperament, being quiet, sensitive and artistic, while the rest of the family was more aggressive. He further indicated that when Marilyn became so upset at school, her mother might have silently sympathized with her. He said his wife had also felt embarrassed lest Miss Yee think that the Lum children were poorly controlled.

I was able to reassure Mr. Lum that Miss Yee was apprehensive lest they, the Lums, blame her for the trouble. I added that Marilyn had been one of several highly conforming children who had reacted to the construction noise with panic. Perhaps Mr. Lum, who seemed less disturbed than his wife at Marilyn's upset, could take her to school the next morning. This was not feasible, due to Mr. Lum's early working hours. I then offered to pick Marilyn up myself the following morning. Mr. Lum seemed to welcome the offer; he said that it was worth trying and that he thought his wife would be relieved. He would explain the plan to her. After a few minutes with Marilyn and her sisters, discussing with them the agenda for the next morning and getting their advice on the time I should be at their home, I departed.

Next morning, I found Marilyn in her school dress, her mother a little tentative yet agreeable, the two older sisters very excited and supportive. Mrs. Lum suggested that Marilyn might have become frightened when she tried to go to the bathroom during recess and found it mobbed because it was temporarily the only one in use. She also hesitantly inquired whether Marilyn could perhaps be a ten o'clocker (she was now a nine o'clocker in the school system in which the primary cycle children come either from 8:45 to 1:45 or from 9:45 till 2:50 so that they can receive reading instruction in small groups) so that she could walk to school with her second and third grade sisters, both ten o'clockers. (It crossed my mind that perhaps this mother, like many in her neighborhood, believed that the nine o'clockers were the slower children and that her anxiety about Marilyn, admittedly so close to her, had something to do with the girl's nine o'clock placement. One of the complications of crisis interventions is that the guidance worker is often not able to verify such hunches.)

I promised to talk with Miss Yee and see whether Marilyn could be protected from the general confusion at school by staying in the classroom as much as possible. I also promised to explore the possibilities of a ten o'clock assignment for Marilyn, should she be able to fit into that reading group.

Before we left, Marilyn did get her mother to agree that she would visit her at school at noon and bring her lunch to her—a step which seemed to reflect the mother's need more than the child's. The trip to school was uneventful and Marilyn was very pleased when, on our entering her classroom, her teacher suggested that she show me at the blackboard how she had learned to print her name. Miss Yee soon walked to the door with me and agreed to protect Marilyn from the confusion of the yard and halls until she seemed to have lost her fears. Miss Yee was less sure about making Marilyn a ten o'clocker, since this meant pushing her a little, but she finally agreed to try. (By the end of the year, Marilyn was one of the best readers in the class.)

I kept in close touch with Miss Yee and the Lums for a few days and helped Miss Yee, via phone, to be tolerant of Mrs. Lum's need to be a little protective of Marilyn. Within two or three weeks, any trace of the difficulty had disappeared. While no recurrence of this crisis is expected, I will keep an eye on Marilyn for some time to come.

GAINING ACCESS TO A DEFENSIVE PARENT

The guidance process with James will be discussed chronologically in terms of the guidance worker's steps and focused on the crucial issue, in this case, of gaining effective access to the family and gradually enlisting their active collaboration in work with their boy.

James arrived at School X around Christmas time, in the middle of his first grade year. His brother, a year older, had been in School X all along and seemed to be a well-adjusted boy with many friends, so that the school was not prepared for the disturbed youngster who now confronted them. James seemed disoriented or confused, he daydreamed for long periods then shouted out queer things completely out of context. If another child was reprimanded, James would go into hysterics, screaming that "so and so" shouldn't be bad, wasn't bad, he, James, wasn't bad, etc. These hysterical spells lasted twenty minutes or more and could neither be handled in the classroom nor cut short in any way except by his being sent to the office where he calmed down at once. In an individual testing situation he became very tense, sat and picked an eraser completely apart then anxiously shouted a blanket denial: "Someone else did it, I didn't, good boys don't," etc. Learning was completely out of the question. James' teacher was understandably baffled but was the kind of person who would not intervene prematurely and was willing to wait until the guidance worker could assess the psychosocial dynamics and help work out a plan. James' long periods of daydreaming and his interest in drawing made this possible.

James' mother, at this time, simply denied any evidence of emotional problems in the boy at home. She said the present school was better than the previous one and that James needed special help in reading to catch up. She put great pressure on the teacher to give James extra attention. At this stage, the guidance worker simply acted as a buffer so that the parental and classroom pressures would not be too great for the teacher. The guidance worker continued to observe the interaction for clues as to the meaning of the behavior from James, his mother, and the teacher. An important aspect of this early phase was the guidance worker's willingness to take the mother at face value, rather than trying to force this denying and fragmenting mother (e.g., able to isolate James' school behavior and deny any problems) into admitting problems, seeking psychiatric help, etc. The massiveness of denial, in the face of James' severe pathology, suggested that referral would simply make a bad matter worse, particularly until the guidance worker could begin to make some dynamic sense out of the situation which then might make referral a constructive or useful next step. It should also be noted that the guidance worker had not, at this time, been in the home. This again was in defer-ence to the mother's obvious reluctance.

In the spring, the mother issued a formal invitation for teacher and guidance worker to come to her home for tea. The tea was an elaborate affair, from which James was systematically excluded. No mention was made of the problem. The teacher and guidance worker met the maternal grandparents, with whom the mother and children lived. These grand-parents were strict, religious immigrants from Sweden who had come to the United States when the mother was fourteen or fifteen. It became clear that much of the pressure for academic achievement and denial of behavioral difficulties came from them; and it seemed to the guidance worker that the mother, in planning the tea, was indirectly telling her parents that several school people were concerned about James. On the surface, the motive for the tea seemed to be to bring pressure on the school not to retain James in the first grade since planning about promo-tions was being done in the school at that time. The guidance worker concurred in the mother's plan of having James tutored in a private school during the summer and agreed to defer a decision about grade placement until the end of the summer.

The guidance worker's non-coercive attitude apparently enabled the family to have a family conference in which they all decided that James would not benefit from so much pressure and that he should repeat the first grade, meanwhile having an enjoyable summer and getting off to a better start in the fall. The mother was pleased with the first grade teacher selected for James for the next fall because this teacher had taught James' brother successfully and would, knowing the brother, realize that James' mother was a good mother. Thus, the mother became more trust-ful of the school.

At this point, the mother was willing to give the guidance worker some family history, certainly still incomplete and distorted because of the mother's major use of denial as a defense. James had been born shortly before the violent death of his father. The mother reported this to the guidance worker as an accident but other informants reported a more traumatic end. The marriage had always been turbulent; the mother and boys had spent most of the time at the home of the maternal grand-parents. The mother went through a very upset period following the father's death. During this time the maternal grandmother took care of the boys. James was a fat, happy baby who was very much infantilized until he was three (fed soft foods, carried around all the time, etc.). When he was three, the maternal grandmother became ill and was no longer able to cope with the boys. The mother entered a Junior College to take secretarial courses and put the boys in a publicly supported child care center next door to her school. James reacted to this, not with obvious upset, but with severe restriction of behavior. He sat for hours, day after day, in the middle of the sand box. A year later, the mother got a job and transferred the boys to a child care center nearer her work. They remained in the child care center from 8:30 to 5:00; the mother was able to do things with them only on weekends. During this period, James was becoming harder to reach, less responsive, and the mother was becoming more anxious. The older brother was taken out of the child care center and put into the neighborhood kindergarten when James was four, leaving James alone in the child care center while the brother was cared for by the grandparents after school hours. The mother and the grandparents, however, denied that there was any difference in their attitude toward the two boys. Eventually, when James was in the middle of the first grade at the out-of-district school where the child care center was located, the mother decided to quit her job and placed James in School X, the neighborhood school, where his brother had been all along. It was at the time of James' transfer that I became acquainted with the case and found the mother unable to focus on anything but reading as *the* problem.

By the fall of James' second year in the first grade, the mother approached the problem with heightened trust in the teacher and in the guidance worker and more active collaboration was possible. We could work together on a mutual problem and try to discover constructive solutions in sharp contrast to the incomprehensible boy and the defensive mother of the year before.

James, although still a highly disturbed youngster, has begun to show definite improvement. He is beginning to learn academically at quite a good rate. His hysterical spells have shortened to about five minutes; although they can still not be curbed, he knows that he must go to the office when he gets upset in this way and will do so, returning to class when he has calmed down. He is being encouraged by the teacher to use other children as the models for appropriate behavior. He is no longer a complete social isolate and is currently reported even to have a definite, though tenuous, individual friend—this after the teacher had set up several special projects or work situations for James with other students whom he liked. James is slowly but surely on his way to better adaptive behavior, learning, and the more benign life experiences which, hopefully, will come to him as a result.

This case illustrates access into a difficult situation by means of slowly getting a mother's confidence and enlisting her collaboration in an active team effort with teacher and guidance worker. The guidance worker and the school will have to keep a special eye on James for many more years, using care in his classroom placement, offering supportive help, planning with and for him the timing of supplementary and remedial experiences (reading, art, summer camp, swimming at the Y.M.C.A., and last, but not least, psychotherapy) with the mother's collaboration. Yet, an approach to this family which focused merely or primarily on family pathology without its being integrated with what could be done at school or enlisting the mother's collaboration with the school almost certainly would have failed.

INVOLVING AN EMOTIONALLY DEPRIVED CHILD IN HIS OWN EDUCATION

Willis was a third grade boy with whom continuity of contact and success of guidance work was curtailed by his family's frequent moves which prevented the minimal stability stressed above as important for guidance work. No added community resources could be mobilized for his family, nor was guidance worker contact with the family particularly helpful. Still, various guidance workers were able to be useful to Willis and some of the beneficial results of their interactions persisted through a good deal of stress and social disorganization.

This boy was one of eight or nine children in a family who subsisted on Aid to Families of Dependent Children. A series of fathers and boy friends had rotated through the home. Willis had a speech problem in kindergarten, was slow in learning to read and developed increasingly hostile and defensive attitudes toward school and teachers. In the third grade, he suffered a concussion in a car accident. No residual neurological damage was found but the mother insisted that Willis' behavior problems resulted from the accident. The neurologist tried to refer the mother and boy for psychiatric help, a referral which was, of course, quite meaningless to the mother and almost surely would have been ineffectual. The referral *did* strengthen the mother's conviction that Willis was made "crazy" by the accident. Subsequently the mother persuaded the school that Willis should be on a shortened day because of the "post-traumatic" personality changes. Unfortunately the school acceded to this plan, which deferred a constructive school attack on the problems.

The family moved while Willis was still in the third grade. He went into the room of a very creative, open-minded teacher. The guidance worker saw him for several interviews in an effort to evaluate his hostility, defensiveness and his reading problem. Willis responded with clear evidence of his hunger for an honest relationship, supportive of his ability to grow, hence of his realistic self-esteem, and helpful in counteracting his evil self-image. The guidance worker was able to use material from individual interviews with Willis to help the classroom teacher pattern classroom experiences for him in a constructive way. His presenting areas of competence were beautiful handwriting and art work; these could be used as a means of giving deserved approval and as a base from which to broaden his competence in other areas. Willis responded dramatically. His reading skills improved by a full academic year in three months. His hostility gave way to enthusiasm for the school; he was *the* student who collected forty bags of rags in the neighborhood for the school rag drive. Even the attempted suicide of his mother did not upset the boy's school adjustment.

Willis *was* upset, however, later in the year when another disturbed boy was put into his room, diverting the teacher's focus from Willis to the newcomer. Unfortunately, before this conflict could be worked out, the family moved again. Three years and three schools later, Willis' behavior has become more delinquent outside of school. His mother still attributes all his difficulties to the concussion but threatens him with reform school. Willis is not a serious delinquent yet but he probably will drift in that direction. He is always upset by a move to a new school and clearly suffers from his lack of continuity in relationships both at home and at school.

Even so, Willis' cumulative academic record indicates that he has maintained the academic gains made with the creative and supportive third grade teacher and has continued to make progress in school. Willis' case shows the desperate need of the lower-class child to have more supports, relationships, possibilities for psychological identifications and active efforts on the part of participating adults to correct evil self-image and intervene in their disturbed homes. Only cumulative benign experiences can counter the otherwise cumulative depair, deterioration and hostility which is the realistic reaction of such children to their actual life experience.

NOTES
(Chapter III)

1 Mary A. Sarvis and Blanche Garcia, "Etiological Variables in Autism," *Psychiatry; Journal for the Study of Interpersonal Processes*, Vol. 24, No. 4, November, 1961.
2. Association for Supervision of Curriculum Development, Washington, D.C., 1962. Perceiving, Behaving, Becoming.

ADDITIONAL READINGS
(Chapter III)

Ackerman, N. *The Psychodynamics of Family Life.* New York: Basic Books, 1958.

Allen, Frederick H. *Positive Aspects of Child Psychiatry.* New York: W. W. Norton, Inc., 1963.

Bower, E. M. "Primary Prevention in a School Setting," in G. Caplan, ed., *Prevention of Mental Disorders in Children.* New York: Basic Books, 1961, pp. 353-378.

Caplan, Gerald, ed. *Emotional Problems of Early Childhood.* New York: Basic Books, Inc.

Caplan, Gerald, *et al., Prevention of Mental Disorders in Children.* Basic Books, 1961.

Erikson, E. H. *Childhood and Society.* New York: Norton, 1950.

Sarvis, M. A., and Blanche Garcia, "Etiological Variables in Autism," *Psychiatry,* Vol. 24, No. 4, November 1961, pp. 307-317.

CHAPTER IV

A Theoretical Rationale for Task-Oriented Guidance

We have stated earlier that the guidance worker can have no set method of operating or preconceived recommendations. This does not imply the lack of a theoretical frame of reference. In this chapter, we hope to spell out a theoretical position which deals with the more common issues in school guidance work without closing any doors to new knowledge nor adhering to any orthodoxies.

Guidance workers come from a variety of backgrounds. Each of these background fields tends to lean on theoretical formulations relevant to its core teaching concepts and history. Just as guidance workers are sometimes tempted to simplify their task by over-structuring it, so do they sometimes look for a "miracle" theory that ends the anxiety and ambiguity of theoretical complexities. Where, then, can guidance workers take their theoretical stand?

We are concerned with life as an unfolding of complex potentialities, subject to the vicissitudes of adaptive/maladaptive integrations and open to intervention anywhere along its continuum.

We find in Erik Erikson's "Childhood and Society" the essential building blocks of a theoretical frame of reference, which encompasses biological, psychological and sociological determinants of behavior dynamically integrated into a meaningful whole. We guard against the "either-or" kind of thinking, so prevalent today, which tends to give the impression that sociological variables somehow contradict or minimize psychodynamic variables, disorders of communication, for instance, seem to minimize genetic factors, etc. Such dichotomies do a great disservice to the understanding of the multiple, mutually interrelated variables we feel need to be considered in each case.

Against this background, we view our role as providing support to "coping" efforts on the part of the child, the family, the school and the community. Data from the field of child development suggest that individuals have, in general, much more ability and flexibility in coping with developmental, familial and sociological problems than would be anticipated from a study of a clinical patient population. The Institute for Human Development at the University of California conducted a longitudinal study in which the experimental sample comprised every third census birth in Berkeley, California, for eighteen months beginning in January, 1928. Participants in the study included, among others, psychodynamically oriented clinicians (including psychoanalysts) and projective data were obtained throughout so that overt behavior was not the only dimension being studied. In the early years of this project, there was considerable hope that, with information about psychodynamics, family patterns and inner stress in the subjects, accurate predictions could be made about adult personality organization. This hope has not been substantially realized but an exciting recognition of the complexity and vigor of coping mechanisms has been highlighted by the follow-up studies done, again in depth, when the experimental subjects were in their thirties. Only a few of the data can be reported in this chapter but J. W. Macfarlane[1] reports that predictions during preschool and school years were about seventy percent erroneous. Nearly fifty percent of the subjects "turned out better than any of us predicted and . . . ten percent . . . turned out *far* better than predicted" (italics hers). In twenty percent of the experimental subjects, "early records [and those] up to age eighteen showed great promise on the basis of high ability or talents—artistic and athletic—and/or easy and successful family and social relationships, followed by later adult appraisals, showing failure to live up to potential or strained dissatisfaction with their lives or showing far less depth and substantiality of character than predicted."[2] Macfarlane says further, "it seems clear that we overweighted the troublesome and the pathogenic aspects and underweighted elements that were maturity-inducing. Since most personality theory has been derived from work with pathological groups, we were oversensitized to these aspects in respect both to overt and covert patterning and inadequately sensitized to the stabilizing and maturity-inducing aspects. Data on these last two aspects were available, but we failed to give them due weight so preoccupied were we with current dilemmas."[3] She further states that the investigators overestimated the durability of well-learned, characteristic and habitual response patterns over a period of time. "It appears that no matter how habitual these patterns were, if they were coping devices . . . which no longer were effective for desired ends in changed situations and with changing physiologies, by the vast majority [of subjects] they were dropped or modified."[4] Macfarlane also stresses the fact that important psycho-dynamic changes in personality occurred throughout the entire observational period with these subjects and through many varieties of experience rather than primarily only in the preschool years and in relation to family psychodynamics. As further reports of this longitudinal study are published, a valuable theoretical rationale for public school guidance work and other efforts to help children cope will be substantiated.

A provocative and important study by Lois Barclay Murphy[5] on pre-school children also illustrates dramatically the wide variation in coping mechanisms, their general success and their relationship to the temperament, experiences and life style of the various children studied.

What emerges from these studies is a focus on ego strengths as well as ego defects, a more balanced view of adaptation and child growth and development as a basis for guidance work's theory and practice. Escalona has stated it thus:

> One of the primary ego functions that sustain adaptation, and that provide means of coping with stress and of overcoming obstacles, is the capacity for formal structured learning. . . . The experience of learning, and the perception of the self as one who *can* learn, generates a sense of the self as an active being, and a sense of the self as the carrier of power and competence. It also makes available a source of pleasure and of satisfaction that is not directly dependent upon the quality of interpersonal relationships. Last, not least, each instance of successful learning makes the world more intelligible.[6]

Escalona's view fits with the more active intervention role expected of today's guidance worker.

Guidance interventions supportive of coping efforts incorporate many technical skills and the contributions of many workers in the behavioral sciences.

In order to outline what is in reality a very complex picture, it is perhaps useful to focus in turn on the coping efforts of each of the participants in the educational enterprise and to review in cursory fashion some of the better known theories and techniques from the behavioral sciences available to these participants in promoting their own effectiveness.

First, the teacher. He may well ask himself: what is an effective classroom climate to promote children's learning? What is an effective curriculum? What are effective interventions with individual children? with groups of children? Should the children's learning be controlled by the teacher? Does such teacher control facilitate student motivation? How? The recent contributions of Skinner and his followers represent one view. They highlight the usefulness of rewarding successful learning behaviors very concretely and in a planned, consistent manner. Once the child is secure in his success, rewards are gradually withdrawn. The hope is that motivation for a given piece of behavior has become internalized. The "rewarding" process may be repeated to encourage increasingly difficult task performance. The teacher may see himself as a "classroom engineer." If the teacher is clearly ready to assume responsibility for planning a very detailed step by step approach to each student's learning and behavior and is prepared to "start where the student is," (and this kind of engineered approach suits the teacher's own personality and style), then such an approach can indeed be useful in the classroom.

If the teacher starts from the point of view that "controls come from within," as Fritz Redl has described so graphically, then the teachers' efforts might most wisely be expended in developing techniques supportive of such inner controls. Prominent among such techniques is the "life-space interview" developed by Redl and his associates.[7]

There is, in addition, an increasing volume of literature exploring "non-authoritarian approaches to teaching" and techniques for getting students involved in their own problem-solving. If the teacher starts from the point of view that teaching/learning is a joint task requiring joint problem-solving, then the teacher will seek to acquire useful techniques such as role playing; open-ended discussions with the class; game-theory applications derived from Eric Berne's formulations;[8] and other planned approaches to teacher-student communication. In order to become an effective resource person in a non-authoritarian classroom, a teacher may have to master the skills of the "participant observer," a role developed by anthropologists in their field studies and one found useful by other behavioral scientists. Skill as a participant observer will enable the teacher to decide when and how to share observed problems with the class as a whole, an individual child or a small group of children. Once the problem is shared, steps can be developed to work at its solution.

To summarize, teachers may find many techniques derived from the behavioral sciences useful in their search for effectiveness. They need an opportunity to examine alternatives and to "try them on for size." In these efforts, they may find an ally in the guidance worker assigned to their school.

The skills the child needs to learn in order to make him a successful student are also receiving attention. They are, of course, interactional with those of the teacher described above and with those of the parent, to follow.

How children learn prompts the following questions: "What is readiness for learning?" "How is it acquired?" "How can it be measured?" "How can it be built on?" These questions are asked in two quarters, especially. First, they are asked by those concerned with early childhood education in Head-Start and similar programs. One school of thought emphasizes the need to help the child discover what he already knows, including the reality of his living situation which may be quite at variance with that of his teacher. The most eloquent spokesman for this point of view is Sylvia Ashton Warner in her famous book *Teacher*.[9] Just as the middle-class child has been allowed in the past to "share" his family's outing to the zoo with his classmates, the ghetto child may now be allowed to "share" openly the experiences he acquires in his own home and neighborhood without negative feedback from his teacher. Speaking, expressing oneself, vocabulary building, reading and writing are then developed from the child's own experiences expressed in his own language. The teacher gradually enlarges on the child's world without alienating him from it.

Others, equally concerned, emphasize their belief that the child is lacking in verbal background, and that he needs to be systematically trained to speak in standard English sentences prior to first grade if possible. Bereiter and Engleman[10] are the most articulate spokesmen for this point of view to date. Their book, *Teaching Disadvantaged Children in the Preschool*, describes how teachers can build systematic language development into their programs.

Still others address themselves to the issue of perceptual development in ghetto children and in young children in general and build a curriculum structured to include manipulative and perceptual tasks of all kinds to prepare children for more formal learning. Montessori techniques are often used in this context.

These concerns with effective manipulative and perceptual skills, as well as speech and communications skills in young children, are shared by an increasing number of professionals who are involved with learning failures due to developmental problems of the child and/or to minimal cerebral dysfunction in children. A literature is rapidly developing which includes this dimension. Well-known authors in this field are Cruikshank, Kephart, Frostig and many others. While the bulk of their present efforts may relate most directly to special education, the implications for child development and for teaching normal children are obvious. Underpinning many efforts in analyzing how a child learns are the theoretical formulations of Jean Piaget who describes the sequential nature of the development of a child's thought processes in such landmark works as *The Construction of Reality in the Child*.[11] Just as teachers can use many approaches to plan a more effective teaching program, so children appear able to use many alternative techniques to enhance their own sense of mastery through learning.

In Chapter III, we discussed the changing position of parents vis-à-vis the schools and their increased self-confidence, after a period of almost universal parental guilt.

Parents have become more effective in securing services for children who were inadequately served before—the severely disturbed, the severely neurologically handicapped, the severely mentally retarded, and, in many ghetto and poverty-stricken areas, the severely undereducated. In the process, they have had to deal with the educational establishment and often they have learned how to work with a system which previously had ignored their children's needs. While hostility tends to be a part of such interactions, some form of collaboration also tends to emerge. Thus parent effectiveness is enhanced.

"Parent effectiveness" is the theme of many efforts of parents in these complex times. One program actually carries this name and aims to train parents to listen more carefully to what their children are saying or acting out, so that mutual problem-solving can occur. This program is an adaptation of Carl Rogers' client-centered counseling technique, and hopes to increase parents' listening skills. Some parents become involved in sensitivity training and encounter experiences, again to broaden their own repertoire of emotional responses and to improve their parent-child and family communications.[12]

For another group of parents, the need seems to be to learn how to set the stage for their children's learning. Robert Hess, in a very interesting piece of research, found that lower-class parents, or those originally from lower-class backgrounds, are apt not to give their children directional cues in problem-solving as more middle-class parents would. The child is left dangling between a parent who wants him to learn, and a task which he has no idea how to accomplish. The child's resultant position tends to be one of passive dependency on the demanding adult but also one of helplessness or hostility toward the task. So far, we have seen few, if any, efforts at helping such parents become more effective parents, except perhaps as a few of them become teacher aides and learn by doing. There appears to be a promising field for further work here.[13]

In the past, we have tended to be far too general in supporting parent effectiveness. Cumulative present evidence seems to suggest that parents often can be encouraged to overcome their own sense of inadequacy by taking very concrete but appropriate steps with their children. Encouraged by a positive response, they can gradually enlarge the scope of their efforts.

Having surveyed how teachers, children and parents are trying out new ways to master their separate but complementary tasks, let us now turn to the guidance worker whose role, by definition, is to restore the effectiveness of those teachers, children and parents whose interactions have somehow run into trouble. As we have described in Chapter I, several models of guidance work have existed in the past, none of which coped realistically with the actual complexities of the task. Whether guidance workers concentrated on a few very disturbed children, a few very recalcitrant families, or on a large volume of psychological testing without appropriate followup, their work was marginal to the educational enterprise.

A number of efforts are under way to test more effective guidance models. Perhaps most influential for school psychology and school social work has been the work of Gerald Caplan[14] who has developed the concept of "mental health consultation" to the schools.

Caplan has been instrumental in helping guidance workers to break out of the straight-jacket of the clinical model, and has helped free them from this too narrow focus. He has also demonstrated that mental health consultants can be drawn from a variety of clinical fields such as psychiatry, psychology, psychiatric social work and other related fields. We have some reservations about mental health consultation as an adequate model for guidance work which we shall discuss in Chapter V. Nevertheless, Caplan's work represents an important milestone in the theory of guidance work.

In her recent book, *Psychological Consultation in the Schools*,[15] Ruth Newman describes a project which draws on Caplan's consultation concepts and on Redl's work with children. Newman emphasizes, as we do, the value of regular, on-going contacts with a given school, the need to start where the school is, to counteract magical expectations by being very visible in one's interventions, etc. Perhaps we go further than she into a synthesis of both the clinical and the consultative aspects of guidance work via the interactional, collaborative model we propose. Our emphasis on collaboration derives from our experience of having been an on-going part of a school system for a number of years, and having found ourselves most effective when we have been on equal footing with educators and parents within a given school community, rather than when we have been viewed as outside experts. Thus, step by step, a theoretical rationale for guidance work is being developed.

Though theoretical differences persist, it is heartening to find many areas of practical agreement among pupil personnel workers. Concerns revolve around developing viable models for guidance work, hence viable models for training guidance workers in the skills they will need on the job. All pupil personnel professions are concerned with their need to gain recognition and secure support via legislative action. These concerns seem to us to foreshadow the need for much greater interprofessional communication and collaboration.

The Interprofessional Research Commission on Pupil Personnel Services constitutes a step in the right direction at the national level. At the present time, this commission is in a relatively inactive state but it would seem to behoove the various pupil personnel professions to lend support to such a duly constituted body whose efforts might well provide the firm ground the pupil personnel field desperately needs in order to develop a broadly realistic technology, a more general visibility and a resultant acceptance into the mainstream of education. We hope this book makes a small contribution in that direction.

In summary, it should be clear that, for the present, no one theory, no one technical approach, no one "specialist" can be viewed as *"the solution"* for guidance work's complex theoretical and practical tasks.

The guidance worker needs to be a theoretical "generalist" profoundly committed to humanist values and to a dynamic view of human development. He needs to be willing to use any technical intervention that will prove useful at a given time, and any collaborative alliances which will strengthen a given child's chances to become a more competent person. He needs to be aware of gaps in his own knowledge and gaps in professional knowledge available to him. He needs a strong commitment to the development of his own competence, and appreciation for the competence of others with whom he works. Only such respect for competence can help transcend present differences in points of view, in temperament and in role perception.

NOTES
(Chapter IV)

1. Jean Walker Macfarlane, "From Infancy to Adulthood," *Childhood Education*, March, 1963, p. 4.
2. *Ibid.*
3. *Ibid.*, p. 5.
4. *Ibid.*
5. Lois Barclay Murphy, *The Widening World of Childhood*, Basic Books, Inc., New York, 1962.
6. Sibylle K. Escalona, "Mental Health, The Educational Process and the Schools," *American Journal of Orthopsychiatry*, Vol. XXXVII, No. 1, (January, 1967), p. 2.
7. Fritz Redl and D. Wineman, *Controls from Within* (Glencoe: Free Press, 1957).
8. Eric Berne, *Games People Play* (New York: Grove Press, 1964).
9. Sylvia Ashton Warner, *Teacher*
10. Carl Bereiter and Siegfried Engelman, *Teaching Disadvantaged Children in the Preschool* (New York: Prentice Hall, 1966).
11. Jean Piaget, *The Construction of Reality in the Child* (New York: Basic Books, 1954).
12. Thomas Gordon, *Parent Effectiveness Training*. 110 South Euclid Avenue, Pasadena, Calif.
13. Robert Hess and Virginia Shipman, "Early Blocks in Children's Learning," *Children*. (September-October, 1965).
14. Gerald Caplan, "Mental Health Consultation in Schools," in: *The Elements of a Community Mental Health Program* (New York: Milbank Memorial Fund, 1956), pp. 77-86.

15. Ruth G. Newman, *Psychological Consultation in the Schools* (New York: Basic Books, Inc., 1967).

ADDITIONAL READINGS
(Chapter IV)

Ashton Warner, Sylvia. *Teacher*

Bereiter, Carl and Siegfried Engelman. *Teaching Disadvantaged Children in the Preschool.* New York: Prentice-Hall, 1966.

Berne, Eric. *Games People Play.* New York: Grove Press, 1964.

Cruickshank, William M., ed. *A Teaching Method for Brain-Injured and Hyperactive Children.* Syracuse, New York: Syracuse University Press, 1961.

Erikson, Erik. *Childhood and Society,* rev. ed. New York: W. W. Norton and Co., 1963.

Frostig, M., and Horne, D. *The Frostig Program for the Development of Visual Perception: Teacher's Guide,* Chicago, Follett Publishing Co., 1964.

Glasser, William. *Reality Therapy.* New York: Harper and Row, 1965.

Hess, Robert D., and Virginia Shipman, "Early Blocks to Children's Learning," *Children,* September-October, 1965.

Holt, John. How Children Learn. New York: Pitman Publishing Corporation, 1967.

Holt, John. How Children Fail. New York: Delta Books, 1964.

Kephart, Newell C. *The Slow Learner in the Classroom.* Charles E. Merrill Books, Inc., 1960.

Krumboltz, John D., ed. *Revolution in Counseling: Implications of Behavioral Science.* Boston: Houghton-Mifflin, 1966.

Maier, Henry W. *Three Theories of Child Development.* New York: Harper and Row, Publishers, 1965.

Peter, Laurence J. *Prescriptive Teaching.* New York: McGraw Hill Book Company, 1965.

Piaget, Jean. *The Origin of Intelligence in Children.* New York: International Universities Press, 1952.

Piaget, Jean. *The Construction of Reality in the Child.* New York: Basic Books, 1954.

Redl, Fritz and D. Wineman. *Controls from Within.* Glencoe: Free Press, 1957.

Sarvis, M. A., S. De Wees and Ruth F. Johnson. "A Concept of Ego-Oriented Psychotherapy," *Psychiatry,* Vol. 22, No. 3, August, 1959.

Skinner, B. F. *Science and Human Behavior.* New York: The Free Press, 1953.

Wolpe, Joseph and A. A. Lazarus. *Behavior Therapy Techniques.* New York: Pergamon Press, 1966.

CHAPTER V

Consultation by Outside Experts

The psychiatric or any other* consultant in a task-oriented guidance department such as we have been discussing, works with the guidance department in a way largely analogous to the way in which the guidance worker works in the schools. That is to say, the consultant is the more peripheral or less involved psychosocial expert within the department who can act as a troubleshooter when the individual worker or the department as a whole finds itself impeded in the guidance task. Such a way of operating is somewhat different from the historical models which we will now describe.

Psychiatric consultation to public school guidance departments developed within the same historical conceptual framework as that which influenced the development of guidance departments in their work with children and schools. Guidance departments organized themselves first around direct services to children in terms of the children's psychopathology and then often swung to an almost exclusive focus on work with teachers. Psychiatric consultation has tended to be similarly polarized. At first psychiatrists were used to discuss the psychopathology and psychodynamics of individual cases. The psychiatric consultant was not part of the ongoing guidance department function and tended to be relatively uninformed or uninvolved in the concrete educational process—with respect either to its opportunities or its limitations. The usefulness of the psychiatric consultant within this frame of reference was quite limited.

Another school of psychiatric consultation developed, in which the

---

* Mental health consultation is now being offered by various mental health professionals, not only psychiatrists. In addition, specialized consultation may be offered by social scientists interested in the schools as a social system, and by other specialized personnel such as neurologists, etc. The model described in this chapter seems to us to be relevant to all mental health consultation regardless of professional discipline.

focus of the psychiatric consultant's concern was on the anxieties of the guidance worker. In our experience, the emphasis here was not on "what makes Johnny tick" but (to the guidance worker) on "why does this case make you anxious?" This second approach seems even less task-oriented than the first. In the first approach, focussed on the psychopathology in a given child, the experienced guidance worker could often visualize a practical application from the discussion. The worker-centered approach, on the other hand, almost completely ignored the guidance worker's actual task and the realistic stress or anxiety related to it. Historically, this emphasis on worker anxiety occurred not only in guidance but in social work training, psychoanalytic training and other fields as well. For a time, consultants and supervisors seemed to lose sight of the fact that the task itself might cause anxiety in the worker and that there could be realistic anxieties, for instance those related to inexperience, etc. At present, in all these disciplines, there seems to be a swing away from a primary focus on the worker's personal problems toward a more empirical and realistic assessment of the worker's task.[1] Thus, unless a worker's anxiety or defensiveness is producing a *typical* or *persistent* blind spot with respect to the worker's function in a given situation, worker anxiety is dealt with only in respect to the aspects of the task which would be anxiety provoking for almost any worker. For instance, the guidance worker has little of the structure and protected atmosphere of the clinic within which safe realm he can feel secure. He deals daily with the ambivalence of educators toward guidance work and with educators' anxieties—for instance about the education of children in a classroom where one or two or five emotionally upset children are impeding the progress of other children. The guidance worker has to face, moreover, the lack of clear cultural definition of his role and the ambivalence of the culture towards his services. He has to cope with his own ambiguous status within the school power and status hierarchy. His position, to use a military analogy, is that of the front line medical corpsman rather than that of a worker in a base hospital. The psychiatric consultant should inform himself of these task-related anxieties as concretely as possible and should relate to the guidance worker interpretatively, educationally or supportively in terms of them.

This way of conceptualizing the task of the psychiatric consultant can, of course, result in role diffusion for the psychiatrist and in the idea that he should do anything anybody wants him to as long as it is supportive and encouraging to the guidance worker. There have been several attempts in recent years to counter role diffusion and over-fluidity of function by efforts to structure the role or function of the psychiatric consultant with more precision. Efforts are made, for instance, to differentiate mental health education from consultation. It seems to us that these more precise structural differentiations are not very realistic or operational in terms of the needs of most present-day institutions such as schools, health departments, hospitals, probation departments, children's institutions, etc. As in the case of the guidance worker, rigid structuring of role may temporarily lower the psychiatric consultant's anxiety but we feel that it will represent a false solution since over a period of time it will not adequately meet the operational needs of the guidance department.

If we introduce a functional or operational model in place of the rigidly structural one, how are over-fluidity of role, false reassurance, etc. to be avoided? This has been discussed earlier in the chapter on how the guidance worker works with principals and teachers; we think the same frame of reference applies for the psychiatric consultant. He comes to this task with a certain set of professional competencies and principles, with certain idiosyncracies of personality and style. He is interacting with a staff which also has characteristic task-oriented skills, concepts and anxieties. There are certain limits for the psychiatric consultant, as for the guidance worker, inherent in the psycho-social troubleshooter role within the schools: for instance, involvement with administrative authority, such as hiring or firing of teachers, would almost always be detrimental. However, the useful next step for the psychiatric consultant, the particular activities he undertakes with the guidance department, depend largely on the common psychosocial approach, on the concrete task in a given school or school department and on the functional and structural issues to be described below.

When the psychiatrist is inexperienced in general or new to a particular school department, he goes through a period in which the guidance workers test him for common sense, readiness to learn, special skills and personal integrity, just as the guidance worker goes through a similar trial experience at a new school site. Often the early use of the psychiatric consultant is around particular individual cases just as the early use of the guidance worker is apt to be in terms of particular children in a new school. Neither professional person has yet shown that he knows enough about the ongoing task or is sufficiently trustworthy in how he would handle complicated situations. As the psychiatric consultant learns more about the educational process and about guidance work, the level and focus of the discussion change. Primary interest in individual psychopathology shifts to more complex issues, such as: given certain problems and vulnerabilities in the child, in his environment and in his interaction with the school, what specific relationships can be utilized, what inner resources of the child can be strengthened, what school originated stresses can be diminished for the student so that his educational growth can be supported and improved?

The psychiatrist must take into account the traditions and practices of his guidance department, the backgrounds, experience and competence of its guidance workers, the administrative policies and personnel of the school department, etc. He is not merely the passive "victim" of these circumstances, of course; the adaptation is an active interactional process' in which every participant will influence every other toward a progressively more constructive implementation of the educational process.

The function of the psychiatric consultant is also influenced by structural factors such as whether he consults regularly and how much time he spends on the task. Occasional consultation or crisis consultation only mean, for instance, that he will be more peripheral to the guidance department, less a participant in the continuing process.

Also, the psychiatric consultant, like all other members of the school district, is a member of the power and status hierarchy. He will be met by a reputation: for instance, the reputation that he will be a magical problem solver, that he will be omnipotent, that he will be of little practical help, that he will use his technical skills to dissect and lay bare staff vulnerabilities. The psychiatric consultant must be aware of whatever reputation has been assigned to him, and must work to modify others' views of him in a more realistic direction. To some extent, the psychiatrist can structure his role with respect to the power and status hierarchy. For instance, he can choose to go in the direction of high status as an expert with administrative authorities versus working to make himself a more integrated (less special status) member of the guidance department. In our experience, focussing primarily on psychiatric consultation to high administrative echelons (e.g. assistant superintendents, principals, etc.) is not a particularly effective way of operating for two reasons. (1) Theoretical psychiatric information given to top administrators does not trickle down effectively to the classroom teacher because it does not help the teacher concretely to any great extent with particular children who are in difficulty. Thus, general information about school phobias given to an administrator is not apt to be useful to his teacher with a particular personality and background who has a particular phobic child with a particular set of experiences, family situation, etc. (2) Mental health education and psychosocial information are even apt to be frustrating to educators when they are not linked to actual legwork by the guidance department, that is to active psychosocial diagnosis of impediments in the educational process and implementing plans for overcoming them.

However, if sophisticated top echelon personnel are willing to introduce the psychosocial dimension consciously and deliberately into their policy-making system-wide problem solving, then a highly skillful consultant can be a tremendous asset and can truly act as a change agent. A few districts are beginning to grant mental health or other social science consultants this amount of trust and power.[2]

So far we have discussed the role of the psychiatric consultant in relation to a whole guidance department, where he is working in various ways with individuals, groups or the staff as a whole. In some school departments this is not the case. Psychiatric consultants in school departments where the consultant is only asked to meet with workers on an individual basis function in a way that is more analogous to that of supervisors in social agencies. Such psychiatric consultants are not integrated into the guidance department interaction with the schools; while the particular supervisory relationship may be mutually constructive to the participants, it has limited influence on the worker's total task.

The psychiatric consultant has several areas of function. He gives information, such as information on psychoanalytic theory, on clinical material, on central nervous system problems, and on sociological studies of lower-class children. Sometimes this information is discussed in terms of particular cases or groups of children, sometimes not. A staff may vary from one year to the next on how formal they wish case presentations to be, how informal around a group of cases, how structured with regard to bringing salient school people into the meeting, etc. As indicated above, specialists other than a psychiatrist may fill these roles. The consultant has the responsibility of helping the guidance staff to keep up to date in terms of general theoretical models and advances in the behavioral sciences.

A complementary function for the psychiatric consultant is to learn from guidance workers and from guidance department meetings about school department policies, e.g. current attitudes toward discipline, toward programs for the gifted, toward special classes for the emotionally disturbed, etc. The psychiatric consultant is not expected to become an educational specialist and should not presume to be so but he is expected to learn the educational task in such a way that his participation in it, in terms of individual children or problems or situations, can be an integrative and not a discordant one.

In the same way that information-giving enlarges the mutual horizons of psychiatric consultant and guidance worker, psychological identification with each other's roles and tasks is mutually supportive. The guidance worker is helped to maintain identification with the more abstract but all important dynamic psychological goals which lend meaning to his work, but which tend to be eroded by the day to day fatigue, efforts and expedience of the job. The psychiatric consultant is helped to identify with guidance as an integral part of the educational process and as a distinct, expert, social/psychological discipline and also with the purposes and operations of a public school department which must balance individual and group needs, expedience, budget, personnel, history, and useful next step in a way which is quite different from psychiatric practice.

The psychiatric consultant has several additional roles. (a) A worker who is completely new or inexperienced needs to get his bearings in terms of the concrete dimensions of the job and usually finds the psychiatric consultant either too threatening or the consultant's knowledge of the practical job and particular school situation too general to be of much help. This worker usually gets more help from his supervisor, department head, school principals or colleagues than from the psychiatric consultant. However, once the guidance worker has a general grasp of the structure of his job and his own task in its practical applications and begins to try to relate it or integrate it with general personality theory, the psychiatric consultant can be of use to him. The psychiatric consultant must be aware that psychoanalytic theory and language must be translatable and applicable to the concrete guidance tasks and are often not helpful at an abstract theoretical level. It is relevant for the psychiatric consultant and the guidance department to define and to clarify a common vocabulary which will enable new insights to be communicated in both directions.

We stress this two-way communication because the psychiatric consultant is not a more powerful guidance worker nor a guidance worker a more diluted psychiatrist; their roles are different, their skills are different, though complementary in the common area of psychosocial information and viewpoint.

The psychiatric consultant does not, of course, limit his contribution to general theoretical issues and their application to guidance work. He is also called upon to assist in the diagnosis of particular cases, in the planning for particular children, in discussing and clarifying the interaction with particular schools, etc. Occasionally, depending on the time he has available for consultation, he may see an individual student, for instance an adolescent in an acute schizophrenic reaction, either to help the family plan the useful next step or to plan with the guidance worker on how to proceed with school and family. The small amount of time alloted to most psychiatric consultants makes such direct services rare, however.

(b) The psychiatric consultant can also play a supportive role when the guidance department as a whole is anxious because of an adverse climate in the schools, uncertainty about new administrative procedures or appointments, retirement of a key person on the staff, etc. In such times, technical or theoretical issues may be much less relevant to the staff and to the staff/psychiatric consultant interaction than recognition of and supportive help with the difficult psychological situation.

(c) The psychiatric consultant may have a supportive, as well as an informational role in direct service to school faculties by participation in faculty meetings, workshops, etc. We will use this category of service to distinguish objective information or mental health education from task-oriented psychiatric consultation. A consultant from the outside, unrelated to the continuing processes and typical problems or tasks of the agency being consulted with, is largely restricted to crisis consultation of one kind or another. He is vulnerable to being used for manipulative ends of which he has no knowledge, such as to support the exclusion of Johnny Doe from school without knowing that a low-morale, hostile faculty is using Johnny as a scapegoat in their fight with a principal who seems to them to be hopelessly over-permissive. Even if his sophistication and focus are such that he could not be caught in this kind of trap, he is still —except for the crisis situation—restricted to general mental health education or to a discussion in general of school anxieties because he cannot possibly be sufficiently aware of the infinity of concrete, complex interactions, forces (rivalries, hopes for promotion, etc.), and emotional relationships which comprise the ongoing life of a school.

On the other hand, a psychiatric consultant may be of use to his guidance department in an informational and supportive role to the schools if he, as a member of that school and guidance department, is willing to enlarge his role to include work with school faculties. He now speaks from within the educational team of that public school district. He goes to a particular school when the school's guidance worker feels it would be advantageous to do so—when both morale and informational level in the school warrant it. This may be either at points of low morale when the guidance worker role needs to be supported or at levels of high morale when teachers are ready for an increasingly sophisticated level of information and psychosocial inference or implications. The guidance worker and the psychiatric consultant work together on what should be emphasized in a given school situation and on how the psychiatric consultant should present his topic so as to further effective guidance work in that school.

(d) The psychiatric consultant, lastly, plays a supportive role *vis à vis* the guidance department and its policies with the administrative staff. He may be asked to give an opinion on or to participate in administrative plans at various levels, depending on the school department. He may, at times, be taken as the representative of the guidance department, although when this role would involve knowledge of the detailed, concrete problems of a given department, the guidance department administrator or supervisor should properly be the person concerned. Nonetheless, in talks to the Principals' Club, in conferences with assistant superintendents, in cooperative meetings with curriculum people, attendance personnel, members of other special services departments, etc., the psychiatric consultant can be of significant support to the guidance department and its role.

It will be seen in summary that we consider the psychiatric consultant's task to be largely operational and interactional with the guidance worker rather than rigidly pre-structured. Structure, such as the regularity of contact with the guidance staff, influences the psychiatric consultant's operation but, on the whole, he operates in the same educational, supportive and clarifying role with the guidance worker as the guidance worker does with the school. It has been our experience that the psychiatric consultant should maintain a continuing relationship with the guidance department for most effective service. This is also true of the guidance worker in his ongoing relationship with his schools. This kind of integral involvement can raise theoretical issues, like over-identification or sibling rivalry, but, in our opinion, the task-oriented approach to either guidance work or psychiatric consultation so largely neutralizes these issues that they are almost always irrelevant. Of course, the personality, style and temperament of the psychiatric consultant influence his way of operating with a guidance department, for instance in terms of the status differential or lack of it with which he feels comfortable or the emotional distance or closeness with which he operates. We feel that such factors are important and that the psychiatric consultant should take his own temperament, style, etc. into account but should recognize that they are idiosyncratic, personal considerations and should not be rationalized in theoretical or structural terms.

While the psychiatric consultant should relate himself to the guidance process, he, like the guidance worker, should maintain his own professional identity. We have said that a guidance worker, for instance, operating without a centrally-organized base and without consistent professional association with his colleagues might lose his professional identity and become an extension of or absorbed into the educational model. Similarly the psychiatric consultant must remain a consultant and not become absorbed into his guidance department too totalistically. Role differentiation and individual professional identification are important in serving collaborative rather than symbiotic relationships.

Guidance work is usually macroscopic rather than microscopic in nature, earthy rather than esoteric, concerned with the useful next step rather than absolute concepts of optimal mental health or even perfect trouble shooting. Like politics, it is the art of the possible. Psychiatric consultation should be similarly oriented: the esoteric or overly microscopic psychiatric frame of reference is incongruous to the task.

Lastly, whatever the reasons for which a psychiatrist elects to serve as psychiatric consultant for a guidance department, he must realize that the experience, like any other human relationship, will be one of mixed feelings and varying levels of technical interest or accomplishment. The psychiatric consultant must be organically involved, rather than expecting to be constantly interested or fascinated with his task. He must go through periods of boredom, tedium, estrangement, etc., as well as periods of mutual enlightenment, excitement and creative collaboration. The same is true of psychotherapy, friendship, marriage and most other durable human transactions. Only with an ongoing, long-term commitment will this creative collaboration be accomplished.

In contrast with the point of view presented so far, the recent literature emphasizes a model of consultation which takes place in the absence of, as a substitute for and sometimes in ignorance of the availability of resources for psycho-social legwork within a given school system. This type of consultation process seems to us to act as a sensitizing process which brings the unmet needs of children and teachers out in the open and shows how general such needs are. These consultants, if they do a skillful job, may receive very positive feedback from their consultees. The consultant may conclude that his intervention is *sufficient* to handle the problems of children taught by teachers he has worked with. In our experience, this does not hold true. On the contrary, more aware and sensitized teachers, while they may no longer contribute actively to a child's difficulty, may insist more vocally on getting help with the child's problems. No matter how devoted, teachers have neither the skills nor the job structure which enables them to solve by themselves educational problems related to a child's severe developmental deviation from the norm, a child's severe emotional crisis due to a family break up, a child's severe lethargy due to poverty and malnutrition, etc. No outside time-and-goal limited consultant can work effectively to build *into* the system those resources that will assist sensitized teachers to work at the *resolution* of the underlying problems now exposed to view.

When the outside consultant leaves, he may, with luck, leave a group of people behind who have become so strengthened by his consultation that they can carry on and work toward the needed changes in their district. Because change is slow, however, and resistances are often deeply entrenched, the sensitized teachers may become actually more discouraged and less able to cope with their day-to-day work situation. Intervention that seemed helpful in the short-run may be disruptive in the long-run unless coordinated with those who can pick up change efforts where the outside consultant leaves off. In our view, demonstration and consultation projects should not be considered as completed until their demonstrations result in expanded services for children built into the ongoing structure of the school district where the consultation or the demonstration project took place.

The scarcity of trained staff available to develop programs is a critical issue but the lack of manpower should not lead to pseudo-solutions. Discussion on the national level of ways to increase dramatically the numbers of guidance staff and their effectiveness would seem to be an essential next step. Consultation is not a substitute for needed child development services in the schools and the larger community. We need to face the fact that a child development oriented model of guidance intervention is a needed on-going component of a modern school system. Information-giving or even attitude-changing efforts directed at significant community agents, in the absence of leg work intervention, will *not*, in our opinion, accomplish the needed job. Legwork, in isolation from feedback to the educational decision-makers, is no longer a viable model for guidance workers, either. The outside consultant brings an important perspective and has a useful contribution to make. However, by virtue of his role definition, even when he is aware of the total complexity of the situation, his efforts cannot substitute for the on-going need for guidance services within a school system.

NOTES
(Chapter V)

1. Beulah Parker, "Psychiatric Consultation for Non-psychiatric Professional Workers," U.S. Public Health Service Publication No. 588, Public Health Monograph No. 53, Washington D. C.: Department of Health, Education and Welfare, 1958. 23 pp.
2. Irving N. Berlin, "On the Learning of Mental Health Consultation with School Administrators," Paper presented at the 39th Annual Meeting of the American Orthopsychiatric Association, Los Angeles, California, March, 1962. Available from author.

ADDITIONAL READINGS
(Chapter V)

Berlin, Irving N., "Mental Health Consultation in Schools as a Means of Communicating Mental Health Principles," *Journal of the American Academy of Child Psychiatry*, Vol. 1, No. 4 (October 1962) 671-679.
Berlin, Irving N., "What Help Can Education Expect from the Mental Health Specialist," *California Journal of Elementary Education*, Vol. 31, No. 1 (August 1962) 45-53.
Caplan, Gerald. "Mental Health Consultation in Schools"; in *The Elements of a Community Mental Health Program*. New York: Milbank Memorial Fund, 1956, pp. 77-86.

Parker, Beulah. "Psychiatric Consultation for Nonpsychiatric Professional Workers." U.S. Public Health Service Publication No. 588, Public Health Monograph No. 53. Washington, D.C.: Department of Health, Education and Welfare, 1958. 23 pp.

Rapoport, Lydia, ed. *Consultation in Social Work Practice.* New York: National Association of Social Workers, 1963.

Sarvis, M. A., "Unique Functions of Public School Guidance Programs," *Mental Hygiene,* Vol. 38, No. 2, April 1954, pp. 285-298.

CHAPTER VI

The Guidance Worker's Back-up Resources within the Schools and in the Community

The guidance worker has many people with whom he can collaborate in furthering the psychosocial development of children. These potential collaborators can be classified into three categories: (1) School people, both educators and ancillary personnel, such as nurses, custodians, supervisors, psychological testers and educational research people, speech teachers, remedial reading teachers, home instruction teachers and other special services people, playground directors, cafeteria helpers, etc. (2) People who work in community agencies which are not formal treatment agencies or where formal treatment is only a part of the agency task.* Agencies falling into this category are probation departments, juvenile courts, hospitals, residential treatment homes, child placement and protective agencies and recreation departments. (3) Finally, formal treatment facilities, such as psychiatric clinics, therapists in private practice, and family service agencies will be useful collaborators in meeting the needs of a small number of emotionally upset children and families.

Why do we put the formal treatment agency at the bottom of our list of resources, when the historical view and much current practice would put it at the top, as the most important resource? We do so because, from the point of view of the guidance worker, only an infinitesimal number of his psychologically upset children and families will see formal, long-term treatment as a useful next step for them. We will document this fact below and then will discuss some of the misconceptions which led

---

* These people will be referred to as "agency workers" to differentiate them from "formal treatment workers" even though the latter often also work in agencies.

61

psychosocial workers to think of formal treatment as the most important resource.

Woodward[1] sums up the statistics from New York State which show the small number of emotionally upset, referred patients who stay in formal treatment agencies for long-term psychiatric treatment. He says: "Let me cite a few pertinent facts: in the first place, of more than forty-eight thousand patients whose service was terminated in the outpatient clinics of New York State in the past year (1959), sixty-nine percent received only diagnostic or referral service, and thirty-one percent received some form of treatment. Moreover, forty-two percent of these treated patients withdrew from the clinic without the blessing of staff, and in a good number of clinics which stress treatment and select only patients who are believed to be well-motivated for fairly intensive treatment over a period of six months to two years, over fifty percent do not get beyond the fifth interview. It appears likely from these facts that the treatment efforts of clinics are being skewed in the direction of the staff's biases about therapy, rather than being based on a fully realistic assessment of the patient's needs, goals, and limitations. Doubtless, many psychiatric social workers (and other psychiatric workers) share this bias that favors narrow selection of patients suitable for depth therapy and the grand though ephemeral outcome of 'cure'."

Are Woodward's figures merely a reflection of rigidity in the New York State outpatient clinics, as he implies? From the experience of one of us,[2] who worked in two psychiatric clinics explicitly dedicated to trying to broaden the treatment range, we do not think so. In both of these clinics, one associated with a student health service in a large university and the other with a large pre-paid health plan, there was easy access to the psychiatric clinic. Patients were seen promptly on request, usually within a week. Even so, only 12.7 percent of the adult patients (in the pre-paid health plan clinic) continued in treatment for eleven visits or more.* The staff in both of these clinics felt that the briefer, intermittent, more focussed and "as necessary" contacts with patients were useful and productive in working with patients. Yet the percentage of patients requesting long-term formal treatment approaches that of Woodward.

---

* Figures from the Student Health Clinic were 22.5 percent in the 11-24 visit category but only 3.5 percent in the twenty-five visit and over category, whereas the prepaid health plan clinic saw 6.2 percent of its patients twenty-five times or more.

Similarly, a psychiatric emergency service in New York City[3] found that only ten percent of their patients accepted a referral for longer-term treatment.

Many workers in the psychosocial disciplines assume that the lower-class patient is the major "resister" of referral for formal treatment. In our opinion, this is untrue. It is true that we find the referral of lower-class families to formal treatment agencies is seldom helpful, except with a major crisis, like a psychotic episode. Yet guidance workers find that, even in middle-class areas, only "one in a hundred" families finds long-term formal treatment the useful next step. Such a referral for treatment is often the outcome of many years of guidance or other task-oriented work with the family.*

Why then, do some guidance workers and other psychosocial workers continue to focus primarily on referral to formal treatment in dealing with upset children or families? We think there are several reasons for this.

(1) Referral for treatment tends to be made on the basis of severity of psychopathology, rather than in terms of "motivation" or the useful next step. This criterion is meaningless: if anything, the relationship between severity of psychopathology (except with commitable psychoses) and treatibility tends to be inverse. The most disturbed families are apt to be the least successful referrals and the most in need of task-oriented handling within a concrete, practical life situation. The psychosocial worker may refer such families on the grounds that they need the more "high powered" or "uncovering" kind of treatment offered by the formal treatment agency. In metropolitan areas, where intellectual comprehension of psychoanalytic theories tends to facilitate parental compliance, the family may actually accept such a referral, yet real leverage in the situation has not been achieved if formal treatment was not actually the useful next step. In lower-class families, the incongruity of treatment is the most clearcut and marked because it is not obscured by intellectual compliance.

(2) The guidance worker may think of referral as an alternative to the guidance worker's own efforts to diagnose and troubleshoot the road-

---

* This is an epidemiological statement. In a guidance load of 300 children, around ten will be referred to treatment as the useful next step. For such children, treatment may be not only helpful but life-saving. Treatment agencies which broaden their scope and make services as prompt and flexible as possible may increase this percentage somewhat.

blocks in the educational interaction for a child. (We mention guidance workers specifically but this also holds true for all other agency workers outside of formal treatment agencies.) If a child has been successfully referred, the guidance worker may feel he can wash his hands of him. Nothing could be further from the truth. The guidance worker still has the responsibility for helping the child to cope with the school situation in an adaptive or integrative way. (Clinics sometimes fall into a similar trap when they tell guidance workers that their child patient should be handled by the schools "just like anyone else," overlooking the leverage which could be contributed by skillful guidance and school handling.) Guidance work consists of implementing adaptive functions in an actual life situation: the school. Treatment with an uncovering goal seeks to overcome intrapsychic roadblocks which keep the patient from adaptive collaboration with others in his particular life task. At the same time that a treatment agency is trying to help a boy with his oedipal problems with his over-protective mother, the guidance worker and school are trying to place the boy, perhaps, with a gentle man teacher, to find a big brother for him, and in any suitable way to provide step-wise experiences which will promote the growth of independence, learning and better relationships with peers. The two approaches are not competitive or alternative but mutually reinforcing.

(3) Guidance workers sometimes seek to force motivation by measures which, within this context, are punitive, such as a shortened school day or exclusion from school until the family has been "successfully" in treatment. This use of such measures (which may sometimes be helpful for other reasons), is self-defeating. Families are not "motivated" by such means; they are made more resistive to treatment and now tend to regard the school as a punitive agent so that they are less accessible to task-oriented guidance help. Educators also will be less accessible to collaborative efforts for educational planning because they will tend to typecast the child as a reject or one who should not be in public school. The child is often set on the road to permanent exclusion from school.

(4) A fourth point, which influences both referral to formal treatment and collaboration with other agencies is the assumption that the patient or client flows in a frictionless way from agency to agency, wherever directed, until the one is found which meets his needs. The concept of the free flow of the patient to the agency best organized (from the community viewpoint) to meet his needs ignores the personal

transaction, transferences and counter-transferences, resentments about being transferred, fragmentation of personality and similar problems which confront the patient who seeks to explore the community resources most useful to him.

(5) Worker and agency idiosyncracies and policies, differing theoretical biases and differences of professional judgment make it profoundly important that the guidance worker not set overly explicit goals for the patient he is referring. The behavioral sciences are still at a stage of development in which highly competent professionals may assess the useful next step for a patient quite differently. The hands of a receiving agency may be tied if a patient has been referred unquestionably for psychonalysis, for instance, when the receiving agency may believe that a different goal, such as improved identification would be more helpful. At our present stage of professional development, referral should be in terms of "Why don't you talk over the situation with Mr. So and So and see what might be a useful way to proceed?"

Having dealt with misconceptions and problems in the process of referral to formal treatment, let us turn to collaboration between the guidance worker and the schools or with the agency worker where formal treatment is not the sole, explicit concern. These collaborative efforts comprise the bulk of the guidance worker's endeavors beyond his work with the child, family, teacher and principal. Schools and agencies are involved with children in task-oriented interactions not related to formal treatment. The child is on probation, he wants to learn to play ball, he has difficulty reading, he has been placed in a foster home, he is required by law to attend school, he went to a teen-age medical clinic because of his acne. These interactions are valuable for the guidance worker in explicitly and/or indirectly helping to further the psychosocial development of children.

The guidance worker's first consideration is with his collaborators in the schools. Here, the people who might be involved in psychosocial collaboration with the guidance worker all have their own core responsibilities which are not guidance work. The teacher must teach, the principal must administer his school, the nurse must be responsible for health problems and the secretary must perform her secretarial functions. These core professional identities should not be blurred by an effort to define these people as "junior guidance workers." Once this difference in role is acknowledged, however, the stage is set for recognizing the important part such people can play in furthering the psychosocial development of students. The school nurse is an uncommonly good example to illustrate the collaboration of the guidance worker with ancillary personnel in the schools. Children's emotional stress is often expressed in the form of physiological symptoms and complaints. The nurse, therefore, among her recurrently complaining or frequently absent children, is apt to see a number whose problems are primarily emotional, where no physical medical remedy will suffice. Teachers, meanwhile, will be putting pressure on the nurse to do something to stop the child's complaint of headaches or the child's frequent absences for "upset stomach" or whatever, since these interfere with the child's progress in school. The nurse usually takes the first commonsense steps, such as talking the situation over with the child and his parents. Once these steps have failed, however, the nurse can either fall back on rigid structuring of her medical role, saying that the family is uncooperative in terms of medical planning, or can broaden her concept of her role to include herself as a member of the general psychosocial trouble-shooting team. The guidance worker will try to support and educate the nurse in this latter role. If the nurse can adopt this role, she becomes an ideal person to find a means of access into the family's emotional problems and to help the guidance worker plan the useful next steps.

The school nurse, if she accepts a place on the psychosocial trouble-shooting team, can also be an important friend and supporter of the troubled, lonesome children who find their way to her office with various minor complaints. At times, it is useful for the nurse and the guidance worker to plan a more systematic relationship between such a child and the nurse by making the child a nurse's helper on a regular or intermittent (at times of stress) basis.

Sometimes, often at the junior high school level, physical symptom formation is a half-way stage from delinquent acting out to more internalized neurotic symptoms. The school nurse who understands this transitional stage will be able to tolerate it and to support the student, for instance by making him an aide, instead of dismissing his complaints as imaginary, considering him an impostor, or declaring that such a supportive role falls outside the proper function of a school nurse.

The guidance worker can extend this way of working with the school nurse endlessly to other educational personnel. If his own core role is respected, any school person can become a creative collaborator in the psychosocial process with children.

There are also school programs which can be set up to advance the needs of children. These vary from time to time and from school to school. The following examples illustrate the range of projects which can be set up in any task-oriented school district.

In a school which had some middle-class children with severe reading retardation, the guidance worker, curriculum supervisor and a worker from adult education collaborated. The guidance worker worked with the children in groups to correct low self-esteem, to build morale and to provide pre-reading experiences. The curriculum supervisor worked with the classroom teachers on special instructional aids, methods and materials; the worker from adult education worked with the parents in groups. The parents also saw this worker individually at least twice during the course of the project. The school released the guidance worker from other duties in order to have her participate in this project. The children, in general, benefitted.

A junior high school established an adjustment class in which academically defeated students could be actively helped to regain self-esteem and to attain some academic skills in an atmosphere where there were realistic standards and limits both in terms of the students' abilities and in terms of the school's ability to integrate them. With an unusually gifted teacher, several students who, otherwise, would have faced exemption, were able to remain in school and to begin to learn. One of the most rebellious and refractory nonlearners twice requested his guidance worker to get him into summer school so that he could improve his reading. Similar adjustment classes, in which academically retarded and apathetic or rebellious students are scheduled for at least several periods a day with the same teacher, have been successful in several junior high schools.

Teacher sponsorship represents another way in which the guidance worker can enlist the help of school people in the psychosocial task. A teacher sponsor is a person chosen, with his concurrence, by the guidance worker and vice-principal to be the special friend and trouble-shooter for a child in difficulties. He may do various things for and with the student, both academic and personal. However, he has two core tasks: (1) When "his" student is in disciplinary or academic difficulty at school, he may ask to see his sponsor instead of his regular counselor or the vice principal, since the sponsor may know him and his problems better than they. This choice has administrative support. (2) More importantly, the teacher sponsor undertakes to defend the reputation of the student and to correct the distortions which, especially at the secondary school level, can quickly snowball into a false but stubbornly believed image. This does not mean that the sponsor tries to sell a false positive reputation but merely that he corrects distortions, gets things into perspective and speaks from the side of the student when lunchroom or smokingroom gossip begins to get out of hand.

Collaboration between guidance workers and agency workers is similar to the collaboration with people within the schools. Once the guidance worker and the agency worker recognize each other's core role and task-oriented responsibilities, collaborative efforts can begin. We will give examples of collaboration with a probation officer and with foster home placement workers.

In the junior high school adjustment class mentioned above, many of the students were on probation. The guidance worker-probation officer relationship was such that they could collaborate closely with a minimum of red-tape or formal conferences. The probation officer's authority often made it possible to hold a student in school during periods of personal crisis or to get him back very promptly if he stayed away (before the student would lose face as a more chronic absentee). At other times, the potential of the adjustment class for motivating students and helping them academically provided leverage for the probation officer's counseling.

An added advantage to the collaboration was that, if exemption of a student became necessary, the reasons for it were clear to both workers and a continuing plan could be worked out for combating and counteracting further deterioration in the multi-problem situation which underlay the student's failures both at school and in the community.

It seems that collaboration between guidance departments and probation officers could be further extended in many communities by a mutual systematic approach to learning, especially reading, problems. It is well known that many predelinquent and delinquent adolescents suffer from severe reading problems. Counseling, perhaps group counseling around problems of evil self-image, lowered self-esteem and antagonistic attitudes might be conducted under the aegis of the probation department, while school offered remedial academic work and the two approaches were integrated.

Another group of children who face predictable hazards in the school setting are children in foster homes. Many such children suffer from lowered self-esteem and a sense of rootlessness because of their previous life experiences. The foster home placement in itself creates hazards not usually encountered by a child in his own home. Diffusion of authority may occur because both foster home parents and foster home worker have contact with the school. Triangles may develop; foster parents and teacher against agency worker or agency worker and teacher against foster home parent. If the child becomes involved in a school problem (minor stealing of lunches and academic passivity are common examples), there is a very real hazard that the problem may be "handled" by moving the child to yet another foster home rather than dealing with it and him in a task-oriented way. This may occur because the foster parents often find school failure and criticism from school people harder to bear than would the child's own parents while the sanctions against moving the child out of their home are much less.

A guidance worker who is alerted to an impending foster home placement and to the predictable hazards, can help to avoid them or to handle them constructively. The school can be kept from stereotyping the foster home child while being prepared for the fact that he is probably under stress and may have some difficulties. The guidance worker can suggest placement of the child with a particularly good teacher, can support the teacher and the child through the adjustment period and can serve as coordinator among school, foster home parent and agency worker.

Let us restate an important point. We have said that the guidance worker respects the core identity and job of other specialists and does not try to make them "junior guidance workers." He works in different ways in various schools and in liaison with various agencies depending on the tasks, issues, agencies, personalities and situations involved. The guidance worker does not try to freeze his work into pre-set structure, for instance by saying that all principals should be used as identification figures. He says, rather, that Principal A might function that way with Boy B if B could be made an unofficial Man Friday. However, he recognizes that, with Principal X and Boy Y, such a plan probably would not work and might backfire. One school secretary or school nurse might go out of her way to be friendly with shy girls; another might find this quite beyond her psychosocial skills or outside the scope of her job as she sees it.

Projects and ways of collaborating could be proliferated endlessly.

The pitfall involved is that of overly generalized structural planning, such as "All nurses will now do such and such," "teacher sponsors will be used in all junior high schools," or "the above model should serve as a model for all remedial reading projects." This approach would freeze collaboration into nonpersonalized, incongruous models which would be inapplicable in many situations. The presence of a gifted teacher in a school may enable the principal and guidance worker to plan that certain disturbed junior high school students should spend several periods a day with him. This classroom may end if the teacher leaves. The inexperienced or non task-oriented guidance worker may be dismayed by such a collapse of collaborative efforts. However, guidance collaboration depends on the styles, temperaments, skills and interests of all collaborating personnel and on the structure of the school or agency involved. It depends on timing. It depends on the readiness of a school and on how well the guidance worker is integrated into school function. It depends on the problems of the given children and on the particular issues involved. Creative collaboration focusses on just these concrete data and does not permit itself to be codified into rule books or preset plans. Changes in points of access and methods of functioning are recognized as part of the living organism of the school and community.

Collaborative program planning and development between agencies seems a useful next step in tackling the multitude of needs we meet in our public school population. Too many agency efforts still take place in isolation from each other. At times, subtle or overt competition exists between agencies for the tax dollar or the United Fund dollar. The division of labor between public and private agencies is seldom viewed as a whole and the separate programs are seldom so organized as to be mutually reinforcing for the benefit of their clientele.

Under the present conditions of crisis in education and in all programs for youth, a new spirit of cooperative planning seems to be in the offing and deserves our most earnest attention. Only through such renewed efforts can the promise of the Community Mental Health movement and of the Community Action Programs of the Office of Economic Development be realized via a new technology aimed at developing collaborative programs. Institutions within the community—schools, medical facilities, housing departments, vocational and employment services need to look at their interdependency and need to develop a joint task-orientation which strengthens children and their families in their most basic functions—

maintaining an adequate home; obtaining a relevant education; securing a meaningful job; utilizing appropriate health services, etc. When these tasks are viewed as interlocking, then merely offering a service is no longer enough. It becomes imperative to make such services available where people are—at home; at school; at work; at play rather than to expect people to go in search of services they may not know exist nor know how to relate to their needs. Such interagency task-forces do not have to be a dream for the future. Examples begin to be available and the following one, while exciting in its organic growth and potential, is hopefully not unique.

This example is the "Teenage Mother Program" developed by the San Francisco Unified School District from a model pioneered by the Oakland School District in collaboration with the Oakland Y.W.C.A.[4]

The purpose of the program is to allow pregnant school-age girls to continue their education, thus maintaining them within the mainstream of life for their age group. It goes without saying that school-age pregnant girls represent a population at risk and that the community has a stake not only in their continued education but also in their preparation for parenthood, their plans for their economic future and that of their babies-to-be, their relations to their families and to the putative father and his family, etc., in short, their functioning as an on-going member of society, rather than their becoming another casualty in the struggle for an adequate life.

None of the above is of course new. What needs attention, beyond recognizing the problem, is the technology for mobilizing society's resources in such a way as to cumulatively provide the structure within which the pregnant school-age girl can resolve her crisis constructively rather than destructively. The provision of continued schooling is an essential first step. By itself, it is not likely to be enough. It becomes necessary to involve those agencies whose services are going to be needed, such as health facilities and welfare services, at a point where their early availability can be most meaningful to the girl. A common problem of teenage pregnancies has been inadequate and delayed pre-natal care, resulting in a high rate of difficult births with resultant damage to the baby and long-term problems associated with the baby's birth defects. It therefore becomes useful to the medical profession to gain access to the teen-age pregnant girl as early as possible. Likewise, a teen-age pregnant girl is often ill prepared to become financially and emotionally independent. She needs help in the development of vocational and parental skills. The sooner counseling in this direction is started, the less likely that the girl will settle for a life of dependency. Again, self-interest dictates early, constructive and sustained intervention by a welfare worker. Health and welfare thus have a great interest in reaching the pregnant girl early. A school setting is a logical point of access. What is implicit in all the above is that self-interest—not just the often maligned humanitarian interest—of health and welfare agencies is involved in problem-solving the situation of the school-age pregnant girl. This self-interest seems to be served most effectively and organically, if the structure of the pregnant girl's school experience includes health and welfare counseling as a routine part of her education. This presupposes close collaborative planning, at each school site, for a comprehensive approach to each girl in the program. Issues such as "how do I take care of my baby?" and "how do I support myself and my baby?" are not peripheral to the girl's continued education, they are the most relevant issues around which her education can proceed. It goes without saying that this implies a high degree of trust, communication and motivation in all those, whatever their professional home base, collaborating in providing services to the teen-age pregnant girl. It takes skillful coordination by people able to reconcile the often divergent viewpoints and priorities of the teacher, the doctor, the welfare worker, and others and to order these priorities flexibly to meet the needs of each girl. Just putting services next to each other does not constitute such an integration and leaves much to be desired.

The following services are integrated to bring needed assistance to the five hundred girls who, on the average, become pregnant while attending the San Francisco schools each year. A mere listing does not convey how these services operate in a mutually complementary fashion. As stated above, these agencies have become involved because they saw their own self-interest in reaching these girls earlier and more consistently and they find that the girls are using their services more intelligently.

Agencies which have been involved for the year 1966-67 were as follows:

1. Youth Guidance Center and California Youth Authority, along with school and Welfare department staffs, assisted in the identification and supervision of possible applicants.

2. Mt. Zion, Children's, San Francisco General and other hospitals

provided medical services to girls, as well as housing for two of the educational centers.

3. San Francisco Department of Social Services provided one female and one male social worker to work with the girls, their mothers, siblings and putative fathers if the families were on AFDC. Cases were transferred to these two workers for a minimum two-year period to assure continuity. Emphasis was placed on planning for the future of expectant mother, expected baby, putative father and their respective families.

4. San Francisco Department of Public Health, U.C. Medical School, and Planned Parenthood provided nurses to give group instruction in prenatal and post-natal care.

5. San Francisco Recreation Department and YWCA provided space in which three educational centers operate, telephone costs and desk space for the director.

6. California Congress, Parents and Teachers, Second District, provided money to pay for nutritional snacks supplied to girls at centers, mid-mornings.

7. Langley Porter Neuropsychiatric Institute provided a psychiatric consultant to assist staff in making professionally sound decisions regarding girls.

8. San Francisco State College and University of California School of Social Welfare provided graduate students in counselling and social welfare to participate in various parts of the program as part of their training in their respective professions.

9. Dy-Dee Wash and interested private individuals provided 800 diapers and 500 pounds of baby clothes plus sums of money for special needs of individual girls.

10. San Francisco Unified School District provided salary of social-work director, clerical service and incidental office expenses. State funds for the education of the physically handicapped paid the teachers' salaries.

11. Economic Opportunity Council provided one part-time recreation worker for the educational center located in a recreation facility.

Within the confines of public education, there are many groups of students whose needs can only be met through integrated services from the community. Co-existence of health and welfare agencies with the public schools is no longer an effective way to provide services. Collaborative, mutually supportive planning of services and availability of services where children's needs are most obvious—in their homes and their schools—depends on our developing a technology for mutual problem solving. Guidance workers and other school personnel who know at first hand where the students' needs are, may be in a strategic position to help initiate, coordinate and monitor such pioneering efforts.

NOTES
(Chapter VI)

1. Luther E. Woodward, *Changing Roles of Psychiatric Social Workers in Outpatient Clinics*, mimeographed material presented at the Psychiatric Social Work Section of the National Conference of Social Welfare, Atlantic City, June, 1960.
2. Mary A. Sarvis, Sally Dewees and Ruth F. Johnson, "A Concept of Ego-oriented Psychotherapy," *Psychiatry*, 22:3, August 1959.
3. Donald M. Coleman and Israel Zwerling, "The Psychiatric Emergency Clinic: A Flexible Way of Meeting Community Mental Health Needs," *The Amer. J. of Psychiat.*, Vol. 115, No. 11, May 1959.
4. Mimeographed report, "Teenage mother program" available from Division of Pupil Services, San Francisco Unified School District.

ADDITIONAL READINGS
(Chapter VI)

Alderson, John J. "The Relationship of School Social Work to Child Welfare Services," *Child Welfare*, Vol. 44, No. 9.
Anderson, M. F., and N. Gibson. "Community Approach to the High School Dropout," *Education*, Vol. 87, March 1967, pp. 431-433.
Brown, Saul L. "Coordinating Professional Efforts for Children with School Problems," *Children*, Vol. 15, No. 6, November-December 1968, pp. 214-218.
Gitterman, Alex. *The Neighborhood Center, Social Work Service and the Public School*. New York: United Neighborhood Houses, 1968.
Nebo, John C. "The School Social Worker as Community Organizer," *Social Work*, Vol. 8; No. 1, January, 1963, 99-105.
Woodward, Luther E., "Changing Roles of Psychiatric Social Workers in Out-patient Clinics," presented at the Psychiatric Social Work Section Meeting, National Conference of Social Welfare, Atlantic City, June, 1960.

CHAPTER VII

The Guidance Worker in the Ghetto School

When this book was first conceived, poor children and their education had received little public attention. Guidance workers universally felt overwhelmed by the problem of making even a small dent on the needs of such children and by the numbers of children involved. Case material and the chapters on groups illustrate some guidance efforts to find techniques for more effective intervention. In the meantime, dating from Riessman's, *The Education of the Culturally Deprived Child,*[1] and within the national climate of the civil rights movement, a great deal of attention has been focused in this direction. We welcome these major efforts but view them only as beginning steps. The dangers of premature generalizations and the development of fads, as a substitute for the massive amount of leg work needed, are obvious. Political implications are complex. We will try to limit ourselves to presenting a psychosocial point of view which corresponds to our experience with these children and families, as well as with the school staffs who teach them.

There are some clues about how such work should proceed in terms of the dynamic factors involved. It is known that such work will not be particularly effective unless the core psychodynamic problem of the deprived and persecuted child is first coped with. This core psychodynamic problem comprises his evil self-image, a caricature of the stereotype imposed on him by the culture,[2] and his consequent tendency to be mistrustful, suspicious or paranoid toward the persecuting culture, and its representative, the teacher. Both these dynamic issues, of course, may be warded off by various defensive maneuvers, such as apathy, rebelliousness, lack of achievement, alienation, and amputation of personal ability. Evil self-image is aggravated, for lower-class boys—particularly those of Negro families—by the absence of stable, valued male identification. Most lower-class boys respond to this devaluation of male self-esteem by denial in the form of "hypermasculine" defenses, such as fighting, swaggering, truculence, etc. Any approach to children from this background must, therefore, include efforts to eradicate evil self-image, reverse paranoid attitudes and provide new identifications. The black power movement may speed up this process.

A tremendous amount of recently published material addresses itself to the key problem of how to better educate the ghetto child. The term "ghetto" itself implies separateness and social isolation. It has recently acquired a pejorative meaning which has also attached itself to the ghetto school, its teachers and its students. They, in turn, tend to believe that ghetto schools *are* inferior. This seems to lower the teacher's own expectations of their ability to teach, and their students' ability to learn. Thus, a vicious cycle is set up. Yet one is impressed with the *variation* of motivation and achievement from classroom to classroom in the *same* ghetto school depending on the hopefulness and effectiveness of the teacher to "get through" to his students and to get them involved in their own education. Just as Riesmann has pointed out, this seems less the result of a given technique than a function of the teacher's determination. One common denominator, though, seems to be emerging among those teachers who are determined to succeed, and that is a movement toward much greater individualization of their students.

This individualization can take many forms.

1. Changes in the classroom involving more individualized assignments, workbooks, creative projects, planning and evaluation. The goal is to get each child involved in *his own* education, to gain satisfaction from his own successes, to praise achievement honestly, to take set-backs for granted, in short to help the child develop realistic self-esteem supported by tangible evidences of successful problem-solving on his part. This also involves training in the prideful care of individual workbooks and materials, a training impossible to give when such workbooks are withheld from ghetto children because "they would not know how to care for them." Thus, teachers so committed change the climate in their classrooms to one of positive expectations and implement these expectations through the use (and the training in the use of) individualized and appropriate teaching materials and classroom procedures.

An interesting systematic approach to helping ghetto children become "learners" has been developed by Kellam and Schiff[3] in the Woodlawn area of Chicago. After a great deal of preliminary work, especially to secure the involvement of the community via an advisory board of the whole spectrum of community members, Kellam and Schiff developed a program in every first grade of six target schools. Led by teachers supported by mental health personnel, the program consisted of weekly classroom discussions with all the students of that first grade. The goal was to help them and their teachers become aware of roadblocks to learning. Two trends emerged in these discussions: "The children . . . often invoked their parents as the reason for their inability to do better. They cannot be successful, say the first graders, because mother is mixed up, or there was a family quarrel, or for some reason trouble in the family did not permit them to do their work or to come to school. Another prominent theme encountered in the Classroom Meetings is that of the 'Peter Pan' phenomenon. The children often take the position that the reason that they are not doing their job in first grade is because they are 'too young'."

Whether or not one agrees that these children are in an "identity crisis related to their role transition," as Kellam and Schiff believe, the message is clear that teachers, children and parents all need to develop a joint technology in making learners out of ghetto children. Such is also the conclusion of Mario D. Fantini in his article on "Alternatives for Urban School Reform,"[4] which underscores the need for system-wide restructuring of the educational experience in the core city and the rearranging of collaborative relationships between professionals and parents on behalf of the education of children.

2. Because both teachers and students in ghetto schools have experienced (or are fighting against the experience of) failure, they need allies. These allies may be extra teachers assigned to share the task, as in some Elementary-Secondary Education Act funded programs; they may be paid parent aides assigned to help with non-academic tasks in the classroom; they may be volunteers from the community; they may be upper-grade students eager to help younger children and thus gain status for themselves, etc. The common task for all these "helpers" is to assist with the individualized educational program set up by the classroom teacher. The children, who previously were confirmed in their negative self-image, need massive positive reinforcement from many sources *before* one can expect them to believe their own experienced success. The negative self-image is so deeply entrenched that, even after a highly successful experience in a highly motivated classroom, such children will eventually—even quickly—

backslide if they suspect that their next teacher does not view them as capable of adequate learning.

3. Because there is this tendency to backslide whenever the teacher experiences a sense of defeat or expects little of his students, a massive program of in-service support for teachers seems essential. In the past, such efforts have largely been focused on changing teacher attitudes via human relations speakers, sensitivity-training sessions and the like. While this approach has no doubt reached some teachers and made them conscious of their perhaps unwittingly negative expectations of their students, it has not replaced a failing model of education with a more positive model. It has seemed to result in a moralizing approach rather than a problem-solving approach. Along with self-awareness, it has sometimes increased guilt and a feeling of helplessness. We would like to suggest a change in format for in-service training from a focus merely on changing attitudes to a focus on changed practices, changed educational materials, changed classroom procedures, changed discipline rules, all with the goal of a more relevant education for ghetto school youngsters and their teachers. Our experience as guidance workers leads us to believe that, regardless of teacher values, teachers want to be successful and derive pleasure from achievement, their own and their students'. More successful teaching and learning will result in more humane values for education, rather than the other way around.

4. More successful teaching and learning is also the most effective bridge between school and community. One reason most middle-class parents are not afraid to come to school and participate in PTA's etc., is because they see, by and large, that their children are being successfully taught. The teacher's efforts are thus echoed positively in the child's home. The reverse is true in the ghetto. Classroom failure breeds distrust in the home and interferes with even minimal communication. Ghetto parents need to see tangible results in order to believe that their children are being educated. They want their children to know their ABC's, their multiplication tables, their spelling words. Once trust is established via tangible results, ghetto parents can become eager participants in school affairs. If such results are not forthcoming, ghetto parents seem more and more determined to take over the running of their neighborhood schools.

5. Time and change: Increasingly, we hear that we are running out of time. We also hear that financial support is lacking to bring about the needed major revamping of our educational establishment. The sense of

futility which has so long pervaded the ghetto appears to be spreading to the community at large while the ghetto is preparing to fight its own battles. The problem has become one of an intensive search, adequately financed, for more meaningful solutions to the problems of education in the core city.

We have sketched in a very general way how guidance workers in the ghetto school see its problems and the alternatives for change. What role can guidance workers play, what specific skills can they bring to bear?

First of all, guidance workers are constantly engaged in helping people change. They are less afraid of change than the general population because they have worked with orderly change processes in the past. They are therefore in a good position to support those administrators, teachers, parents and students in a given school who are looking for better solutions to educational problems. Guidance workers are highly sensitized to ambivalences, rivalries, projections, distortions and free-floating anxieties that inevitably accompany the process of change. They know the hard work involved and distrust "flights into health," the sudden over-optimism which conceals the fear of getting truly involved.

Not being educators themselves, they should not presume to advance "solutions," but should clearly encourage everyone in the problem-solving process so that genuine, relevant solutions *can* emerge out of joint efforts. Guidance workers are under great pressure to become aligned with those who have given up hope that education can change through the efforts of educators themselves. They are being attacked for being members of the educational establishment. It is our belief that forces exist *within* education as surely as they exist in the community, forces that are committed to making education more relevant to all those involved in it. Just as guidance workers are bridge people and sometimes anchor men in resolving the difficulties in the interaction between individual students and their teachers, and their parents, so perhaps guidance workers can use their relevant skills in this larger arena.

They can share the emotional load with teachers who are willing to try new ways. They can help students and parents communicate their grievances to those interested in listening. They can assist teachers with home visiting and interviewing skills, thus encouraging the schools to learn how to communicate with their community. They can teach skills in matching school helpers most suitably, for instance a student "big brother" to a student "little brother," a community volunteer to the teacher she is to assist. They can act as resource people during staff discussions, using their "third ear" to discover underlying issues that might interfere with true communication. They can demonstrate the usefulness of extending their own effectiveness—without being overprotective of their roles as specialists—by working closely with "new career" people who are assisting in the classroom and as home-school liaison workers. They can modify supervision techniques in the training of such "new career" staff who often resist more traditional forms of staff development but may feel comfortable when worked with in small groups of their peers.

They can be available for emotional first aid when a teacher suddenly feels "he has had it." Last, but not least, they need to continue doing "guidance work" for it would be ironical to write off all problems of individual children in ghetto schools as being the result of inadequate education, thus denying them the individual psychological trouble-shooting available to their more affluent contemporaries in more middle-class schools.

More than anywhere else, the guidance worker in a ghetto school needs to be positive, flexible, able to tune in on many levels of anxiety. By his own attitude, he needs to convey realistic hope and a determination to "stick it out." Because of the high level of anxiety on all sides, and because of the omnipresent danger of distortion and distrust, it would seem important that the guidance worker be ever accessible and locally available in ghetto schools, since negative reactions tend to snowball very rapidly. If a guidance worker is assigned to a ghetto school full time, many "human relations" aspects of the school operation may well be delegated to him as these duties have become too complex and numerous to be "tacked on" to the multitude of more conventional responsibilities carried out by teachers and especially administrators.

Guidance work in a ghetto school may not suit the personality and stamina of each person trained for the guidance task. It behooves the guidance worker to be completely honest with himself before he accepts such a taxing assignment. If he does, he will need the support of his peers as well as that of the mental health consultant. Ready availability of support to prevent despair, promote problem solving, and face complexities never quite confronted before is an essential back-up service to guidance workers in ghetto schools.

NOTES
(Chapter VII)

1. Frank Riessman, *The Education of the Culturally Deprived Child* (New York: Harper, 1962).
2. Erik Erikson, "Ego Identity and Historical Change," *The Psychoanalytic Study of the Child*, Vol. II, (New York: International Universities Press, 1946), pp. 359-396.
3. Sheppard G. Kellam and Sheldon K. Schiff, "Adaptation and Mental Illness in the First Grade Classrooms of an Urban Community," *Psychiatric Research Report 21*, American Psychiatric Association, April, 1967.
4. Mario D. Fantini, "Alternatives for Urban School Reform," *The Harvard Educational Review*, Vol. 38, No. 1, Winter, 1968.

ADDITIONAL READINGS
(Chapter VII)

Coleman, James S., *et al. Equality of Educational Opportunity.* Washington, D.C.: U. S. Government Printing Office, 1966.

Conant, James B. *Slums and Suburbs.* New York: McGraw Hill, 1961.

Deshler, Betty. "The School-Community Agent in the Detroit Public Schools." Great Cities Project, Detroit Public Schools, February 1965 (mimeo.).

Erikson, Erik. "Ego Identity and Historical Change," *The Psychoanalytic Study of the Child*, Vol. II. New York: International Universities Press, 1946, pp. 359-396.

Fantini, Mario D. "Alternatives for Urban School Reform," *The Harvard Educational Review*, Vol. 38, No. 1, Winter 1968.

Fantl, Berta, "Integrating Social and Psychological Theories in Social Work Practice," *Smith College Studies in Social Work*, Jerome Cohen, ed. Vol. XXXVI, No. 3. Northampton: Smith College School for Social Work, June 1964.

Fishman, Jacob R., *et al. Training for New Careers.* Washington, D.C.: Howard University, 1965.

Grier, William H. and Price M. Cobbs. *Black Rage.* New York: Basic Books, Inc., 1968.

Hellmuth, J., ed. *The Disadvantaged Child*, Vols. I and II. Seattle: Special Child Publications, 1967, 1968.

Kellam, Sheppard G., and Sheldon K. Schiff. "Adaptation and Mental Illness in the First Grade Classrooms of an Urban Community," *Psychiatric Research Report 21*, American Psychiatric Association, April 1967.

Kellam, Sheppard G., and Sheldon K. Schiff. The Woodlawn First Grade Program. I. Concept of Mental Health; Periodic Measurement and Study; Evaluation of a Community-Wide Prevention and Early Treatment Program. (In preparation.)

Pearl, Arthur and Frank Riessman. *New Careers for the Poor.* New York: Free Press, 1965.

Pearl, Arthur and Frank Riessman, eds. *Mental Health of the Poor.* Glencoe: The Free Press, 1964.

Riessman, Frank. *The Education of the Culturally Deprived Child.* New York: Harper, 1962.

Roberts, Joan I., ed. *School Children in the Urban Slum.* New York: The Free Press, 1967.

Schiff, S. K. and S. G. Kellam: The Woodlawn First Grade Mental Health Program. II. Rationale, Implementation and Evolution of a Community-Wide Program of Prevention and Early Treatment in First Grade. (In Preparation.)

CHAPTER VIII

Typical Guidance Interventions

INTRODUCTION

This chapter and the six which follow deal with case material which ranges from typical guidance interventions, through work with severely disturbed children and work with groups, to the complications in working with students at the secondary level. Seven collaborators from different backgrounds (psychiatric social work, psychology, attendance work) contributed the cases, in addition to the two authors. They are: Helen E. Ausenbaum, M.S.W.; Emerson F. Blodgett, Ed.D.; Lorraine G. Corden, M.S.W.; Mary Addams Hulbert, Ph.B.; Leslie H. Mitchell, Ph.D. in Child Development; Elizabeth D. Morrison, M.S.W. and Frances D. Skiles, B.A. These workers represent a range in backgrounds and levels of training commonly found in guidance departments. With the exception of Mrs. Frances Skiles, they all worked under the title of Guidance Consultant. Mrs. Skiles worked as a Supervisor of Child Welfare and Attendance. We have tried to preserve individual variations in style, both in writing and in ways of working, since we feel that it is very important to emphasize that workers must operate in terms of their own temperaments, backgrounds and flairs, rather than trying to overstandardize their approaches.

The cases range from those in which a minimum of information was available to those in which a good deal of psychodynamic understanding was acquired in the course of long-term contact with the child and family. This range is deliberate. The cases in which only superficial data are available are included to emphasize the fact that this is the guidance worker's *modus operandi:* he does not wait for a detailed psychosocial work-up but intervenes at many levels, usually as promptly as possible in terms of a point of access into a situation. Once this point of access is achieved, the guidance worker can progressively gain further understanding of psychodynamics and cultural factors so that his interventions become more and more informed and more nearly precise, if the case in question requires this kind of long-term intervention and help.

The cases reported comprise about sixty per cent Caucasian and forty per cent non-Caucasian and represent the whole socio-economic range. We think that this is a reasonably accurate sample of the usual guidance load in northern metropolitan areas, (prior to the advent of ESEA funded services) although if it were possible to meet the needs of relationship-hungry, culturally deprived children through guidance services alone (which, we believe, it is not), the percentage of these children would naturally increase.

TYPICAL GUIDANCE INTERVENTIONS

Duncan

Duncan, a Negro boy, was referred in the third grade because he "seems to live in a world of fantasy, yet seems intelligent. He is unable to work independently. Has a short attention span. Has no friends, seldom participates in classroom or playground." An early Stanford Binet intelligence test gave Duncan a minimal score of 88 and indicated that he responded extremely well to praise, perking up emotionally and increasing his attention span.

He was seen fairly frequently in the spring semester after referral. He had unusually attractive features but was sleepy-eyed and walked as if in a trance as we went from the office to the room where I saw him. Even on warm days he wore his jacket buttoned close (as has been true of so many "closed-in" children). He tried to answer all questions but did so mechanically and with as brief a response as possible. This did not seem at all a hostile child but rather one who was trying to answer from a long way off. He repeatedly drew pictures of a lone airplane in an expanse of blue sky—always very carefully, first with pencil, then filled in with crayon. Conversation was extremely difficult for him; he responded to comments in almost a whisper and a stutter, with unusually flat affect. His left hand lay lifelessly in his lap as he drew; he seemed uncertain about what to do with the eraser crumbs until I brushed them off for him. Eventually, he talked enough so that I could discover that he could read almost all of the captions under bulletin board exhibits. He said he wanted to be a jet pilot. I asked where he would go. "To New York, Chicago,

Miami." Throughout this period, I saw the teacher from time to time. There was practically no change in Duncan's classroom behavior, though both the teacher and I believed we had seen a flicker of a smile at times and a slightly lessened "sleep-walking" appearance.

I did not manage to get a home call made until the end of the term. It had been known at school that Duncan lived with his grandmother, who had a son about a year younger than Duncan. He also had a brother and a sister who lived with his own mother, fairly nearby. My interview with the grandmother was not productive, aside from learning that she seemed to take Duncan as a sort of joke. She responded to my concern rather flippantly. An older girl (I think the "big cousin" referred to by Duncan as one he liked and who attended junior college) seemed more genuinely interested. The grandmother said that Duncan had been with her since birth. He had not been a quiet baby but by the age of two or three lacked energy and was found to be so anemic that he required a blood transfusion. Recently, he had been given "a tonic" and seemed to have more energy but he still dreamed around and didn't talk much. Duncan's mother was always very quiet, does perfect work but is slow. She made A and B grades in high school and works currently as a clerk-typist. The brother and sister go to a nearby school and Duncan sees them often, especially on weekends. The mother expects a new baby soon. (Duncan had seemed to me to be confused about his family relationships but communication was so minimal it was difficult to know.) Duncan's father sees him on rare occasions and bought him a bicycle last Christmas. "He is a drinker and a user of dope." Duncan calls his grandfather "Daddy." The grandfather, "a very nice churchman, is fond of Duncan." Duncan and his seven-year-old uncle fight a great deal.

The grandmother and three teenage girls, whose relationship was not clear, were all very attractive of feature. There seemed to be a warm relationship among them, but I got the impression that Duncan was relatively isolated in the family. When I tried to talk about some of the things which would help Duncan over the summer, the grandmother said she and her husband were "getting on" (in years) and couldn't do much for him; however, the oldest girl did appear interested.

When school opened in the fall, Duncan was, if anything, more withdrawn than in the previous year (mother's new baby?). I saw him several times in preparation for an attempt to give him the Children's Apperception Test. I showed him the pictures and asked if he would make up stories. He was reluctant. I did not press him but had them on the table near him the next time I saw him, and got busy with something else for a time. He listlessly picked them up. I don't recall whether it was the next time that he said he was willing to tell a story but, when he did try, it was a painful experience for me. He sat nervously fingering the picture for about five minutes, during which I said little, except to reassure him that it took time for imaginations to work and that I would be quiet and let him get started. I really thought he was not going to be able to. Finally, he took several great, deep breaths, as if he were going to plunge into cold water, and started, in a barely audible voice. However, the story unfolded rather smoothly with relatively little hesitation. I was greatly pleased with the maturity of the vocabulary and the well-structured story. When he finished, he said, "I'd like to change it," whereupon he retold the story with a slightly changed focus.

The next several sessions (which were not necessarily on consecutive weeks) were spent on other pictures. The stories continued to be well-constructed. Each dealt with a little animal who tried to be independent and strong but always was taught a painful lesson, in that rebuke, punishment or defeat invariably followed such efforts. It was during the period of the story-telling that Duncan began obviously to reach out for relationships with his classmates and began timidly to volunteer in class. It was not long before we persuaded him to try Instrumental Music.

And it was not long before it became evident that he did not want to be differentiated from his classmates by coming to see me, even though he still expressed a desire to come. His participation in class and on the playground has steadily increased. I have maintained a hall, playground or lunchroom contact in terms of a wave or brief conversation. By this year Duncan even waves spontaneously at his former teachers and calls "Hi!" to them.

Bob

Bob was in the third or fourth grade when referred. He was one of the few Caucasian children in an almost entirely Negro school. His problem was stated as "Crying, leaving school to go home, little or no work though of average intelligence, wetting—odor causing rejection and teasing—very nervous. Communication with others, poor." The home situation was seen initially as poor. The mother and father had violent quarrels, knives were used at times, both drank some, the father more frequently.

Bob is the oldest of four children: a younger brother and sister are in classes for the mentally retarded. The youngest seems to be of normal intelligence. The mother seems to be intellectually limited.

I made frequent home calls in terms of trying to help the parents handle the situation in ways other than beating Bob and taking him screaming back to school. The parents' relationship also came up for discussion. I often went to get Bob myself and persuaded him to come back to school—usually. A change of teachers helped. The new teacher was one who had empathy with Bob, yet could be firm when the need arose, and one who was willing to keep going in spite of slow progress. With great effort on the part of the school and on my part, Bob developed some trust in relationships over a period of two years, though he was still severely blocked in communication.

When he reached junior high school level, knowing he would not be able to adjust to the aggressiveness of the school in his district and, therefore, that it would become virtually impossible to keep him in school, I arranged for him to attend another school. This was arranged through a medical recommendation so as to avoid a neighborhood reaction that the transfer was due to racial prejudice. Even so, the three years of junior high school were touch-and-go. I continued my contacts with Bob and the family as frequently as possible. The school often called me on complaints that Bob had cut school, had some fights and was showing some "defiance." The last was usually the result of being corrected or pressured with Bob having no way to respond because of his very limited verbal communication. I worked with Bob on specific techniques for handling himself in these situations; I enlisted the help of the shop teacher and of the principal, who had both developed an interest in Bob.

Eventually, graduation time arrived. Bob obviously really wanted to "cross the stage." but was petrified at the idea. He had no suitable clothes, his parents did not plan to come. The principal rustled up a dark suit belonging to his own son. I arranged to take Bob home after the ceremonies (because the distance was too great for him to travel at night and he was fearful in his home neighborhood after dark). Bob was, by now, a tall, handsome, Scandinavian-appearing boy. As he crossed the stage, one could *feel* his effort to make it. The principal said that Bob had grasped his hand as if it were a life-line. Afterwards, I took him out for a treat and tried to get him to invite others, but he couldn't. For the first time in all these years, he really talked: he was excited and pleased that he'd "made it"; he spoke of his feelings as he crossed the stage.

Bob did not last long in high school where there was no constant follow-up. I tried to do what I could but it was too sketchy. He came back to see me when he was about nineteen. He was able to talk quite freely about his experiences, was reasonably well-poised and self-confident. He does not plan to finish high school.

Ronnie

Ronnie, a fourth grade upper-middle class Caucasian boy of superior mental ability enrolled in a new school. This followed his family's move because of the father's promotion to a junior executive position. Ronnie shortly began to express extreme dislike for his teacher and everything about the new school. He refused to respond when given directions and frequently lay on the floor kicking and screaming.

When the principal telephoned the home, Ronnie's father told her that the boy was very distressed at the recent death of his grandmother, who had lived with the family. He asked that special, kind consideration be given Ronnie at school. Ronnie's teacher was experienced and well able to deal with disturbed children who need firm control. In this instance, she was literally immobilized because of the father's statement and because Ronnie's behavior became more violent daily. The conscientious principal feared that use of regular procedures might precipitate a more extreme reaction, even a "nervous breakdown." She asked for help from the guidance worker. The principal was beginning her second year of experience as an administrator and had worked with the guidance worker during the preceding year.

The guidance worker's brief observation of the boy in class revealed a nice looking, well developed lad, busy at his seat. The teacher was asked to send him to the nurse's office where the guidance worker would wait to meet him. Ronnie came down the hall muttering and kicking the floor. He was introduced to the guidance worker by the principal, looked at her keenly and shouted, "NO," when it was suggested that they become further acquainted. The principal's anxiety was vividly expressed in her face as she hovered near the guidance worker. Head turned away, Ronnie listened carefully to the guidance worker as it was explained that she knew many children here and wanted to know him, too; that after talking with her a few minutes he would return to his classroom. She said she was interested to see whether anything could be done to help him get well started in the new school. As she talked, Ronnie moved away a little, leaned against a counter and put his head on his arm, watching covertly with a petulant expression. When the guidance worker moved from his sight, he jerked his head up and after seeing her, dropped it again to his arm with a triumphant smile. When the guidance worker was sure that Ronnie was not really frightened, she remarked casually that she didn't believe she had any more time to talk to him today, and that he might return to class. At this, Ronnie looked up surprised and, with a sheepish air, walked quietly back to class. The guidance worker had terminated the interview because the principal so clearly expected an explosion that she dared not leave Ronnie alone with the guidance worker. At the same time, Ronnie's continued resistance further heightened her anxiety. She was not reassured by gestures indicating that the guidance worker was able to continue alone with Ronnie. In view of the boy's apparent attempts to manipulate the adults, it was not thought wise to allow him to witness the principal being reassured about him.

The principal was dejected when Ronnie left and said nothing had been accomplished. The guidance worker agreed that Ronnie had not been induced to say much, but suggested that if we thought about what he did, we might get some helpful clues to the meaning of his behavior. As the discussion continued, the principal commented that she noticed Ronnie listened hard, and she believed he knew there was nothing to be afraid of. Could it be that he was "bluffing?" This idea did not coincide with her idea of a child about to break down emotionally. In what she had just seen, there was not so much lack of self-control as something else. Then, hopefully, she asked if his behavior might be "good old three-year-old tantrums." The guidance worker suggested that we continue study, but right now try out that idea, since children who are either emotionally sick or well need to feel that adults will control them and protect them from being too swamped by strong feelings. The principal, now animated, said she would talk to the teacher who would know just how to proceed. As for herself, it would be such a relief to work on the problem this way, even if it took several months to help Ronnie over it.

The guidance worker met with both of Ronnie's parents at their home two days later. The father was embarrassed by the need to confer, but was interested in helping and fairly objective in attitude. The mother was very protective of Ronnie and critical of school handling. No significant developmental data was obtained. Ronnie is essentially an "only" child, although he has an adult brother in the home. The guidance worker suggested to the parents that they visit school and get to know the teacher and principal so that information would not have to be exchanged between home and school only through Ronnie and the guidance worker, or by phone. This was difficult for both parents to face.

During the eight remaining months of the year, the guidance worker, principal and teacher had a number of conferences. At first, these had to do with confirming our tentative diagnosis of Ronnie's behavior difficulties and supporting the teacher in handling them. Several ideas of involving the mother in a productive working relationship with the school were tried before deciding to communicate chiefly with the father. Ronnie continued to have tantrums, but usually everyone at school was hopeful that he would behave satisfactorily in time. At two "low points" when the teacher felt she had exhausted her own resources, the consultant had interviews with Ronnie at her request. On both occasions he expressed discouragement that the rages interfered with his popularity, and on both occasions he was helped to evaluate his progress and to try again.

During Ronnie's fifth grade year with the same teacher, he made a great deal of improvement, with concurrent change in the mother's attitude to one of cooperation. It was with mutual regret that Ronnie and his teacher parted, when the family moved again after the father once more was promoted.

Jimmy

The principal of a 99% Caucasian school referred twelve year old, sixth grade Jimmy, a boy of Chinese ancestry, born in America. Jimmy was a bright, potentially gifted, friendly boy. However, he caused trouble in the classroom because he is "noisy, mutters, slams desk top, swears, has temper tantrums. When the teacher asks him to stay after school, he runs out. He doesn't complete his work. He is dressed in ragged clothes and is ill-kempt." Jimmy's father had told the principal, "You have to beat him up." When Jimmy was paddled once, he became quiet and obedient but this did not seem to be an appropriate solution to the problem. The father said he did not know what to do about the problem. The school knew that Jimmy was the oldest of six children. His father spoke good English, though with an accent; his mother's English was very broken.

I observed Jimmy in class. He was a short boy with heavy, dark hair who wore very thick-lensed glasses and held his books close to his eyes. (His vision without glasses is 20/50 in both eyes.) He remained in the classroom at recess, *intently* studying the dictionary and talking with the other children who stayed in the room. During class work after recess, he muttered to himself (without reference to others about him—not attention-getting behavior nor hostile to the teacher). When the teacher told him to stop, he responded. He volunteered frequently in class and was obviously trying hard. When he answered "yes" or "no," he got halfway out of his seat; for long answers, he got up and stood beside his seat. (He was the only child who did this—apparently because of home training or Chinese School.) His answers were always correct, but his language was very laborious. (Query: Is he now working with the speech teacher?)

On the basis of this information and classroom observation, I could suggest to the teacher and principal that Jimmy's "muttering" probably fitted in with his standing to recite, both probably being the behavior demanded in Chinese School (where chanting the lesson aloud is expected) rather than symptoms of a rebellious attitude. This fitted in with their own feeling that Jimmy was a friendly boy.

I had a feeling that I had remembered Jimmy from previous years in another school. This turned out to be the case. He had entered school in a 98% Negro school in a poorer section of the city. His father at that time had been a laborer in a laundry. His mother was a "child bride" from China. Jimmy was originally referred in the first grade for severe temper tantrums. I had made a home call but the mother and I were almost completely unable to communicate with each other.

The speech teacher in Jimmy's school reported that he had been with her for his first four years in school and had been "at all times a controversial figure. . . . Earlier such a tortured child—so devalued . . . his relationship with me meant a lot to him. I was a helper in a supportive role." Some of Jimmy's earlier school experiences had been unfortunate; when he was taken home for misbehavior at school he acted "as if he was being cast out of heaven—he had a sit-down strike and wept." He had had better relationships with his teachers in the last three years.

Next, in separate conferences with Jimmy and with his father, I discovered that the family had risen, through tremendous labor and frugality, very rapidly in the economic scale. The father now owned and operated both a restaurant and a five-dwelling apartment house. Jimmy sold the afternoon paper downtown (probably the reason he "ran away" when the teacher tried to make him stay after school). He went to Chinese school from 6-8 p.m. Before and after Chinese school, he helped his father in the restaurant, going home with his father at 10 p.m.

With this knowledge, now, of a bright, highly motivated but tremendously pressed and harassed boy in a family where everyone was apparently working 14 to 16 hours a day, the school image of Jimmy's behavior could be radically altered. It was seen that he needed maximum rest, support and respite at school, minimal expectations for homework but active academic encouragement. By the end of the year, the teacher reported that his academic work was inconsistent but "very good when he does it—now most of the time. . . . He is showing much improvement though his temper makes this progress somewhat inconsistent." His difficulties were "getting along with others and not disintegrating when he is late or when children chafe him into a temper tantrum and swearing. He throws tantrums over being tardy, being late with his banking, not being chosen for a kickball team, being reprimanded for continuous talking in class. He needs firm but kind guidance constantly. If you can calm him down after a tantrum and discuss the problem calmly and softly, he responds very well and temper tantrums get further and further apart."

I am also the guidance worker in the junior high school Jimmy will attend, so that I will continue to keep an eye on him and help him and/or the school as needed. In the latter part of his sixth grade year, I talked with Jimmy about behavior, such as the muttering which might be open to misinterpretation, and urged him to try to become sufficiently aware of this automatic behavior so that he could control it. I also talked with the junior high school people about Jimmy's background and the meaning of the behavior which otherwise might be unintelligible and therefore disturbing to them.

Mary

Mary was a quiet, well-behaved, intelligent Negro girl who was referred to the guidance worker in her elementary school by her sixth grade teacher because her unexpected stealing had thrown the teacher into a panic. I knew her first in seventh grade. At this time, she was stealing in a way which seemed to signify an obvious desire to get caught;

she was telling fantastic lies and she was not achieving to ability. The previous guidance worker had the impression that Mary felt it was her fate to follow in her mother's footsteps and was depressed by it. The mother had been alcoholic and sexually promiscuous; the history suggested that she was an intelligent but emotionally disturbed person. Her five children, all of whom seemed brighter than average, were very much attached to her in spite of her neglect of them. At the time of referral, Mary and her siblings had lived with a paternal aunt for several years. The aunt, who was illiterate and probably less intelligent than the girl, seemed to be baffled and frightened by Mary's behavior.

Mary's first year in junior high school was difficult for all concerned. There were a number of crises involving stealing, lying, and poor school work. I arranged for one teacher to sponsor her in order to obtain closer contact and improved identification. Mary failed seventh grade and the aunt therefore refused to let her go to YWCA camp, despite my efforts. I think I managed to persuade Mary that her academic failure was not too much of a disgrace and that she might be in a better position for doing good high school work by repeating: she was young for seventh grade, very small and immature physically. My contacts with the aunt were not frequent enough to be fruitful; she was quite negative and pessimistic about Mary.

In Mary's second year of junior high school, repeating the seventh grade, her identification with the teacher sponsor and with me improved. There were fewer episodes of a major sort. I tried again for YWCA camp, feeling that this experience away from home might give the needed perspective to Mary for changing her self-concept to a more positive one. She went, and came back literally "bubbling over" with enthusiasm about her experiences. She found that she had been, in her words, "the life of the group." She had attached herself to a young counselor of whom she had grown very fond.

Her grades were much better during the eighth grade: she made the scholarship honor roll twice and hoped also to make the citizenship honor roll, but I think did not. The YWCA sent a note to the aunt to let her know of Mary's good adjustment at camp—undoubtedly a help to the aunt in viewing Mary more positively. There were two major crises during this year: she once stole some earrings, which I helped her to return. At another time she came to school quite badly bruised, saying her aunt had beaten her with a broom. Her aunt came to school the same day on some pretext and stated that Mary had fallen off her bicycle. There was evidence of maturation on Mary's part despite these crises. However, she deceived her aunt about her grade level by altering her report card, letting the aunt believe that she was graduating. She had bought graduation clothes, so that it was not until after the ceremony that the aunt discovered the facts of the matter. Both the aunt and the school were understandably furious.

Arrangements were again made for Mary to attend the YWCA camp with her aunt's reluctant permission. I am not the guidance worker at Mary's school this year, but I phoned the aunt in February to see how Mary was progressing. The aunt said, "Mary was talking about you just the other day. I'm very pleased with her. She used to be so scarey-like, now she's flirtful-like and I have to calm her down. Camp started her off being more brave. The fearful accent she had is almost gone. I got her ice skates for Christmas, so she goes ice skating with her brothers and sisters. She is even into womanhood and is so nice and delicate about caring for herself. I was so worried she'd be untidy—you'd be surprised how nice she is. I'm proud of all of them now. I was worried a long time. I had a nervous breakdown right after they came to live with us and I'm really just getting over it. I just conked out and couldn't do anything —I just sat and shook. But now they are fine: the baby is doing real good in school. Morton is finishing high school and they say that if every boy was like him, the school would be a pleasure. The oldest boy went into the Army and is staying with my sister in Sacramento; he has a civil service job." Nothing has been heard from the mother for over a year. Presumably, the mother will not re-establish a stable role in this family. However, Mary seems to have made strides in overcoming her negative, self-destructive identification with her mother.

It would be foolish to predict any child's future, but Mary, now about to graduate from junior high school, may be on the road to her stated goal, that of becoming a school teacher. I have seen her every three or four weeks during the past four years with more intensive follow-up (once a week visits, phone calls, etc.) during crises. She will continue to be followed in high school, by me rather than by the regular guidance worker in her high school, though we will coordinate information and the regular guidance worker will work with the school people if problems there arise.

Gloria

Gloria X, a Caucasian girl, was the second of four children, who lived in a neighborhood served by a small, stable, elementary school where most of the teachers had been content to remain for many years, becoming extremely well-acquainted with the families in their school district. Gloria was referred to the guidance worker when she was in the third grade because she was irritable, whiny at times, did not finish her school work, and did not have many friends. The school knew that Gloria's older brother, Hubert, had been accelerated and was now in the gifted class of a junior high school, while Gloria's intelligence tested within the average range. Bobby X was in the first grade in the same elementary school, and Debby X would be entering kindergarten next fall. Mr. X was a TV technician. Gloria's teacher was upset because of a recent crisis: Gloria had been kept after school to finish some work, whereupon the mother had come to school and "blown up" in an exceedingly angry way at the teacher for doing such a thing without notifying the family.

Mrs. X was a Brownie leader and often at school. She knew all the teachers and the way the school operated, hence her angry outburst was even more inexplicable to Gloria's teacher. When Mrs. X came to school, she always brought Debby, the pre-schooler, with her. They made an unusual appearance: Mrs. X was tall, gaunt, and emaciated while Debby, an animated little girl, had no hair at all, either on scalp or eyebrows.

The guidance worker was asked by the teacher and principal to talk with Mrs. X as an aid to understanding Gloria. The principal also asked the guidance worker to find out more about Debby, since it seemed that such an unusual looking child might have social difficulties when she entered kindergarten.

The interview took place in the X home because the guidance worker hoped that Mrs. X would find it easier to express herself there. Debby played nearby. Mrs. X was worried by the guidance worker's interest because she did not want Gloria to be considered "a problem child" by school people and she felt guilty about having gotten angry. She said her husband made invidious comparisons between Gloria and her older brother, Hubert. The father felt that Gloria's relative lack of academic prowess was related to the mother's babying of her and Gloria's lack of persistence with homework. Mrs. X tried to protect Gloria from her father's pressure but, when the teacher seemed to imply the same criticism by keeping Gloria after school, the mother displaced the conflict with her husband on to the teacher, hence the hysterical quality of her anger.

Mrs. X was encouraged to take a firm stand with her husband if she felt her approach was right. She readily agreed to do this, saying that it was her tendency to adjust herself to others rather than to insist, if the latter would be unpleasant. In this sense, she felt she had been failing Gloria. She said that Mr. X would agree if she were firm.

Mrs. X said she had been trying to combat her tendency to be "easy-going" by activities like the Brownie work, which is hard for her. She has continued with it because it is important to Gloria and she believes that it increases Gloria's security at school with the other children. Hesitantly, she said that it also had a personal value, for it gave her something to think about so that she spent less time being preoccupied with family troubles. She indirectly hinted at difficulties with her husband. Then, rather impulsively, she confessed that she often got very angry at Mr. X because he criticized her. She gave two or three examples of this in regard to her discipline of the children, which Mr. X considered too mild. The children had been witnesses to the disagreements and Mrs. X felt quite guilty about this. She was concerned about Gloria's confused reaction to her parents' dissension and "hated to think" that it might be responsible for some of the girl's school problems. Thoughtfully, she said that her husband was not in good health and she supposed that she wasn't helping matters by "flying off the handle." Mr. X, she said, had a painful, chronic leg injury from a mine explosion in World War II.

Mrs. X then timidly said that she had told the guidance worker a good deal about the family but that if it would help Gloria, maybe it was all right. She was assured that the family difficulties would not be discussed at school but the understanding the guidance worker had gained would be of definite help in school planning. Mrs. X said she would try to be more controlled, but she didn't know what else to do. The guidance worker wondered if Mrs. X could talk to Gloria about her father's health, helping her to see that upsets at home did not necessarily indicate that Gloria was at fault. Mrs. X said with surprise that she had been so preoccupied she had not thought of this but, obviously Gloria needed to hear it. She remarked that it wouldn't hurt if she were a little less personal about things herself. At this point, Mrs. X was ready to terminate the interview and she indicated that she would not need to talk with the guidance worker again. Whenever Debby had been mentioned, Mrs. X spoke of her as if she were in no way different from other children.

In discussing the interview with the teacher and the principal, the guidance worker first made it clear that Mrs. X harbored no resentment against the teacher, had reacted angrily in the crisis because she was under stress, and now felt sorry for her outburst. The stress was described as Mr. X's health. Mrs. X was presented as a loving and perceptive parent. They were informed that some of Gloria's problems were related to the same stress, as well as to her relative academic inferiority to Hubert. The guidance worker suggested that the teacher give Gloria as much encouragement and individual recognition as possible in the ordinary classroom routine. The teacher was relieved, but remained dubious about seeing Mrs. X again. In a separate conference with the principal, he was told that the guidance worker had not discussed Debby's hairlessness because the mother had ignored all leads to that topic and the guidance worker had felt, therefore, that a direct approach would have been too threatening to the mother, especially as Debby was not yet in school. The principal had agreed that a frontal approach would have been unwise.

The teacher still tended to avoid Mrs. X until, at one of the guidance worker's weekly visits to the school, she reported that Mrs. X had apologized for getting angry. The teacher had more conviction about giving Gloria recognition after this, and, during a period in which Mr. X was in a veterans' hospital for prolonged orthopedic procedures, she became very positive in her attitude toward Gloria. Gloria responded by working hard, became more friendly toward other children, and was elected to a class office. Her whining and crying disappeared, but she continued to be irritable at times.

As the teacher's anxiety subsided, the principal turned more openly to his concerns about Debby. He attempted several times to broach the subject of Debby's hairlessness with Mrs. X, but the mother always appeared oblivious of his meaning. The guidance worker suggested that consideration of Debby's medical problem be deferred until the spring enrollment of kindergarteners a few weeks in the future. Perhaps at this times Mrs. X would offer some explanation or plan in filling out medical forms.

Kindergarten pre-registration took place but Mrs. X did not indicate that she was aware of Debby in any special way. The principal felt frustrated by this and wondered what it might signify in the relationship of mother and child. He believed that somehow Mrs. X must be induced to face the situation, for two mothers in the PTA has expressed concern about Debby's entering school, fearing that she might have some kind of disease. The guidance worker suggested that the school nurse, an effective, warm person, approach the matter directly with Mrs. X, bringing up the possibility of a wig for Debby.

The nurse reported that Mrs. X had been surprised that anyone thought Debby's condition might be a social or emotional problem for her. Mrs. X said she had believed that, if she and the other family members made no issue of it, Debby's reactions would be normal and self-confident. She was able to see that Debby's age-mates might not respond so objectively. Mrs. X said she had been told by her doctor that Debby's congenital condition would someday necessitate her wearing a wig but, at this point, due to Mr. X's recent return to work, purchase of such an expensive item would be difficult. The nurse was able to locate a financial resource, with Mrs. X's approval, and Debby later made a good kindergarten adjustment, arrayed in blond pigtails.

Betsy

Betsy, an adopted Japanese-Negro orphan, attended a small elementary school in an area of the city which was undergoing a rapid change from all Caucasian professional and business people to one which included a number of Negro families with civil service jobs. Some of the school faculty members, who had been in the school a long time, were disturbed by the fact that there was higher tension among the children, with more fighting on the playground. The principal was new to the school. She was experienced as a vice principal in a similar area of the city and at once became effective in enhancing faculty morale. The guidance worker was beginning the third year of work in this school.

Betsy's first grade teacher, a motherly woman about to retire, became aware of the fact that the child had injuries from time to time (such as a lump on the head) for which explanations seemed guarded or somewhat unrealistic. Betsy learned well and was a quiet, conforming youngster at school. The teacher spoke to the guidance worker about Betsy during one of the guidance worker's weekly visits in the school. She was somewhat apologetic about bringing up the matter, for nothing she knew would support the idea that Betsy was being struck. The guidance worker encouraged her to schedule a routine conference with Betsy's mother or father and follow up any leads they might give to further understanding Betsy.

The teacher found that both parents responded when she asked for a conference. They were a pleasant, dignified middle class Negro couple, but appeared to be at odds about Betsy. They were guarded in conversation with the teacher; expressed a desire for help from "a specialist" in regard to Betsy. The teacher gave them the guidance worker's name and told them they would be telephoned for an appointment.

The guidance worker interviewed Mrs. Q., Betsy's mother, promptly because her anxiety was clear when she was contacted by phone. Mrs. Q. was controlled, but had a driven quality and much guilt and masked hostility. She said that Mr. Q. disapproves of her critical attitude toward Betsy. Mr. and Mrs. Q. have adopted Betsy and a boy, who is currently enrolled in kindergarten. Mrs. Q. stated that she has never had any special difficulty with the brother, nor has Mr. Q. She gave a good deal of information about Betsy.

Mr. Q. fills a technical position in the Armed Forces. When he and his wife were in Japan, they obtained their son, a Japanese-Negro infant, for adoption. When he was several months old, the adoption agency phoned late one afternoon and asked the parents to take Betsy for a few days until a plan could be made for her. She had just then been returned to the agency from an adoptive home. Mr. and Mrs. Q. agreed to this and shortly received Betsy, then between three and four years old. She was in a filthy condition, her body covered with bruises, sores and scars. She behaved in a thoroughly cowed manner, spoke only Japanese, of which the Q.'s had little knowledge. Both parents were shocked and they deeply pitied the child. They continued to keep her week after week, as the agency was not able to arrange other care. At last the Q's were approached as to their willingness to keep Betsy permanently, with the explanation that nothing but institutional care could otherwise be provided. Mr. Q. reacted strongly against the idea of Betsy's going to an institution and wanted to adopt her. Mrs. Q. had marked reservations about adoption of Betsy, for the child maintained a rather distant attitude toward Mrs. Q., while responding affectionately to Mr. Q. There was a psychiatric evaluation of Betsy and the couple were reportedly told that in time Betsy should, with loving care, adapt satisfactorily to the family. With this, and in response to Mr. Q.'s desire, the adoption was completed about a year after Betsy came to them. Shortly after, the family came to the United States and eventually settled in their present home.

Returning to Betsy's early experiences, Mrs. Q. said she had learned from the agency that Betsy had been given to the agency when she was two years old because her own Japanese mother no longer wanted her after her Negro father left. Betsy was then, at age two, in a seriously neglected and undernourished condition. After a brief period of care in a foster home, it was believed she was mentally retarded and she was placed in an institution for retarded girls. There, a matron became interested in Betsy and was instrumental in helping to determine that she was not retarded. The child was then placed for adoption with a couple having no other children. The wife was Japanese, the husband American Negro. Not long after the placement, the adoptive father was sent to Korea, returning in several months to find Betsy in an abused condition. In addition she had been exposed to a questionable moral situation. The husband gathered Betsy up just as she was and took her back to the agency.

Mrs. Q. gave these details in a sober, almost sorrowful way. She emphasized that she and Mr. Q. have done all that is possible to help Betsy overcome the past. They feel that she is an intelligent, healthy child and Mr. Q. sees no problem in her emotional relationships. As soon as he goes to work, however, Betsy becomes highly resistant to direction. Mrs. Q. cannot get her out of bed, dressed, or fed without a terrific struggle. Once Betsy is at school, or anywhere out of the home, she behaves in an exemplary fashion. When Betsy returns from school, the difficulties are resumed until Mr. Q. comes home. Mrs. Q. gave the impression that Betsy almost consciously plays the parents against each other. Without saying that she has struck Betsy, Mrs. Q. said that she has lost patience completely and is barely controlling her feelings about Betsy, saying she can hardly believe she could feel this way about any child. Rather desperately she said maybe Betsy was "not right" from a psychiatric standpoint. She gave the example that Betsy sometimes isolates herself from Mrs. Q. and the brother to the extent of watching lines on the TV screen for prolonged periods.

The guidance worker maintained a receptive attitude during Mrs. Q.'s description, indicating recognition of the very real difficulties Mrs. Q. had in coping with Betsy and in maintaining her self-concept of a good mother. It was pointed out that Betsy is having no problems in regard to learning or school behavior, so that it would seem advisable for the family to seek counseling on a consecutive basis from a community agency other than the school, if they wish it. Mrs. Q. indicated that Mr. Q. has urged her to get help and has said he will accompany her. He was called out of town today or would have met with the guidance worker. Mrs. Q. seemed to feel, however, that confronting the problem by seeking help on a regular basis would, by implication, prove her own inadequacy. The guidance worker pointed out that Mrs. Q. seemed to have no difficulty with her son but with Betsy, who had experienced so much that was painful before coming to the Q.'s, special help could very understandably be necessary. Mrs. Q. remarked that most of Betsy's early unhappy experiences seemed to be with women, maybe this had something to do with Mrs. Q.'s present problems with her. She asked how to go about obtaining help.

Mrs. Q. was given a general description of fee and non-fee services available in the community and those available in a local military hospital. She preferred to apply at the hospital, but did not know how to proceed. It was suggested that she take Betsy there for a pediatric examination, give the doctor a description of the problem and ask him to refer her to the proper department. Mrs. Q. said that she would do this immediately because the situation, she felt was now at the stage of emergency.

Betsy's teacher and principal were told that the Q's had been referred for counseling because of problems in the family relationships, which were not described. It was suggested that the school handling continue in the same way.

About three weeks after the interview with Mrs. Q., the guidance worker called her to find out whether she had been successful in obtaining help. Mrs. Q. said that she had done nothing yet because she and her husband were busy with various business matters, which needed to be completed before Mr. Q. went overseas. As soon as he left she would have the use of the car and she planned to begin counseling then.

School closed for the summer shortly after this. In the fall the guidance worker learned that Mrs. Q. had started interviews at the hospital because a letter came to the school asking information on Betsy's school adjustment. Betsy was no longer enrolled there. The guidance worker learned that she was now enrolled in second grade in another school assigned to the guidance worker. Checking there it was found that, as before, Betsy's school behavior and academic progress were satisfactory in every respect. The principal and teacher of this large school were told that the Q.'s had been referred by the consultant for counseling because of home problems with Betsy which had not been manifest in school during the previous year.

Mrs. Q. asked to have Betsy excused from school several times to keep appointments at the hospital, then told Betsy's new teacher that she was continuing regular interviews, while Betsy was not to go anymore. Betsy has since run away from home several times, spending varying amounts of time at a detention center. When she returns to school, her behavior continues good as before. Beyond conferring with her teacher briefly when each runaway occurred, the guidance worker has given no further service.

Jerry

School Z, a middle class, largely Caucasian school, has a pleasant, amiable man principal. He has a planned approach to teacher development, i.e., he encourages teachers, in the field of guidance, to discuss prospective referrals, so that he can help them think through other steps that might be taken before referral.

He seems to encourage teachers to seek help primarily from him. He has definite ideas regarding discipline and prides himself on working with children who have had problems at other schools.

This principal makes few referrals but wants his guidance worker to be around. He believes that this is what teachers like. The morale of his school seems good; the faculty seems stable; the teachers come from a wide range of socio-cultural backgrounds. However, guidance work is peripheral in this school, as in some others, and severe cases may be referred much too late. This was true in the case of Jerry, which did not come to the guidance worker's attention until the child was in the fourth grade when the situation had reached the point of no return. The guidance worker was asked to sit in on an exemption conference with the parents of the boy. Following the exemption, a review of the boy's record indicated that he had evidenced severe disturbance even upon entering kindergarten.

He was described then as behaving like a little animal. He urinated in the classroom, needed to be watched constantly, often went into the girl's bathroom, pulled up girls' dresses. He seemed unhappy except when involved in music. He was not upset if he could sing or play rhythm instruments. He did not seem dull and would come out with amazing statements. Because of "immaturity," he was retained in kindergarten, remaining with the same teacher. His mother was not happy about the retention, feeling that it was a reflection on the family.

The teacher felt that the boy was starved for affection, that he was neglected and rejected by his family after they began to believe that he was not bright like his brothers. As a result, the teacher indulged the boy during his second year in kindergarten. Although she and the other children felt sorry for him, the children started calling his "crazy." Bizarre behavior continued to be reported through the next few years. By the fourth grade, his teacher did not feel that it was safe to leave him unsupervised; when corrected on the playground he would run away.

When the case was finally referred, not only had the school reached a complete impasse but referral by the guidance worker to a child guidance clinic and later to a children's treatment institution proved "too little and too late": the child is now in a state psychiatric hospital.

Petrucchio

Petrucchio was a boy whose real name was as incongruous to his Chinese background as the pseudonym I have chosen. When I first knew him, he was in junior high school and had come to the United States from China only recently. He was still having great difficulty with the American language. The guidance worker at his elementary school, where he had been referred for fighting, had set up a good relationship with Petruccio. He readily shifted this to me, though he also kept contact with the previous worker by sending messages and cards to her through me.

Petrucchio came from a large family. The older boys and the father had come to the United States many years earlier but the mother, Petrucchio and two other younger children had followed them just three years ago. I made a home call but was unable to obtain much information. The mother could speak only a few words of English and the older boys, who were present, were not willing to help out—perhaps feeling that Petrucchio's problems were the business of the parents. (This is in marked contrast, for instance, to our lower-class Negro families where older siblings and relatives are often major sources of information and support in working with a child who is having problems.) The home was in a poor section of town where there was a mixture of several nationalities and races. There were many evidences of Chinese culture in the home and the mother looked as if she had walked off a Chinese painting: she was tall, statuesque and had the clear, translucent skin so frequently seen on the paintings of Chinese women on silk scrolls.

The older boys did finally explain how I could get in touch with the father, who worked for an import-export firm in a nearby city. Eventually, when I talked with the father, it became evident that Petrucchio was considered the "black sheep" of the family—this was the way it was and there seemed little I could say that was going to change the family's conviction. When I knew Petrucchio better, I made one other attempt to involve the father in the situation but was unsuccessful.

The school personnel were interested and worked with a reasonable degree of success during Petrucchio's junior high school days to instill self-respect and a degree of self-confidence. He posed only a moderate problem in terms of behavior, getting into occasional fights because of teasing. Academically, he struggled and made good progress, considering the language handicap. He managed to find jobs to earn money for clothes and spending money.

During the three years of junior high school, I saw Petrucchio as frequently as possible, encouraging, listening (he liked to talk and have his English corrected), and, in general, along with several teachers, trying to provide the approval and the limits which his family seemed unwilling to give. It was my impression that, though he attended Chinese school after regular school hours, he tried to become Americanized faster than his family could tolerate. His problems seemed more related to his "culture straddle" and his rejection by the family than to deep-seated intrapsychic difficulties. Petrucchio's awareness of the acculturation problem and his disidentification with the family were documented by his request that his name in school be changed from Petrucchio to Johnny, which was done. I think he would have changed his last name to Smith, had it been possible.

High school, however, proved to be Johnny's Waterloo. (At that time there was no regular guidance follow-up in the high schools.) In spite of my protests that he was still too unfamiliar with the language, he signed up for a college preparatory course. He was intelligent enough to handle it but he could not manage the lag in understanding the English language. He was still working at the odd jobs he seemed always able to find, so that study time was at a minimum. After the second report card period, I tried in vain to get him to change his program, for he had begun to show signs of stress by beginning to cut school and to ally himself with a fringe delinquent group. He often lied to me about his school adjustment and could not come to terms with the concept that it would be hard for me to help him unless we could approach his problems without such an urgent need to "save face" and impress me with a more pleasing picture of the situation.

However, Johnny seemed to have a positive concept of our relationship. He frequently left messages at my office for me to call him; when I tried, I almost always got someone in the home who did not speak English (I think the older boys had married Chinese girls who had been brought over from China). For two years, the struggle to keep Johnny in school continued. He was so disappointed that he had not been able to handle the college preparatory course that he could not accept any other program; he lost interest in school. Around this time, he became closely associated with a brilliant Negro boy who was rebelling against all authority and particularly against educational authority. Having reached 16 years of age, they both managed to get jobs and to quit school.

Johnny continued to keep in touch with me from time to time but I was never able to get him to return to school. When he was about seventeen, he went into the Service. I received two letters from him when he was stationed in Korea. They did not say a great deal but it did seem that he was working toward maturity and some self-realization.

Referral for formal treatment

Brad and Kent W., middle class Caucasian boys, (and the case of Peter to follow) represent a category of children with internalized neurotic problems for whom referral to psychiatric treatment is by no means as simple or automatic as it might theoretically appear.* In some cases, the parents themselves seek treatment but when, as in the W. family, the problems of the children are warded off, denied or projected for a period of years, the guidance worker avoids giving the family an ultimatum about treatment and works to facilitate the boys' educational progress in the same way as he does with other children whose problems are more situational or less classically neurotic.

---

* See Chapter Six.

Brad and Kent W.

As the guidance worker at X school, I had become acquainted with the W. boys and their mother years ago. First Brad, the older, caused concern to his second grade teacher because he was constantly playing with rubber bands, often teased other children, did not seem to care whether he pleased the teacher or not, did not seem to respond to either praise or punishment and, in short, was hard to get next to. Yet, when he wanted to, Brad could do work far beyond his grade level. The teacher was particularly exasperated because his mother, during a conference, stated that she knew Brad had troubles but if his present teacher could just understand him, as his previous teacher had not. . . . After all, he was not a juvenile delinquent, was he? Besides, in private schools, like the one she had attended, they taught the children much more. Maybe Brad was bored.

Kent, just one year younger than Brad, came to my attention when he had a tantrum at school because his teacher had asked him to do a piece of work over again. Up to this point, he had maintained a rigid pose (in the first grade) that he could be his own teacher, knew all about what the teacher was teaching the class, was doing perfect work. How dare she criticize him! Kent was indeed a very bright boy but one who was physically immature, so that his coordination, his handwriting and his skill at games were poor. With the active support of his mother, he belittled skill at games but his handwriting gave him trouble and caused the tantrum. His very sensitive teacher, instead of reacting with counter-rejection, made it her business to become more acquainted with Kent's mother. The teacher sat through the mother's typical diatribe against Kent's previous teacher and against public education, then asked for the mother's help in coping with Kent's rigid need to be perfect and his refusals to try anything he had not mastered completely. Mrs. W. then indicated her real concern and her puzzlement as to how to help him— she agreed that he showed the same tendencies at home. The teacher suggested that both she and the mother talk with me, the guidance worker, thus bringing me officially into the picture. (This unusually perceptive and tactful teacher realized that referral of the mother alone would only have created antagonism—that she and the mother both should talk with the guidance worker in the framework of a common task.)

From then on, I followed both boys, essentially running interference between this critical mother and the boys' teachers. A home call confirmed my hunch that both boys were reacting to the atmosphere in the home where they were expected to accommodate themselves to the interests (highly intellectual) and to the aversions (to noise and confusion) of their mother. They were thus set apart from and lacked the skills to deal with the run-of-the-mill middle class boys in the neighborhood. Brad seemed to "solve" the problem by going in for a great deal of surreptitious playing at school (like the rubber band play), a pattern which persisted whether he was placed with an average class or with a gifted group. Kent continued to be perfectionistic. He was occasionally so handicapped by his need to do things right that he was almost dropped from his accelerated class because the teacher could hardly bear to watch him torture himself. Referral for uncovering psychological treatment might seem theoretically to be an obvious step, yet it seemed clear that the intensity of the mother's denial and projection of the problem would have not only defeated successful referral but also have defeated or aborted the successful rapprochement with the guidance worker.

When I had my occasional contacts with the boys' mother, their need for the more usual boyish outlets and for some relatively unstructured fun was often discussed but was not pressed too hard, since I felt my main function was that of buffer and of relatively trusted bridge between home and school.

Eventually, when Kent was in the fifth grade, perhaps because his teacher stressed her opinion that regular boys are good at games as well as at book work, Kent became increasingly upset and openly sarcastic toward the teacher and his classmates. He also would burst into tears at the slightest mistake on his part. He apparently carried these moods home and became increasingly irritable with his mother, whose favorite he was. One day, over a minor incident, he seemed almost in despair to his mother and finally told her, amidst tears that, at his age, it was just as important for a boy to make friends and be good at games as it was for him to read and write well.

The next day I had a call from Mrs. W. Kent, she felt, needed help. She had tried to do what she could. She did not want to see him grow up this unhappy. Did I know a good psychiatrist? I did and I referred her to him, having confirmed first with the psychiatrist that he had time available.* The psychiatrist is very pleased with the way in which this bright, insightful boy is working on his internalized problems.

In the meantime, I have continued to play the role of trouble-shooter. Kent's teacher has found ways to avoid needling him, which she had sometimes done without realizing it, and Mrs. W. has been more understanding of Kent's teacher's predicaments in working with him. Occasionally, too, Mrs. W. has needed support in her determination to continue Kent's psychiatric treatment. At times, when she wondered what was going on in the treatment sessions, when she found it terribly difficult to be left out of the treatment relationship, or to let go of Kent, she called me for reassurance.

Brad, the older boy, is now ready to go into junior high school. He has continued to play and to "goof-off" inappropriately. His involvement with education is peripheral. He shows evidence that he might like to ally himself with a pre-delinquent group, except that he is so immature that the group will not accept him. His mother is not able to empathize with him as well as she does with Kent and one feels that, if Brad made one false public move, the mother would consolidate opinion against him. Thus, when Mrs. W. told me that she thought of boarding school for Brad, I was initially startled but then supportive of the plan. Unless the whole family were to be involved in therapy so that the family balance could be shifted—a highly improbable contingency—it seems likely that Kent will continue successfully in treatment but that Brad will be able to benefit more from an alteration in his twenty-four hour environment and an opportunity for new identifications.

Lastly, it should be emphasized that if I had pushed harder toward therapy early, it is doubtful that I could have played even this marginal role in the education of these two boys.

Peter

Ten year old Peter, a boy of Caucasian background, and his older brother attended a middle-class elementary school. Their mother was a widow with limited financial resources. Neither boy presented a school

---

* It is our policy, as it is in most public agencies, to refer either through the family doctor or to a list of several suitable therapists. However, occasionally, when there is enough information and a good match is crucial, the guidance worker must make a specific referral. We suspect that this is widely done, though little discussed.

problem but the mother asked for help from the guidance worker because she worried about Peter's compulsivity and fearfulness. He was a compulsive hand-washer and had other compulsive symptoms—his clothes had to be arranged in a given pattern, he checked and re-checked to see that doors were locked, etc. He was a sleepwalker and had some food fads. He also was fearful of going to school or to any activity outside the home unless his brother went with him. Once at school, however, Peter entered into activities readily, was very good at sports and in instrumental music. He was very well liked by his peers, according to his teacher and principal, although his mother said that he complained that he felt he was not liked and often wept bitterly about it. His academic work was good, though probably somewhat below his capacity. The mother requested help because she considered the symptoms serious, even though she had been advised by her family doctor and by a friend to ignore the symptoms and to force Peter to do things without his brother's presence so that "he'll outgrow it."

I talked with the mother, who seemed to have considerable insight into the nature of the problem and the psychodynamics in the family which might be relevant. The mother had married a professional actor who was often on tour so that the family traveled a great deal when the boys were young. The father was quite erratic but dependent on and loving to his wife. Financially, he was improvident, having made and gone through several fortunes without setting aside any savings or making any investments. When traveling, the family stayed at very expensive hotels and lived luxuriously; the mother, who had come from modest circumstances, was never comfortable in this way of life. Also, she was eager to have a settled place in which to bring up the boys. Eventually, when the boys reached school age, they and the mother stayed with the maternal grandmother, except that the mother went off with her husband on trips from time to time. The grandmother was an extremely meticulous person who kept the boys washed within an inch of their lives. At the same time, she overindulged and infantilized them. The grandmother also relegated the mother to the role of one of the children in the home.

When Peter was eight, the father died of a heart attack. Peter and his brother had been very fond of their father, though I felt that their relationship seemed more like that of boys to their big brother than to their father. About a year later, the grandmother became ill and was ill for many months before she died of cancer. This was very upsetting for all concerned. Before the grandmother's death, the mother had been trying to establish her role as the actual parent. Now, she was precipitously thrust into the role of the *only* parent. She felt insecure and uncertain, leaned on friends from whom she got varying advice and, because of the almost precocious maturity of Peter's older brother, leaned on him. He became the "man of the family" while Peter became "the child."

Peter's symptoms did not fully crystallize until the death of his grandmother, although there had been evidences of fearfulness before. At the time I saw the mother, she felt that the symptoms were subsiding to some degree.

This boy was discussed with the psychiatric consultant, who felt that psychotherapy was urgently indicated for Peter before the acute neurotic symptoms, relating in part to the traumatic events in his life, had been diverted into chronic characterological patterns. I saw the mother for a second time, reported the opinion of the psychiatric consultant and felt that the mother was interested in following through. She proposed to get a job which would enable her to finance treatment for Peter. I gave her the names of several therapists.

A year later, no move had been made. Peter's brother had gone on to junior high school. Peter, left on his own, had slipped into a pattern of increasing absences from school, during which he stayed at home for various minor or imagined ailments. His academic work has deteriorated, his involvement in learning and in school has lessened and the school is considering retaining, rather than promoting him. The mother, although superficially amenable, was not ready for a psychiatric referral.

CHAPTER IX

Guidance Work with Severely Disturbed Children and Families

Whether a severely disturbed child can be managed within the framework of his neighborhood school depends not only on the nature of the child's behavior but also, very concretely, on the specific school situation: the principal's attitude, the personalities and special skills of teachers available, the number of other disturbed children in the school, the school's value orientation with respect to difficult children, the rate of socioeconomic change in the neighborhood and similar factors. One child might be helped to operate successfully in the neighborhood school. Another might, out of necessity or expedience, be allowed to go into a class for the mentally retarded, even though the guidance worker felt that the child's lowered I.Q. score probably reflected the emotional disturbance rather than the child's true intellectual potential. The guidance worker's task, in this latter and less desirable event, would be to work with the child and the special class situation to prevent consolidation of the child's attitude or reputation as chronically or "actually" mentally retarded and to promote the child's growth so that a return to the regular classroom could be facilitated as soon as possible. It is undeniable that some emotionally disturbed children do "solve" their problems and show marked reduction in anxiety by "factoring out" at a mentally retarded level; essentially these children amputate the problem (and also their potential) by reducing their aspirations and their level of intellectual functioning. The guidance worker makes every effort to avoid this "solution" for the child and to help in step-wise planning which will enable him to handle his problems and return to more optimal functioning.

Some school departments have or visualize the development of special classes throughout the school system in which emotionally disturbed and neurologically handicapped children could be placed. We feel that even severely disturbed children are sometimes not best handled in this way. The presence of such classes may serve as a temptation for teachers and others to refer a child there rather than exerting their own efforts or using their own best ingenuity within the framework of the regular neighborhood school. Children, therefore, may be manipulated into such special classes, just as some children are now manipulated into classes for the mentally retarded, e.g. by taking a sulky or withholding test result as a literal measurement of intellectual potential.

There is another major reason for opposing the widespread use of segregated, self-contained classes for emotionally disturbed children. This is the serious danger that the child will identify with or model himself after more seriously disturbed children. Thus, a child may be encouraged to act "crazy" or "dumb" as a means of "solving" his anxieties over his realistic problems.[1] This danger will be seen clearly in the case of Jenny, where special class placement probably would have been disastrous. Several children in the Hayes family, on the other hand, might have benefited if a special class placement had been possible because it might have short-circuited the merry-go-round of suspension, disciplinary management and aggravation, in the family, of paranoid attitudes.

Thus, we do not feel that special classes for emotionally disturbed and/or neurologically handicapped children should become a routine way of handling children in the public schools. Such classes should be available but referral of a given child should not be on the basis of the medical or psychiatric diagnosis. There are two major reasons for such a referral. The most important of these is a positive educational indication that the child needs *special educational approaches,* which cannot be provided in his regular classroom. The second reason for referral, as in the case of the Hayes boys, is that a vicious circle has become so self-perpetuating and evil reputations so entrenched that a self-fulfilling prophecy has become established and no reasonable guidance efforts are likely to prevent the victims of this prophecy from acting in the way they are expected to. (This latter category will diminish in proportion to the amount of guidance time available in a given school to combat and moderate such vicious circles.)

The question will be raised by some whether such long-term, time consuming work with *one* disturbed youngster or family is either possible or desirable when guidance workers are constantly confronted with loads far too large to manage. It is our belief that intensive work with a few very disturbed children and families counteracts the worker's own tendency to abandon child development and clinical model identifications in favor of that of an expeditor, and provides the challenge needed to keep complex interviewing and treatment skills alive. It also keeps alive in the faculty the commitment to long term goals when the movement of children from teacher to teacher mitigates against such a view. In the case of Jenny and Craig, the whole faculty, while apprehensive at times, took pleasure in their progress and continues to inquire about their welfare, now that they have left their school. In the case of the Hayes family, much was learned that was of value to the guidance worker in her less intensive work with other families presenting similar, though perhaps less extreme problems.

Jenny

Jenny Adorno, a Caucasian girl, was enrolled in kindergarten in Smith School, when she was five years old. The guidance worker was consulted within the first week of school because Jenny's behavior was so bizarre. Jenny wandered around, talked to herself, jumped up and down to go to the drinking fountain. There she laughed and gurgled while she let the water squirt on her face for an hour at a time. She made odd noises and frequently stuck out her tongue continuously for ten minutes or more without apparent cause. She was oblivious to teacher direction, to the other children or to any usual social norms of behavior. She spoke in an infantile, singsong manner and did not use the personal pronoun. Her behavior was repetitive and unrelated to any classroom activity. Jenny's highly competent teacher noted that, on the positive side, Jenny had skills in painting pictures and in rhythms. Since these two activities occur frequently in kindergarten, the teacher was able to get Jenny to paint at work time and to dance at rhythm time in a kind of parallel play which gave a semblance, at least, of conformity on Jenny's part, although it was obvious that she painted and danced only in response to her own preocupations and without regard for the group.

Jenny was so remote that the guidance worker and teacher were not able to gauge how frightened she really was of the school situation until her teacher was absent for a day. When Jenny saw the substitute, she screamed incessantly and uncontrollably until her mother was finally called to take her home.

Jenny was fortunate enough to have entered a school with a very stable middle and upper middle class population. Children in this school were not lost in the mass; a great deal of attention was focussed on each child. This could have been either an asset or a liability, since the teachers in Smith School also implicitly demanded that a sensible pattern be made of a child's behavior so that they could perceive a way of working with the situation. An incomprehensible pattern might have led to earlier exemption in Smith School than in others, where bizarre behavior could be more easily lost in the morass of learning problems and those of social transition and acculturation. Jenny's principal was not apt to panic and had no preconceived moralistic notions. He was anxious to help children, however odd, as long as his teachers were able to cope with the situation.

Jenny's kindergarten teacher was highly skilled and had excellent standing with the other teachers and in the community. She had taught disturbed children before, had a long range view of the function of kindergarten and collaborated closely with the guidance worker. Also, the teacher really liked Jenny and was intrigued by her "Alice in Wonderland" quality and her gracefulness. Despite the difficulties described above, the teacher did not feel that Jenny was mentally retarded (though Jenny's mother did).

The first task or goal facing the guidance worker and the teacher was the issue of whether Jenny could be retained in a public school.

Prior to the screaming episode with the substitute, Jenny's mother, Mrs. Adorno, had been to school several times at the teacher's request. The mother had seemed to be frightened about what the teacher might think of Jenny and, by implication, of her. Mrs. Adorno attributed Jenny's bizarre behavior to several causes, which were not clearly related. (The guidance worker and the school were aware at this time that they were by no means getting the complete history of this problem but purposely refrained from pressing this highly anxious and minimizing mother.) (1) A friend had told the mother that Jenny was not bright. (2) Jenny had been acutely upset by the birth, 9 months earlier, of a little sister. According to Mrs. Adorno, Jenny had stopped speaking altogether, had vomited at the sight of the baby and, when she had recently resumed talking, had done so in the singsong, stilted manner noted by the school. (3) Jenny had been a happy baby until she was two, when her parents had moved into the home of the paternal grandparents. The move had been necessary because Jenny's father had suffered a lengthy illness and the family had therefore had serious financial problems. Mrs. Adorno reported being unhappy about this move. She was extremely conscious of her in-laws' critical attitude toward her and Jenny. Hence she kept Jenny restricted to her bedroom almost constantly but tried to make up for this restriction and her guilty feelings about it by overindulgence and infantilization in other areas. (Jenny's early photographs, recently shown to the guidance worker, confirm the fact that the child's appearance was happy and seemed to be outgoing until her second year, when it changed to the withdrawn, autistic expression she still had at the time she entered school.)

On the basis of this history and Jenny's day of uncontrolled screaming, the guidance worker asked Mrs. Adorno to keep Jenny home during the tense, excited school period which always exists just before Christmas vacation. This did not involve a formal exemption because Jenny was not yet of legal school age. The mother knew that it was part of a plan to integrate Jenny constructively into the school and not a euphemistic first step toward exempting the child permanently.

Several measures were taken while Jenny was at home. (1) An experienced psychologist gave her a Stanford Binet Intelligence Test. Jenny's I.Q. score was 80, which enabled the guidance worker to assure the mother and the school that Jenny was not a dull child (since this I.Q. was obviously influenced by Jenny's emotional problems, hence far too low) and that thoughts of placement in a mentally retarded classroom would be wrongly directed. Jenny's most significant failures on the test were in the areas of common experiences such as "What is a chair . . . a dress . . . a shoe made up of?" Thus, the test offered a clue to the fact that some of Jenny's bizarre behavior might be attributed to lack of experience with reality and/or to the overriding influence of her own fantasy life on her perception of reality. That we gave the test, while Jenny was out of school, also reassured the mother of the school's continuing interest in Jenny and intention of continuing to work with her.

(2) The guidance worker held several conferences with this highly anxious, defensive mother. These conferences were focused on trying to increase Mrs. Adorno's trust in her own judgment and ability to set limits for Jenny. It was hoped that this would help the mother to be more supportive and less appeasing with Jenny and eventually would facilitate the mother's cooperative work with the school.

(3) The guidance worker and Jenny's teacher conferred to plan Jenny's gradual return to school and to anticipate ways in which her behavior could be dealt with. It was decided that Jenny's idiosyncratic

behavior should not be interfered with in general, as long as it did not disrupt the class but that Jenny should gradually be encouraged to join more often and more meaningfully in group activities.

Jenny returned to school after Christmas vacation. She spent a great deal of time playing in the bathroom, pretending to "spit up" and playing in the sink.* Gradually, she seemed to be a little more aware of the group, more apt to come out of the bathroom when another child needed to use it, and better able to take cues from the teacher. She still had no direct personal contact with other children. By May, Jenny had begun to express her autistic fantasies in a repetitive, monotonous identification with Snow White. She dressed up as Snow White during play time, she painted repeated pictures of Snow White and she constantly clutched a Snow White book in her arms, wherever she went. Her other major activity was to hang upside down from the bars of the jungle gym during play periods—a forerunner of her future flamboyant sexual exhibitionism. On the positive side, she had learned the names of the other children in her class and would comment on their absences in an odd, high-pitched voice. She would take part in singing and rhythm games. The children and school faculty had adopted the implicit attitude of Jenny's teacher, that this was a "different" child who, nevertheless, could be helped at school in a relaxed, calm atmosphere.

By the end of this kindergarten year, the first goal for Jenny had been reached: it seemed clear that, at least for the time being, Jenny could be kept in public school and did not need to be exempted. This agreement was not the outcome of a formal decision but, rather, of a tacit agreement that the guidance worker and the school would keep on trying. The teacher was the central strength in the situation. She used all her skills to create an ego-strengthening yet non-pressuring atmosphere for Jenny. She was able to do so because, basically, this was the atmosphere of her total classroom. It was not an uncritically permissive atmosphere but, rather, one in which clearly defined steps (e.g. activities, patterns of doing things) helped each kindergartener, by implication, to modify his own personal ways of doing things in terms of the processes and goals of the group. In Jenny's situation, as far as the teacher was concerned, there

---

* The bathroom has continued to be her refuge up to the present time (end of sixth grade). She retreats there whenever she feels left out, finds coping with the group too difficult or wants to escape from educational tasks she dislikes.

was merely a greater gap to close between the child's idiosyncracies and the group's goals. The teacher, it should be emphasized, had not tried to become a therapist, even though her attitudes and skills helped Jenny toward greater emotional stability.

Skilled and mature teachers in the next several years were able to continue in this role with Jenny while the guidance worker functioned primarily to support and clarify the teacher's efforts and to provide background information which could reduce the trial and error in learning to deal with Jenny. Since these highly skilled and dedicated teachers might have continued to struggle with Jenny past the point of diminishing returns, to the exhaustion of themselves and the class, the guidance worker also took the specific responsibility for deciding with the principal when and if Jenny should no longer be kept in public school. The guidance worker looked for every point at which the teacher could be supported through recognition of concrete, explicitly helpful steps with Jenny. The guidance worker, lastly, acted as a bridge between the teacher and the home and as a planner with the family of useful next steps outside the school, such as tutoring, summer activities, therapy in a community setting, etc.

No formal treatment referral was suggested at this time nor did the guidance worker (though she had the qualifications and experience) attempt to act as a therapist for Jenny or Mrs. Adorno. There were several reasons for this.

(1) The primary job of the guidance worker was to keep roles clear and communication open among teacher, principal, child and family and to stabilize a commitment to Jenny on the part of the school. Direct involvement with Jenny at this time would have beclouded this role and might have resulted in a less stable working relationship with the teacher or in competitiveness between the teacher and guidance worker about who was to be the major helping agent to Jenny.

(2) Jenny seemed to be overwhelmed by her own inner fantasy life. Introducing her to a direct treatment situation might have emphasized the importance of this inner world at a time when it was a primary goal in the school to make the outer world of other children—learning, socially appropriate behavior, and ordinary kindergarten activities meaningful for Jenny.

(3) Mrs. Adorno had responded eagerly to early interviews but had then become more anxious, had seemed to be personally more confused

and finally had withdrawn into a sort of hopelessness, veiled by surface cooperation. This surface cooperation, focused on immediate concrete issues, turned out to be the safest level of work with the mother at this time. Referral of the family to a community treatment agency was out of the question because of the high anxiety level, hopelessness, defensiveness and evidence of barely concealed chaos in the family situation.

Though Jenny was by now firmly established in school, she was by no means ready for the first grade. Therefore, she was retained for the present in kindergarten with the same teacher. She was still extremely preoccupied and very tenuously related to the group; also the structure of a first grade, with its many greater demands for conformity would undoubtedly be too difficult for her.

The next task or goal involved the question of whether Jenny could be *taught*—whether she could learn in a public school classroom of about 30 children. Initially, the guidance worker and the teacher had no clear idea of how to get Jenny more "ready" for first grade but it was assumed that more time with Jenny would provide some cues. She continued to be preoccupied with Snow White fantasies but her relationship with her teacher was close and trusting. Soon, it became apparent that she was more concerned with finding and testing limits. There were numerous episodes in which Jenny ran away from school, hid in high and dangerous places and cried "to find my Mommy." This behavior seemed teasing, rather than desperate. The teacher set firm limits and, when necessary, retrieved Jenny. In several conferences with the mother the teacher emphasized that such behavior was unsafe and could not be permitted. The close cooperation between school and home seemed to be what Jenny wanted and relieved her anxiety somewhat. Jenny's progress in relationships and social reality made it possible, by Christmas of her second year in school, to work out plans for a gradual transfer from kindergarten to first grade.

In terms of her fantasy life, Jenny had turned from Snow White to repetitive, compulsive drawings of "Nose Adornos" (the guidance worker wondered silently if the child symbolically meant "knows Adornos"). Pages of drawing paper and the margins of her textbooks were covered by these "Nose Adorno" pictures. When asked to draw faces, she would reply in her high-pitched, puppet-like voice, "I don't want them to have faces, just a nose."

The first-grade teacher had worked with disturbed children and was not particularly anxious about Jenny's eccentric behavior or compulsive preoccupation with "Nose Adornos." She pointed out classroom routines to Jenny and made it clear that, while the content of Jenny's day might be different from that of other children, she could not disrupt the class. Jenny's fits of screaming were handled firmly and consistently. She was not allowed to get her way by screaming or by the dramatic, inappropriate behavior which had begun by this time. (This behavior was extreme; for instance, Jenny came in late and made a grand entrance to class wearing a Playtex bra outside her dress.) Jenny was not allowed to draw Nose Adornos all over the blackboard.

On the other hand, the class was helped to accept Jenny as a routine member. Extra help was given to Jenny when possible: she was paired with a very stable girl in a lotto game, for instance, and took her turn with the help of this little girl. Thus, slowly, group participation skills were introduced. While formal learning started later, Jenny was now being taught to watch others and to learn vicariously. Her mother's help was enlisted in talking over with Jenny experiences which would interest other children at "sharing time" so that Jenny's long, incomprehensible, bizarre tales were gradually replaced by more human and interesting stories.

Referral for formal treatment was still felt to be inadvisable. The mother could cooperate with the guidance worker and the school only in terms of the most concrete current issues; she still appeased and could not set realistic limits for Jenny at home, although she recognized that Jenny was much better at school, where such limits were set. The mother's inability to say "No" was similar to her inability to be decisive with the elderly grandparents in the tense living situation. For instance, Jenny herself, finally became upset because her mother did not get her to school on time: after years of regular tardiness, Jenny eventually recognized that such behavior made her too conspicuous. Mrs. Adorno still viewed the guidance worker's occasional (three-four times a year) formal conferences with great apprehension, while welcoming more casual contacts, for instance by phone.

The teacher felt that Jenny, by the fall of the next year (Jenny's second semester in first grade), was ready for more formal learning. She worked with Jenny individually during the last twenty-five minutes of the school day. Jenny's protests, e.g. "I'm tired of reading," were countered by the teacher: "This is your reading time." Jenny progressed quite quickly through three pre-primers and one primer. It was difficult at first to get her to relate the printed story to the picture illustrating it—she hated to be confined to a realistic interpretation instead of her fantasies. But eventually, she became surer of her accomplishments in reading and these brought school/home relationships to a new high point, since Jenny read to her family and got great praise from them for it. Jenny's dramatic, isolating and isolated behavior began to drop off, although she still would have appeared psychotic, at times, to an outside observer.

Another milestone, nonetheless, had been passed: it had been demonstrated that Jenny could be taught academically if she had a sufficiently imaginative and gifted teacher. It had also been established that there was a clear relationship between consistent, relevant limits and Jenny's increased ability to tolerate. anxiety when confronted with a focused, ego-building step, such as learning to read. The guidance worker often thought that the task in working with Jenny was analogous to the effort needed to drain a lush but treacherous swamp by criss-crossing it with canals, thus gradually gaining a certain acreage of solid ground. Jenny's teacher observed, for instance, that Jenny would allow herself to read mechanically long before she began to show any interest in the meaning of what she read. She still drew Nose Adornos compulsively and tended to inject personal meanings into all educational processes. She was still largely motivated by immediate narcissistic interests and would not cooperate with tasks where the personal gain was not conspicuously apparent.*

In the second grade, Jenny's repetitive, compulsive drawings shifted from "Nose Adornos" to "Bobby-pin families." (These continued until about the fifth grade.) The "Bobby-pin families" were drawings, literally, of bobby-pins but with elaborations around the U-shaped top and clothes which differentiated family members, including Father, Mother, Jenny and her younger sister, Dora. The "Nose Adornos" had never become so personalized. Jenny also drew repetitively a series of "Lion" families, personifying particularly her relationship with her sister. The Lions looked like Cat drawings but the *dramatis personae* again were made clear by facial expressions. Jenny had to be kept from drawing

---

* She did not, for instance, learn any appreciable amount of arithmetic until sixth grade, when she realized that doing so would expedite her going to Junior High School at the proper age. Then, in a few short months, she mastered the basic concepts taught in the third, fourth and fifth grades.

Bobby-pin families and Lion families all over the blackboard. She scribbled them into the margins of her textbooks and onto her spelling or arithmetic paper. She still spent a great deal of time in the bathroom and still was involved, though rarely, with inappropriate, dramatic behavior like screaming or pulling her dress up and her pants down in the school corridors.

Yet, as she began to read quite well, toward the end of the second grade, both the teacher and the guidance worker felt a qualitative change had occurred in Jenny. Her theme became "I know now that I am somebody by the name of Jenny Adorno but who is this Jenny Adorno?"

Jenny spent the next two years with another excellent teacher, who volunteered to work with her. She established an excellent relationship with the mother (as the previous teachers also had, except that the mother, previously, was more defensive). In the third grade, it first became possible to insist that Jenny, occasionally, do conventional art work. Her early productions were always landscapes without human or animal forms but they were meticulously and artistically done. Conventional art work has progressively played a larger part in Jenny's artistic productions, while the Bobby-pin and Lion drawings have gradually (very slowly) given way.

The third grade teacher felt that Jenny's progress in school and the consolidation of her personality had proceded sufficiently that referral for formal treatment should again be considered. Jenny had progressed from being a chaotic jumble to being a girl with problems, albeit severe ones. The mother was much less hopeless; work with her had progressed from chaotic and apologetic descriptions of family life to task-oriented collaboration on useful next steps for Jenny. It was possible, at this time, to focus explicitly with the mother on the need to support reality and realistic limits in the home. The mother had felt previously that pointing out reality or conventional limits would squelch spontaneity in the children and therefore, she had permitted highly bizarre behavior.

Jenny, despite her improvement, still needed a great deal of individual attention and help. She still daydreamed for hours at a time, resisted academic work in favor of her idiosyncratic drawings, daily tested the teacher to see how much bizarre behavior would be overlooked. The teacher felt that while she could usually get Jenny "back on the track" academically, someone needed to "get at the roots of the problem." The guidance worker concurred in referral because of the improvement in the family situation, the father's improved economic stability, the essential separation of the Adornos from Mr. Adorno's parents (observed during a home visit) and the need to support the teacher's viewpoint. The psychiatric consultant* concurred, although neither consultant nor guidance worker had much hope that the referral would be stably successful. The guidance worker made a home visit to discuss the referral and the receiving agency with the mother and father. The mother was fearful but willing; the father's attitude was that his family had several odd people in it and that Jenny was not *that* different but, that if the guidance worker thought a referral was advisable he would go along with it.

Mrs. Adorno was seen about ten times at a child guidance clinic. She seemed at first to be involving herself in the treatment relationship but then suddenly became anxious, demanded a change of workers and finally mustered her courage to say directly that therapy was too upsetting to her and that Jenny would have to wait to get help of this kind until she was on her own. Mr. Adorno, who had also reacted with panic in his clinic interview, concurred in this decision. Mrs. Adorno told the guidance worker that she knew there were serious problems in the family but that they could not, at this time, afford to have the psychological "apple cart" upset. Having been able to handle this clinic situation directly helped Mrs. Adorno a great deal in her further relationships with the school and the guidance worker. She began to initiate contacts and to anticipate issues which might come up with Jenny at school so that she could "prepare" Jenny.

Jenny, in the meantime, had gone on to fourth grade with much improved reading skills, some spelling ability, greater conscious awareness of classroom expectations and a more directly expressed desire to get along with other students. She had learned to play hopscotch and jumprope but was clumsy and easily upset when children were impatient with her. Her fourth and fifth grades were fairly uneventful from an academic point of view. Her skills improved steadily, although there were still slips, periods of daydreaming, time spent in the bathroom, etc. Her chronic tardiness ceased when Dora, her younger sister, now in first grade, insisted that *she* wanted to be at school on time and put pressure on the

---

* The psychiatric consultant had followed Jenny's progress via the consultation process right from the beginning.

family to expedite morning dressing and breakfast so as to make this possible.

Both Jenny's teacher and her mother pressed the guidance worker, when Jenny was in the fifth grade, to see Jenny weekly because of her continuing difficulties with other children and her problems with reality testing and socially inappropriate behavior. This involved a marked deviation in the guidance worker's role and caused her considerable concern about its appropriateness in a school setting. She and the psychiatric consultant agreed, however, that it was appropriate in this situation and should be tried. The guidance worker met with Jenny after school hours, to underline the fact that their meetings were not part of the usual school routine. It was no longer necessary for the guidance worker to work closely with Jenny's teachers, since daily problems in the classroom had receded into the background. The guidance worker's collaboration with the teacher consisted largely of participating in several parent-teacher conferences focused around efforts to get Jenny to do homework, practice arithmetic, etc.

The guidance worker's individual weekly conferences with Jenny were concerned, for many months, with helping her (through drawings) to differentiate the "old Jenny" and the "new Jenny." These were the words Jenny used. The "Old Jenny" was completely self-centered, unable to handle any frustration, expecting everyone to cater to her. The "new Jenny" was more aware of appropriate behavior, knew you had to take turns at jumprope, for instance. She was the "sensible" Jenny, while the "old Jenny" was the "goofy" Jenny.

Yet, it was very obvious that there had been comfort in "old Jenny's" way of living, which was lacking in "new Jenny's" efforts. There were persistent attempts to get the guidance worker intrigued with the "old Jenny" and, failing in this, to sneak in some of the "old Jenny" via the Bobby-pin drawings, which continued to be highly disturbed in form, though more ego-oriented in content. Jenny's drawings remained symbolic. Finally the guidance worker asked her if she could make a "dictionary" of them. Jenny said that she could. It became clear that she had constructed highly stylized hieroglyphics which expressed various human feelings, such as anger, sadness, or glee.

After the construction of the dictionary which deciphered Jenny's symbolic language, the focus of interviews with her shifted to a direct discussion of feelings and then of the situations which produced severe anxiety for her. Social appropriateness became a major focus—what kinds of hair styles were suitable for junior high school, the level of arithmetic necessary for the seventh grade, how one evaluated realistically one's own emotions and those of others with whom one comes into contact. Jenny's conflicts with her family were discussed in this same vein: was it appropriate for her mother to be angry with her when she dawdled; should Sheila (a girl in the room) pull Jenny's sweater sleeve when Jenny wore the sweater in a sufficiently eccentric way to cause attention and teasing? Should Jenny hide in the bathroom when she feels left out of games? What are the alternatives for her? How could she become more aware of those around her, their feelings and their anxieties? This covered two years' work.

Jenny's future is uncertain. Experience has shown that such children, entering junior high school, may be ignored or rejected by their peers and that no amount of counseling or psychotherapy, at times, can counteract this social isolation and ignominy. Jenny's community, at present, has no groups *for* isolates (for instance in a group work agency) which might help to bridge her gap in relating to other children. Academically, however, Jenny's future in junior high school is reasonably assured if there is careful preplanning of her placement and curriculum. Her problems will be in the area of peer relationships.

An interesting byproduct of the direct work with Jenny has been a great increase in the interaction with Mrs. Adorno. An easy collaborative relationship has developed and there is increasing movement toward freer discussion of Mrs. Adorno's problems. Jenny reports that both her mother and father have begun to insist that it's time that she stopped being a problem at home and that they are both much firmer with her "goofiness." For instance, they finally laid down the law about her drawing "crazy" pictures and are encouraging her to build artistic model cars and to develop similar outlets. The parents are able to discuss Jenny's problems with each other more openly.

It is hard to predict the future. All that one can say is that Jenny now seems motivated to "overcome the bad start" (in her own words) and has developed a good many ego strengths. Her experience in junior high school will be uncertain but it is fair to say that this girl has received maximum support from her elementary school experience.

Craig

Craig is a Negro boy who has been followed by the guidance department from kindergarten on. (He has just finished ninth grade and will continue to high school.) I first knew him in kindergarten because the teacher recognized that his behavior was "not normal." He was very tense, his movements were "wooden," his speech was very infantile and difficult to understand. He talked little, was usually completely detached in the group, grimaced a great deal, made strange noises. Sometimes he hit other children or clutched them and would not let them go— seemingly an attempt at communication. His physical development appeared to be about that of a three year old. His drawings were scribbles. Other children recognized that he was "different" and were tolerant and protective. He attended a high morale elementary school in which the psychologically wise faculty could also accept very unconventional planning for a child who required it.

The mother, when interviewed, gave the following history. Craig was adopted when he was ten weeks old. He seemed to be a happy baby, though he was sick a great deal with colds. When he was just over a year old, he had a high fever with convulsions. He continued to have convulsions till he was about three and a half. He was seen by "nerve specialists" many times and became extremely frightened of anyone wearing a white coat. His development was uneven.

He was taken to a child development center when he was just under three years of age. They reported that his behavior was more like that of an eighteen months old child. "He was confused about language, jibbered and squealed; was stiff, anxious, babyish; no contact with children; much throwing of toys." He improved during the year he attended nursery school there but still appeared retarded. His test results, however, did not substantiate Craig's markedly retarded behavior. After four unsuccessful attempts to examine him, Craig finally obtained the following (minimal) scores on the Gesell Developmental Schedule: at a chronological age of 34 months, his motor age was 30 months, his adaptive age 24-30 months, his language age 24 months plus (he identified pictures at 30 months); his personal-social age 30 months.

By the time he was four, Craig wanted very much to play with other children but the only ones who lived near him were older and ran off and left him. It was at this time that his mother noticed that his movements became wooden, though he had been a tense child before.

Craig was five when the family adopted a year old boy, Joseph. Craig was delighted for a few days, then asked the parents to take the baby back where they had gotten him. He began to hit Joseph and to grab his toys. When Craig was about seven, a girl baby was adopted. By this time, Joseph had become something of a "helper" to Craig when the latter built things, etc. Craig has always been very gentle and protective toward his sister.

At home, Craig spent much time painting, working with his tools and listening to his records, many of which were classical music. He had a number of symptoms which could have indicated brain damage, such as overreaction to certain smells, a tendency to perseveration in speech and action, "jitteriness," and the nature of his learning difficulties. However, he had no temper outbursts and his coordination was good. He has had many neurological examinations and has been given phenobarbital by the family physician.

Craig's kindergarten teacher felt that she could handle the situation with him but I began seeing Craig fairly regularly when he was in the first grade. For many months, he was not willing to leave the classroom with me, so I spent time with him in the classroom, especially during recess periods when the other children were outside. He seemed to enjoy the attention, though he spoke little and kept his distance. He painted "pictures," mostly just large brush strokes with no content. He showed me things in the room and eventually talked about the things he showed me. His speech was difficult for me to understand but I hope I responded correctly—Craig was not a child one would ask to repeat what he had said. By the end of that year, Craig came willingly with me to the room in which I saw children in that school. He always walked on the opposite side of the hall from me, and, for the next two years, kept his literal distance.

There was no marked change in Craig until after a series of remarkable individual sessions. There was a mirror in the interviewing room, because it was used by the speech teacher. Craig sat in front of the mirror, working with clay. He pointed to his reflection and made faces at himself, turned to me and said, "That's me." I asked him what he thought about the boy in the mirror. He responded, "I don't like him . . . I don't like him 'cause he came to our house and stole money." He worked silently with the clay for a while; then, appearing to be unaware of my presence, pointing at himself in the mirror and making faces, he gave forth with a vehement, irrational tirade against himself in which he said several times, "You'll get kilt."

The next week, Craig sat down before the mirror and again paid no attention to me. To his reflection, he said—or rather, shouted—"I thought I kilt you last time I was here! I make a moon . . . (noises and much about moon and killing which I couldn't record). Hey, you! Pow! (Hit at himself.) You don't like it, huh? One of these days right in the kisser. What did you say? Pow! (Loud voice and many noises.) I'm not mad at you any more. I laugh at you—see? I'm not going to like you, though. There's a moon up in the sky. A big, round moon in the sky, and it's going to drop down and get kilt. (He smashed a ball of clay on the floor, saying something about the moon falling.) It came up again and fell on its face. But wait a minute. You kept my best moon—you dirty rat—my best moon—you dirty rat, you dirty monkey, donkey. Now I'm going to do something with the moon. I can't get the moon. Oh, I could kill you! I thought I kilt you the other time I was here!" He continued for the rest of the hour with similarly incoherent expressions of anger and self-directed aggression. He was shouting at himself and his face became flushed. The principal, hearing the shouting, came down to peer in through a small glass window in the door and was taken aback at seeing and hearing the quiet, usually unresponsive Craig acting in so wild a way. In the last five minutes of the interview, after I had told him we'd have to go back to the classroom, it seemed to me that he tried, in a garbled way, to pull his destructive fantasies back into better connection with reality.

In other sessions, he went through much of the same kind of procedure but began to vary it by running around the room with toy airplanes, making noises of airplanes and of crashes. He began to include me by "piloting" his airplane very close to me as he passed.

The teacher and Craig's mother noticed that, during this period, the boy was becoming more communicative and that his expressed desire to remain a baby gradually changed to a desire to be responsible. He shifted from a reluctant to an eager school attender. However, this "opening up" on Craig's part brought about an increase in some of his symptoms, which were very disturbing in the classroom. He began to make a barking noise so frequently that it was almost like a hiccough. The teacher, fond as she was of Craig, found this tic-like barking quite unnerving, though the children—who had, from the beginning, been very tolerant and accepting of Craig—seemed to be able to ignore it. Craig increased his clutching and jumping on other children. Needless to say such behavior required that the guidance worker make clear to the teacher, principal, and even other school personnel that, despite his obstreperousness, Craig was making progress compared with his former behavior.

Fortunately (in terms of being able to help Craig in the school setting), he remained very small and immature physically, so it was possible to keep him for two years in first grade and, again, two years in second. Of course, he was over age for the classroom group but did not appear out of place physically or socially. Fortunately, also, Craig's parents were most understanding and cooperative. When it began to look as if the school might have reached a total impasse, for instance, they would have gone along with a temporary exemption if necessary. Such a total impasse threatened twice, but the school managed to "hang on," even though, for a time, Craig attended school only for half a day.

Craig had made considerable progress in communicating and it began to look, from sessions with him, as if he might be ready to benefit from formal psychotherapy. This was discussed with the family and arranged for. Unfortunately, about the time this plan had been worked out with the community agency involved, the agency lost its child psychiatrist and there was a long delay before they re-opened their child therapy department. This agency was the only possible out-of-school resource for Craig locally, so I continued to see him on a regular basis. He did attend a special summer session in a private school for emotionally disturbed children, where his problems were essentially the same as those observed in the public school.

Craig's behavior at school became more disturbed after he began to break out of his shell of isolation. Everyone agreed that the picture was an encouraging one but that the boy was much more difficult to handle than in his previously isolated, silent state. He went on hitting sprees, "tackling" sprees, and kissing sprees. He continued to make bizarre noises and he sucked his thumb constantly, unless occupied with something like drawing. For almost one year, he talked to an imaginary parakeet on his shoulder or in his hand. (He actually had a pair of parakeets at home and lavished great love and affection on them.) The next year, he carried a "baby" around in his hand and talked to it a great deal. He took this "baby" with him to the summer school mentioned above. His speech was improving rapidly, he appeared to enjoy talking to me and moved into a closer, more direct relationship. His mother reported that he was even talking with some strangers (in stores, etc.) in a quite sensible way.

In one session, he talked to me about a school building which was to be demolished: he had seen the pictures in the paper. It seemed to disturb him; he went to the blackboard and drew the building, then carefully, with the eraser, demolished it bit by bit—he repeated this about three times, then asked about the new building which would be put up and seemed more relaxed.

By the time Craig was in the fourth grade, he was eleven years old, though he appeared to be only eight or nine. He was beginning to read. His drawings were always designs, but beautifully done in great variety of color and form. He could still do no arithmetic. He was somewhat better integrated into the group. However, because of his extreme social and physical immaturity, we arranged for him to repeat fourth grade. By the end of this year, he was thirteen and a half years old and had suddenly begun to grow. Permission from the assistant superintendent was required to keep him another year in elementary school. This was obtained. In the following year, he was placed with a sixth grade because of the inevitable imminence size of junior high school. He had, in repeating the fourth grade, learned to read with fair facility at about third grade level and was improving steadily.

We had not counted on the growth spurt, which brought on adolescent deepening of voice (it had always been husky) and—more than a little incongruous in elementary school—the shadow of a mustache. By now Craig, although he did not enter much into sports, was acting in a much more mature way. He "graduated" from elementary school at the age of fourteen years and five months.

Craig went to a stable, high-morale, middle-class junior high school, which had been prepared to meet a much more serious problem than the boy they encountered. The school was prepared to help him with special programming. Craig presented no problems in his three years of junior high school. He became a sort of "mascot," who was protected by other students. His behavior was not bizarre in any way, he showed no evidence of unusual tension, and he seemed to be a happy boy, but he was definitely retarded in his intellectual functioning. He seemed to have "solved" his severe psychological problems by stable pseudo-retardation. In the ninth grade, he achieved the citizenship honor roll twice and proudly displayed his certificate for this. He is graduating from junior high school at the age of seventeen years and five months, though his immature appearance matches his school placement. He will go on to high school next fall.

The Hayes Family

This case involves a Negro family whose four children all presented very difficult school problems. It will be hard to discuss clearly because it involved not only the family members but also a large number of school personnel, community people, probation officers and the Juvenile Court. "The Hayes" became as synonymous with trouble in the school setting as the name is synonymous with excellence in the world of the theater.

When I first met the family, it consisted of James, nine; Paul, seven; Etta, six; and Mark, four. My first contact with them was in connection with the problems of James, a bright, goodlooking but extremely withdrawn, sullen boy who came to our school from a neighboring town. He had presented a severe problem there, had been seen by their school psychiatrist and followed in their guidance department. The report from them indicated that James' problem was his behavior outside of the classroom—punching others without provocation, fighting on the playground and on the way to and from school, antagonizing other children by taking their balls away from them and throwing the balls over the fence. James and his mother reportedly had "terrific feelings of racial discrimination." The guidance worker in the previous school had set up as good a relationship with James as would have been possible to do. James had responded, problems had dwindled. Now, in the setting of a new school, problems of the same kind flared again.

My first home call, where I saw the mother, was very productive as far as her facts and observations about the two older children, James and Paul, were concerned. She was not hostile with me then and did not become so, toward me, through all the future difficulties—which were multitudinous.

At this time, the family lived in a basement apartment. All the rooms were small and the ceilings low; house-keeping standards were good, though not rigidly immaculate. The mother was very thin, her voice loud and piercing (when Mrs. Hayes phoned school, the principal usually had to hold the receiver some distance from her ear), she talked very fast and compulsively. She reported that she had been very depressed during her pregnancy with James because she was extremely homesick for her own mother. Her mother had told her that if she cried a lot, she'd have a baby who cried a lot. James did cry a lot, the parents had to take turns holding him—he was always "whiney" and had to be near his mother or he would start crying—he slept with his mother until he started walking. He paid little attention to toys, did not "get into things," would sit in his mother's lap for hours. Even at five years, he still wanted the bottle and, when his mother decided he was too old for it, he fixed it for himself. He was always "picky" about what he would eat. In kindergarten, he wanted his own way—he used to change his clothes every day—he was afraid of getting dirty. He used to let others hit him, "now *he* hits too much." He seems to want to do things for his mother around the house, he saves money. His father used to whip him a lot, not so much now. He and his father do some things together, for instance shopping at sales for bargain buys. The mother said James feels that everyone else is permitted to do things he gets punished for. When he is corrected or when he doesn't want to do things, he cries. When asked a question by his parents, he "lowers" his head and says, "I don't know." He feels girls get a better break at school than boys; that his sister gets a better break at home. He complains that the principal and his mother always bring up things he did in the past. Teachers have repeatedly told the mother that James has to have his work too neat.

Paul has always liked to be by himself, has not joined much with other children in play. The mother wonders if his hearing is all right, for he often appears not to hear when spoken to.

The mother gave no early history on Etta or Mark.

James and Paul continued to have severe difficulty in school. After about six months, affairs with them reached such a pitch of crisis that I determined to see the father as well as the mother. By this time, the mother was at sword's point with the principal, who was bending every effort to keep the situation within bounds. The mother would frequently phone, making all sorts of threats to the principal and once carried out her threat to "go to the Board" (The Board of Education). The one saving grace in the whole massive conflict was that the mother did not seem to be hostile to me (from her own history and from later events, I believe this was because she somehow placed me in the position of *her* mother). Each time I saw her, I was able to get her to "simmer down" and accept some of the necessary arrangements for having the boys (at this time, particularly James) sent home when the situation at school became "too hot to handle." Only after meeting the father did I begin to understand why, after I had obtained agreement from the mother for certain procedures, the whole fabric of the plan would fall apart and the mother would call the principal in a screaming rage about the boy or boys being sent home.

I had made arrangements with the mother, who had consulted the father, to make my home call at 5:30, when he arrived home from work. (The school principal had had only one contact with him, when the father had arrived at school late one afternoon with a friend and both had been fairly drunk. Mr. Hayes was somewhat belligerent at that time, but not markedly so.) I arrived before the father got home. When he came in, the mother introduced me. He grunted and went on into the back room. The mother and I went into the living room. Mr. Hayes did not come back until his wife asked him to. He sat on the edge of his chair and glared at me, said nothing as yet, waiting for me to open my big mouth. When I briefly explained the difficulties we were having and our plan of having the boys go home at times when they seemed too upset to be in the school setting, he burst forth on a tirade about the ineffectiveness of modern teachers in controlling children and discrimination against Negro families, then abruptly left the room. He did not return until his wife again called him back. As has been my custom in such situations, I maintained an attitude that would have been appropriate if the royal red carpet had been rolled out for my visit. It worked, at least to a small extent, for I was able to get him to sit for a short time to explain what our long range plans would be and the probable difficulties we (the Hayes and I) would encounter. He continued to maintain that, if the teachers and principals were not so "soft," they could whip the kids, as he did, and make them behave. I made my usual pitch for the steps in developing inner controls, but knew it was only an initial opening of the subject.

The family had expressed their ambition to buy their own home and after a time managed to do so. I made many calls at many points of crisis—and crises were practically weekly, as far as the two boys were concerned. I was careful to call at the home after the father got back from work, so that he would be included. Little by little, the father's hostility lessened, as he became accustomed to my home calls. Shortly after they had moved into their new home, he took me through every inch of it, even into his "shop" where he complained that his boys weren't interested in working with tools—"these modern kids!" During this last year or so, he seems to enjoy a good friendly argument with me on current local or national affairs, topics he brings up with me. He sits back, relaxes and laughs heartily if a returning sally of mine strikes him as spunky or funny.

What became evident in the repeated contact was Mr. Hayes' great bitterness that he had not made more of his life—he had sacrificed his own hope for more education to make this education possible for one of his brothers, who had "gummed up" in the process and not made use of this advantage. Mr. Hayes works as a skilled laborer but hopes his children will not have to "beg" for jobs but will be people to whom others would come for help, for instance dentists or lawyers. Behind his facade of violent hostility and suspiciousness was a poignant, anxious and intellectually competent human being who, for instance, despite his poor formal education, kept himself informed about current events.

But to get back to the earlier picture, we managed to get James on a reasonably even keel with a superb teacher. He was working even beyond his registered potential of above average ability, but the danger signs of intense perfectionism were still present. All of the Hayes children defeated themselves repeatedly on this point: unless a thing could be absolutely perfect, it was not worth trying for—no use at all. The school faculty was alerted to this roadblock for these children and began immediate work to counteract it with the two youngest children, Etta and Mark. They, too, were beginning to present problems similar to, though as yet less severe than, those of their older brothers.

As James became better integrated, Paul became increasingly impossible to contain in the school situation. I attribute this to three things: (1) Paul is probably far less intellectually able than James and James began, with his own better adjustment at school, to "pour it on" Paul. (2) Paul was just hitting the school grade level where academic failure is a severe blow to the ego. (3) Further, the mother, who had been recovering from a hysterectomy, was in an automobile accident and had suffered a concussion, with subsequent headaches, etc. The mother's illness and accident upset the whole family. In spite of the dense, "stainless steel wall" barriers with "outsiders" and the intra-family conflicts, there were very close ties in this family (almost, I feel, on the order of the inbred New England kind).

It eventually became necessary, in the fifth grade, to exempt Paul from school for the rest of the year because of his attacks on other children and his disruption of the classroom. By now, my relationship with the parents was such that they accepted the exemption with relatively little hostility or projection of blame. There was little doubt on the part of the principal and some of the teachers that Paul was, at times, a scapegoat and was blamed unjustly by other children and some teachers, but it was also true that he would deny an act even when seen doing it. It was necessary for me to handle both aspects of this directly and honestly with the parents and the children. I said we all might get blamed by others for things we had not done, that the school was aware of the scapegoating and was trying to check carefully on the actual facts and faults involved in any incident. We were fortunate to have an elementary assistant in the school, so that Paul, while he was out on exemption, could come for an hour each day for help with reading, on which he was completely blocked.* The family could not have afforded to have daily tutoring. Each day, Paul arrived with his brief case of materials and home work. Having Paul out of school was a great relief to the teachers, though there were times when he would appear at school to wreak his vengeance on some one of the other children. The following year, Paul was back in school. He was periodically involved in some intolerable act and had to be sent home, but the school managed to contain him for the greater part of the year.

By Paul's last year in elementary school, his sister, Etta, was presenting a severe school problem of much the same nature. She was a tomboy, "tough," "obstinate," and "sullen." She bullied younger girls, was defiant, and often refused to do her school work. Careful planning to have her placed with teachers who could tolerate this kind of behavior kept crises to a manageable number, though she, too, had to be sent home for a day or two from time to time. James was completing his second year of

---

* Paul's school and some others, at the option of the principal, had the half-time services of a specially skilled teacher who worked with teachers on instructional resources and with individual children or small groups on their academic difficulties, especially reading, in an atmosphere specifically directed toward building self-esteem, helping children to "loosen up" and providing pre-reading experiences with puppets, vocabulary-building games, etc.

junior high and was getting along much better than I had expected, though his problems seemed to be getting worse as the year progressed. Mark, the youngest, presented a milder problem. He was not having academic trouble, aside from the fact that he could tolerate no imperfections and frequently tore up his papers or refused to finish them. For a time he formed a "gang," which he organized to run through the games of younger children, grabbing balls or hitting. I worked with the "gang" as a group for a time toward the end of the year and the school took firm measures to put a stop to the behavior, yet it periodically cropped up.

Because all four Hayes children were in repeated trouble, I started having bi-weekly conferences with the whole family in their home, after Mr. Hayes got home from work. I explained to the parents that one of the great difficulties of their children was their inability to talk with people when they were "on the spot" about their behavior and that the children could not accept correction of any kind without feeling rejected and angry. I hoped that by my trying to get them to talk about things which happened at school or in the neighborhood, I could help them with their feelings and help the parents to be able to talk with the children in a more constructive way, *i.e.*, neither just to beat them nor, on the other hand, just to blame the teacher or school. James was very resistant to coming but his parents insisted. He ducked out at times but was usually present. The others came, although conversations were very difficult to come by. It did become clearly evident that both the mother and father were extremely needling and teasing with the children in much the same way that the children needled and teased other children. I do not feel these interviews were particularly successful in a direct way, though I think there was some carryover in the fact that the children seemed increasingly able to believe that the school was not totally against them and were better able to talk over difficulties which arose, with the principal and teacher. This might have developed anyway, for all their teachers were interested in the problem and the principal was working hard to support his teachers and to develop a positive relationship with the Hayes family. For some teachers, the problems of these children presented a real challenge, for they recognized a kind of personal integrity and intellectual "quality" in the children, which was not easy to define but impressed itself on them.

In the course of our family conferences, the parents came to accept me very well, usually had coffee ready and waiting. The mother frequently commented on whatever dress I was wearing and wanted me to give it to her when I was tired of it. Once when Paul had promised to make some cookies for my next visit but baseball practice intervened, Etta remembered just before I got there and hurriedly made them. She brought in about a dozen very good cookies, a bowl of jello and a cup of coffee—all carefully arranged on the best dishes and on a tray. The mother said it was entirely Etta's idea.

To recapitulate the progress of four years of work by many people: James seemed to be making a marginal behavioral adjustment in junior high and a fairly good academic adjustment. Paul still presented a severe problem but at least the principal and a few of the teachers felt we were making some progress. Whereas, at the beginning, he had presented a silent, impenetrable wall to any "talking with," he later would weep and, by the sixth grade, could tolerate an arm around his shoulder and could try to verbalize his side of the story; he even was willing, at times, to admit that he was at fault. He, even yet, could not achieve a first grade reading level. I was able to interest a retired teacher in Paul and she was helping him weekly without cost to the family.

Etta was the least attractive-looking of the Hayes children (why *would* this have to happen to the girl!). She had a skin allergy which caused a raw-looking, elephant-hide appearance of the neck and arms. Other children teased her, did not like to sit by her or touch her. She had made some progress with an especially skilled teacher, who found that a tacitly acceptable way to get Etta to do something was to say, "Oh, well, I don't think you can do that work anyway, so don't bother," or since Etta could accept no praise, "That's a poor paper," with a grin, since both knew it was good; or, in private, "I guess you wouldn't be able to handle this job because you really don't know how to take care of yourself." Etta usually "bit" on this pseudo-negative approach and "came through." The teacher reported that Etta must be "won over" by the teacher, yet treated with firmness. No issue can be avoided with Etta—she challenges the teacher but respects the teacher only if the teacher wins—Etta has to test to see whether the limits will "give." At the same time, Etta has to be given time for "face-saving."

Mark was presenting more of a problem than he had before, but he was never as difficult as his brothers, and we felt primarily that he was reflecting the tensions of the school and family problems, plus his unremitting perfectionism.

My hope that we were "over the hump" with these children proved false. This last year has been a very bad one as far as James and Paul are concerned. They were both in a multi-problem junior high school where stresses from many sources were causing plummeting morale and near-riot attitudes on the part of the difficult students together with in-creased and (increasingly arbitrary) severity and antagonism from some of the teachers. James reverted to his earlier sullen, defiant and explosive behavior; at ninth grade, this posed real problems. His academic work deteriorated, his defiance and even verbal attacks on teachers were in-tolerable to many, but most difficult to deal with was his growing reputation for being "dangerous," *i.e.* capable of doing bodily harm. (We have wondered if James might have central nervous system damage of some kind.) He then became involved in what appeared to be two unprovoked attacks on other students, also he seemed to be at the bottom of other fights. Eventually he became so disturbed and seemed so dan-gerous that he was committed to a State correctional institution which has psychiatric facilities. (At present writing, James is reported to be home again. The guidance department will continue to work with him in high school.)

Meantime, Paul, who had entered the same junior high school, was not able to "stick it out" past the first three months. He made a real effort to keep out of trouble but the diffusion of authority in junior high school, Paul's lack of academic skills, his impulse-driven tongue ("vile language"), and James' reputation were too much for him to handle and we had to exempt him for the balance of the year. The smoothness of my interview with the parents regarding the exemption was proof of the change of their early attitudes, when all blame was projected onto the school. They faced this crisis very realistically. However, it was fortunate that the retired teacher, whom I mentioned above, was willing to help Paul twice a week instead of once and, at this time, is reporting some small progress in the area of reading: naturally, she is delighted. So was I, when she reported that Paul had seen her in the car as she passed on a nearby street and had waved and grinned—this kind of gesture was, as far as we had seen, unprecedented with Paul. This teacher has developed a good relationship with the family. The mother now tends to lean on her for support when things go wrong—talked to her at length, for instance, when James was sent to the State correctional institution. Her regular appearance at the Hayes home twice a week during these past two years has taken the edge off the many, many difficulties. Paul will return to junior high school next year and further efforts to help him with his adjustment will be made.

Etta, meanwhile, was getting along very badly with her teacher during the first part of the year—so badly, in fact, that consideration was given to either exemption or a change of schools. I did not have the nerve to ask any other school to take her but the gods were with us and another teacher in the same school offered to try. This has worked out remarkably well, for Etta has become fond of his teacher, has dropped much of her tomboyish behavior, dresses more attractively, etc. I do anticipate trouble for her in junior high school next year.

Mark is progressing quite well in view of the difficulties presented by the sibs.

NOTE
(Chapter IX)

1. This also applies to children with a factor of cerebral dysfunction.

CHAPTER X

Minimal Cerebral Dysfunction: a New Dimension for Guidance Workers

Evidence is rapidly accumulating that cerebral dysfunction may play a significant part in the emotional and learning disturbances of some children even in the absence of the more clear-cut classical syndromes such as epilepsy, cerebral palsy, athetosis and the like. In childhood schizophrenia, the estimates of cerebral dysfunction, as a factor, rise as high as 60% to 85%.[1] Guidance workers are becoming aware that a factor of cerebral dysfunction may play a part in many learning, behavioral and neurotic disturbances of childhood. Some examples of this will be discussed below.

First, it should be noted that this diagnosis is a controversial one still, especially when the electroencephalogram is negative, equivocal or controversial (unusual wave patterns where various authors differ on the probable significance).[2] Nevertheless, diagnosis can be educational and/or behavioral, as well as medical; remedial educational and psychological handling can proceed with or without a clear-cut medical diagnosis, although the latter is greatly to be desired and sophisticated pediatricians are using their own clinical acumen rather than basing their judgments entirely on the EEG (electroencephalogram) or on gross neurological abnormalities.

Orton[3] in the late nineteen twenties advanced the hypothesis that subtle cerebral dysfunction played an important role in many learning and other difficulties. He stressed issues of handedness and mixed laterality and related these to brain mechanisms in a manner which was probably not sufficiently complex in terms of the actual interrelationships of functional areas in the cerebral cortex and parts of the mid-brain. His contributions, however, did not serve as a pioneering exploration which would later be elaborated, corrected, and refined. Instead, until rather recently, most authors overlooked cerebral dysfunction as a significant factor in the learning problems of some children.

There seem to have been two major reasons for this. First, doctors often did not detect subtle or complex neurological disturbances because examination of the patient in the usual small examining room did not permit their disclosure and because doctors did not obtain sufficiently detailed developmental histories. Also, if the diagnosis was made, many doctors had an attitude of therapeutic nihilism; they felt that the child's maturation would take care of the situation, they would not prescribe medication in the absence of seizures, or they tended to rely exclusively on phenobarbital.

On the psychological side of things, it will be recalled that this was the period of Anna Freud's *The Ego and the Mechanisms of Defense*.[4] Psychoanalytically-oriented psychological approaches were becoming very popular in the United States and, unfortunately, were dichotomized from organic components in a child's difficulty. Thus, on a gross level, Tom, one of the cases discussed below, was refused treatment in a child guidance clinic on the grounds that his difficulties had been diagnosed as neurological. A more sophisticated child guidance clinic asked why they should be concerned with factors of cerebral dysfunction, since it would not alter their treatment approach in any event. A third cited a child with known cerebral dysfunction and pointed out that psychotherapy alone had helped. These viewpoints contain two fallacies: (1) that neurological factors can be handled by medication alone (without attention to paranoid attitudes, evil self-image, defensive maneuvers) and, (2) lack of recognition of the fact that, although maturation, improved ego strength, etc., can indeed help a child to control aggressive outbursts and other symptoms, this may occur at the expense of unresolved learning difficulties, unfortunate defensive "amputations" of personality and unnecessary expenditure of energy on the part of the patient.

In the cases which follow, it will be seen that the children presented themselves with various kinds of difficulty. Some suffered from aggressive outbursts, particularly in high stimulus situations (lunch hour or recess at school). Others in this category (*e.g.* Hugh) controlled themselves at school but fell apart when they got home. These children often showed evidence of perceptual disturbances: hyperacuity of smell or taste, overreaction to glare, hyperreactivity in the preschool years to noise, etc. One would often think of a temporal lobe locus for the cerebral dysfunction (since the temporal lobe is intimately concerned with perception). A second group of children are most apt to be identified in the early school years when their visual-motor difficulties are seen: they may write their names off the edge of the paper, complain that the letters jump around so that they cannot read, etc. The Bender Gestalt and other tests will demonstrate the visual-motor basis for their difficulties. Yet a third category of children present themselves with neurotic or psychotic symptoms as the chief complaint. These presenting symptoms often mirror some aspect of the psychodynamics: phobias related to fear of aggression, exhibitionism related to severe castration anxiety, compulsivity binding aggression, identification with the female aggressor (when the mother is the primary object relationship for the very young child) and consequent tendency toward effeminacy. A fourth category of children should be investigated for possible cerebral dysfunction: these are the children with severe, sometimes isolated, learning disturbances in the absence of other obvious problems. Severe difficulties with reading are usually noted by educators and, in intellectually capable middle-class youngsters, referred for diagnostic evaluation, where they must be differentiated from children (boys, as a rule) with passive-resistive attitudes toward reading on psychological grounds. Severe difficulties with spelling or arithmetic may be less liable to detection but the student with such difficulties should not be dismissed automatically as disinterested or blocked but should be investigated for cerebral dysfunction influencing these particular skills.

We turn now to a representative sample of cases. The first six cases were seen privately as psychiatric referrals. The other cases were seen as guidance referrals by guidance workers.

Hugh

This patient has been previously reported.[5] He was an unusually bright and lusty infant until the age of nine months, when he suddenly suffered a physiological trauma (presumably a cerebral vascular accident), which caused a violent change in his behavior to that of a classically autistic or schizophrenic baby. He screamed, had aggressive outbursts, hit anyone who came near him, stared into bright lights obsessionally, had to have the vacuum cleaner going for hours at a time, took the bottle only when it was held at arm's length. He was taken to every variety of medical specialist, all of whom felt that the boy was spoiled and the mother over-protective. Psychiatric examination, when the patient was six, revealed the picture of a boy with severe aggressive outbursts and of a severely anxious but not rejective or over-protective mother. An electro-encephalogram disclosed massive focal and degenerative lesions in the left temporal lobe. In the course of further psychiatric treatment, various perceptual disturbances were discovered: Hugh was hyper-reactive to smell and/or taste, had abnormal color dreams and *déjà vu* experiences. This patient, at fifteen years of age, under conditions of stress, had his first *grand mal* seizure.

Tom

A nine year old boy was referred from a rural area because of aggressive outbursts and sadistic behavior. Tom's parents were of lower middle-class background, psychologically naive and did not recount enough psychological disturbance in the family to account for the boy's difficulty. In taking a developmental history on Tom with special attention to problems of perception and coordination, a surprising factor emerged. The mother said that the family had always been unable to understand Tom's aversion to smells—even those usually considered pleasant, such as perfume—because the boy had congenital bony atresia of the posterior nares, which had required operative intervention, so that they would expect him to be relatively insensitive to smell. Tom's electroencephalogram, done with photic stimulation, showed a temporal lobe lesion. There were no historical findings to account for this and multiple congenital anomalies must be considered, as they must be in the case of John.

John

A five year old boy was referred because of a severe phobia about dogs. He was at an age when it was reasonable to assume that his problem was a classical oedipal phobia and the case was handled on this basis. A year later, the mother returned, saying that she had minimized the history of aggressive outbursts. These occurred, as evident in further investigation, in high stimulus situations. This boy alternated between phobic and aggressive behavior. An electroencephalogram, with photic stimulation, disclosed a temporal lobe lesion.

Erik

A fifteen year old boy was referred for sexual exhibitionism. His parents were hearty, extroverted people who felt that they "might have been too much for the boy." Erik had had severe learning problems from an early age and the school people involved had felt that his parents' upward social mobility and aggressive extroversion were the primary cause of the boy's difficulties. The mother expressed similar fears. Yet, when the developmental history was explored, the mother was able, very vividly, to describe Erik's severe handicap in learning to ride a bicycle. This kind of difficulty was not anticipated by the interviewer and was convincing because of its unexpectedness and concrete detail. "You should have seen that day," said the mother. "I'll never forget my husband, sweating like a pig, pushing Erik all day on that bike until he finally caught on." Further evidence of difficulties with coordination was obtained. In this case, psychological (testing) evaluation did not reveal a central nervous system factor in Erik's problems, *i.e.* there was no impairment in visual-motor performance. Neurological and electroencephalographic examinations disclosed, however, that Erik suffered from psychomotor and *petit mal* seizures. Coordination with the school was possible, Erik was placed on medication and began combined tutoring and counselling with a male social worker.

Dick

This boy was referred at the age of fifteen because of severe academic failure, low test results and passive-aggressive behavior toward the school, his parents and life in general. His mother was a woman who, at first, seemed overwhelmingly anxious and over-protective; she emphasized psychodynamic factors. Recalling the case of Hugh, the psychiatrist wondered why the mother's anxiety was so extreme and referred Dick to a pediatric neurologist. A regime of medication was instituted and a workup for specific, remedial educational planning was obtained. This patient has been tutored by a person of special competence with the learning difficulties of children with cerebral dysfunction. He has been kept out of a special class and out of a low-achieving group because of the danger of promoting his feelings of worthlessness or the hopelessness of academic competence. Three years later, Dick is at grade level in school and has become a relatively self-confident, age-appropriate boy.

Matthew

An eight year old boy of Chinese-American background was the youngest child of an attorney. He was a year behind in school, having been so immature in kindergarten that his mother kept him out for a year. His mother described him as impulsive and a severe problem at home because of his aggressive behavior. Matthew had been a premature baby and the family, especially the father, was almost ready to believe that he was retarded. On the other hand, much family turmoil during the boy's preschool years made them wonder if Matthew were reacting to that. The developmental history, the aggressive outbursts and the unevenness of Matthew's behavior made cerebral dysfunction a likely factor in the diagnosis, in addition to neurotic patterns in the family and pseudo-psychotic patterns in the boy. However, in the playroom observation, no clearcut evidence of cerebral dysfunction could be obtained. Matthew showed marked relationship hunger. He acted retarded but could draw a man at the level of his chronological age. His drawing disclosed distorted, damaged body image and Matthew quickly made it "crazy" by filling it, like twisted skeins of twine, with "bones," manufactured by a machine in the bottom of the abdomen. He did these drawings repetitively both for the psychiatrist and for the educational evaluator. In the educational evaluation, when Matthew was set thoroughly at ease by helping to garden and playing with the cat, he could perform on an intelligence test within the normal (average) range. His performance quickly deteriorated under pressure and he acted "crazy." No evidence of cerebral dysfunction could be elicited.

Matthew's case illustrates the importance of a complete diagnostic evaluation.[6] He was referred to a neurologically sophisticated pediatrician, who discovered abnormal neurological signs and made the diagnosis of cerebral palsy or a related neurological situation. Matthew's response to medication was dramatic.

The above cases, presented for diagnostic points, all happen to have been seen by the psychiatric author and are reported elsewhere. They could equally well have been brought to the attention, first, of a guidance worker and the same diagnostic process could have taken place, as demonstrated by the next two cases.

Lisa

Lisa was a beautiful blonde, blue-eyed, pigtailed girl in a small middle-class school which tended to have few guidance problems. The school had an excellent staff and administrator. Lisa, then repeating first grade, was the daughter of an immigrant family from Europe and the only serious problem in the school. The staff and principal felt that she was strange and wanted to be helpful to her. They were particularly perplexed by this attractive young girl's hyperactivity, her obvious need for attention and affection, her severe learning handicaps and her diffuse ways of behaving. They even doubted that she should be allowed to walk to or from school by herself as she appeared to wander and become lost.

Lisa had been known to the guidance worker who had served the school previously. The child had entered school there a few months after her arrival from central Europe. Her English was quaint but clear. She seemed bewildered. There were a large number of realistic factors which made such a reaction plausible: Lisa's halting English and the family's adherence to a religious faith opposed to saluting the flag were two striking ones, which set Lisa, the little foreigner, apart. Then her lunches were "different" and seemed inadequate to the teacher. At first the teacher was very critical of Lisa's strange ways, her restlessness, her difficulty in learning to read. The guidance worker tried to make sense out of the situation and to stall for time for Lisa. Lisa's teacher gradually became much more interested and sympathetic, due largely to the child's own personal appeal. Yet Lisa's problem—her hyperactivity and difficulty in learning—continued.

This guidance worker spoke the native language of Lisa's parents. In a home visit, the guidance worker found the mother afraid of the "authorities," scared that Lisa's father would find out his child was causing trouble, worried about Lisa, who had a tendency to wander away from home as well as from school and had done so even in Europe. Despite the fact that the family had made several moves en route from Europe to California, none of the other children had such difficulties. The guidance worker promised to watch Lisa's progress at the school closely and to work with her until her behavior fitted into a more meaningful pattern. It was arranged that she should walk to and from school with an older sister so that she would not get lost.

The cultural factors in the situation were still not distinct from Lisa's personal problems when summer came. The next fall this school had a new principal and a new guidance worker. Lisa's troubles continued.

The new principal naturally called the parents in for a conference but was shocked to find that their response was to administer a severe beating to the child for the "bad behavior." After several such occurrences, the school stopped calling home and attempted just to hold the girl in school. When the new guidance worker saw the child, he suspected some organic problem. Psychological tests tended to confirm this impression. But communication with the parents was difficult as the guidance worker did not speak their native tongue. The parents showed "cultural shock" and overreacted to every call or visit from the school or guidance worker. They did, however, seem to respond to the idea of taking the girl to a hospital clinic when the possibility of some physical illness was successfully conveyed to them. They were members of a large hospital group insurance plan.

Unfortunately, when the parents took the child for a physical examination, they were seen by an anti-psychiatric pediatrician who reported that the child was the very picture of health (which, in fact, was true if neurological problems were overlooked). A second referral was made to a University diagnostic center. This again involved much explanation to the parents although, by now they were following the guidance worker's recommendations on faith. A neuropsychiatric workup was done at the University Center but, to the confusion of the parents, they were referred back to the first hospital, where they were insured. The findings from the University Center were sent to the first hospital but the parents' cooperation was lost in the transfer as they were not only confused by these switches but seemed to feel that they were "not wanted." Being new citizens and "on trial," they seemed to be particularly vulnerable to such feelings.

The guidance worker discussed the case with a staff pediatrician at the original hospital who was more attuned to psychological problems and their possible origin in central nervous system damage. The guidance worker emphasized his impression that the parents, particularly the mother, did not actually understand as much English as they appeared to. This was new to the pediatrician. He had seen the mother only once and she appeared to follow the conversation, although she did not say much herself and had trouble phrasing what she did say. The pediatrician asked a physician who spoke the parents' language to take over the case.

The mother was overjoyed to find this new contact. After several months of effort, a complete history was finally obtained on the girl. It developed that she had had convulsions during her infancy in Europe. This history fitted in with the neurological impression of organic difficulty.

Medication was started and Lisa improved immensely, although she continued to have learning problems. Even more important than the help to Lisa was the salutary effect on the whole family provided by this contact with a bilingual physician, who was eventually able to persuade the parents to relax about the moral implications of their daughter's behavior.

Louanne

Louanne, a skinny but alert nine year old Negro girl, had been known to another guidance worker in a nearby slum school because her behavior was characterized by temper tantrums, fighting and inability to cope with school routines. She seemed bright enough but her disruptive behavior had resulted in a shortened school day, so that there were gaps in her learning of the three R's. The first worker had attempted to pinpoint the source of Louanne's trouble, presuming that it had to do with her very early childhood, about which little was known. She had been brought North by her maternal grandmother, now dead, while her own mother stayed in the South. Louanne's mother did move North a few months before the grandmother's death and had been caring for Louanne ever since. The shift in family composition had coincided roughly with Louanne's entrance into kindergarten. The mother's attitude, when interviewed by the guidance worker, was almost totally passive. He recorded that he felt like "planting a bomb under her." His hypothesis was that early deprivation and the mother's attitude accounted for Louanne's trouble in school.

Louanne's family moved in the spring of the year she was nine and she enrolled in one of "my" schools. She was placed with a very experienced teacher, who had a reputation for setting clear but kind limits. The class was unusually stable for this neighborhood. We wanted to try Louanne on a full-day schedule. For the remainder of this year, the plan worked beautifully. Two semi-tantrums were handled firmly but kindly by her teacher. Louanne was allowed by the teacher to stay in the classroom during recess, thus avoiding the chaos of a large school yard. She went home at lunch time. Thus there was little unstructured contact or friction with classmates. Louanne was eagerly learning to read and was given a book to study from at home. The teacher found her a pathetically industrious learner and a very likeable girl, despite her difficult behavior.

At the end of the year, Louanne wrote a poignant little letter of thanks to her teacher.

Then came the summer months in a slum neighborhood. Apparently, Louanne's old reputation for fighting was revived. On her first day of school in the fall, she was chased by a group of children and arrived at school in hysterics. A tantrum in class that day could not be handled by the teacher; the principal had to intervene and Louanne was suspended. I made a home call. In terms of our diagnostic hypothesis at that time, I was unable to decide whether Louanne's deterioration was due to her poor relationship with peers or to the lack of care at home during the summer.

But when I started making more regular home calls, usually when Louanne had been in further difficulties at school, I saw the mother's passivity melt away. Her true concern about Louanne became apparent. She was bewildered, particularly because Louanne's behavior at home was that of a reliable mother's helper: a pseudo-adult, perhaps, but certainly not a spoiled, deprived or tantrum-ridden child. As our relationship grew, so grew my wondering. There was no doubt that Louanne was falling apart at the seams in the school situation, but why?

Eventually, I presented this case to the psychiatric consultant who, on the basis of Louanne's interest in learning, her ability to relate, her poignancy, and her inability to tolerate confusion and teasing, felt that the diagnosis of primary behavior disorder was unlikely and suggested a possible diagnosis of temporal lobe brain damage.

This possibility was discussed with the social worker attached to the pediatric service of the hospital where Louanne was getting her medical care. This worker, too, had seen Louanne's family often and was convinced that Louanne's troubles at school were the school's fault. She felt that Louanne had become a scapegoat there. She did not see any point in a neurological work-up. (This family was on Aid to Dependent Children and financially unable to obtain a work-up through other channels.) A letter from our psychiatric consultant to the pediatrician at the hospital brought about a neurological work-up. An electroencephalogram, done with photic stimulation, confirmed the diagnosis of temporal lobe damage. Louanne was to be started on medication.

However, summer had come around again, and Louanne's mother made a short trip South while the girl, not yet on drugs, was left with a neighbor. She became embroiled in a fight with a youngster on the street;

when taken home, she was so panicky that she threatened to jump out of the second story window. The police had to be called, and she was taken to the psychiatric ward of the county hospital for observation. From there, she was committed for ninety days to a State Psychiatric Hospital. Her present status is unknown.

In the diagnosis of a probable factor of cerebral dysfunction, several points should be emphasized. Middle-class families, conversant with popularizations of psychoanalytic theory, tend to distort history and symptoms because of their assumption that the child's difficulty is unquestionably psychogenic. Other middle-class families deny or minimize the child's difficulties but one can say that, whatever defensive stance the family selects, psychogenic etiology is usually assumed.* The guidance worker who is aware of this will require documentation from the parents of some specific relationship between the child's symptoms (such as eruptive-aggressive outbursts) and the psychological patterns in the family. The case of Hugh was striking in the family's assumption that they were to blame for the boy's problems.

Extreme anxiety in the mother may also be a clue to cerebral dysfunction. This anxiety has a catastrophic quality, as if the mother were caught in the midst of an earthquake. Hugh's mother showed this anxiety, prompting the psychiatrist to wonder what she was so anxious about. The medical opinions until then had been of a spoiled boy and an overprotective mother: when the formulation was stood on its head and became "What situation in the boy could make the mother so anxious?" cerebral dysfunction suggested itself.

In lower-class children, such as Louanne, the danger lies in minimizing a careful evaluation and assuming that poverty and a defeated home are the main causative factors in the child's difficulty. As stated earlier, poignancy and relationship hunger along with explosiveness or withdrawal should alert the guidance worker to take a further look.

In summary, evaluation of a child with respect to a factor of cerebral dysfunction should always include a guidance or psychiatric evaluation, an educational evaluation and psychological testing and a medical (pediatric or neurological) work-up. Differences in medical opinion may cause difficult problems for guidance workers at present but it seems likely that

---

* This is changing fast since the appearance in national magazines of articles on minimally brain-damaged children and the development of parent organizations working on behalf of such children.

experimental, neurophysiological findings will disseminate and be reflected in clinical practice relatively soon.

Ideally, psychological testing and educational evaluation should be combined, although some psychologists are not prepared to make concrete educational suggestions. Educational evaluation and recommendations are complex and need to take into account the child's and family's ways of coping with his central nervous system factor.

Specialized diagnostic investigations and appropriate remedial formulations may receive an increased amount of attention in the years just ahead. This may revitalize "testing" as a valuable adjunct to education. Studies of complex learning disabilities could become very useful to special educators involved in the remediation of such disabilities. Identification and remediation of learning disabilities will sooner or later be of interest to regular educators having in their charge youngsters whose educational difficulties have not yet been diagnosed. Such a trend carries the hope that many of the negative coping manoeuvers of youngsters described in the early section of this chapter can be avoided, in so far as these manoeuvers are already a reaction to stress or failure in school as perceived by the child. Early diagnosis and remediation thus become a form of prevention.

This whole concept of prevention is vital to special education, whether via tutoring, part-day attendance in a special small class or full-day attendance in such a class. Special education programs have become somewhat discredited in education, not because of their goals, but because too often they became, or were viewed as, dumping grounds for non-learners.

We feel very strongly, therefore, that a special education program designed to overcome the multitude of behavioral and learning handicaps found among school children with normal potential needs to have built into it adequate safeguards. We need to provide for careful screening and discharge, expert educational diagnosis, special training of teachers and the kind of guidance service documented throughout this book, so that parental feelings, the child's own feelings, peer relationships and the learning handicaps themselves can all be dealt with at the appropriate time. If such safeguards, in-service training and services to teachers are not made available, teachers will soon become discouraged, and the children in their charge will react to their teacher's lack of hopefulness by further impairment of their already damaged self-image and ability to learn. A potentially creative educational effort will have failed.

Teachers of such programs will need to use the guidance worker as a perspective-giver, a coordinator of all the services available to them, the children and the parents and a collaborator in discovering those areas where presently available knowledge and technical skill are unequal to the task at hand. Because of the intensive demands made on special education teachers by the severity of the educational problems of the children in their charge, weekly conferences by guidance workers with such teachers seem necessary and profitable. Much still has to be learned through their joint successes and failures.

The following final examples will show how the guidance worker needs to intervene to help the child develop his own strengths, yet assists in planning remedial measures as indicated.

John has been followed for six years. In the early days of his treatment, educational planning for these children was comparatively crude. The psychiatrist advised that John be taken out of his small, upper-middle class public school, where the attitudes of teachers were hardened against him and where the guidance worker felt ineffective in altering their handling of the boy. (It later became clear that John's first grade teacher might have been used as a lever in this faculty situation, since she liked the boy.) John progressed reasonably well in a small private school, where his diagnosis was known. In the upper elementary grades, he began clowning to avoid feeling helpless or inadequate in learning situations. Informal tutoring by a family friend was not sufficient to remedy his academic difficulties. An educational evaluation was requested when John was in the fourth grade and again when he was in the fifth. From the first evaluation, it was recommended that John be pushed with firm, consistent demands that he perform, and lengthened study periods if he avoided work. In the second evaluation, a specific arithmetical defect, felt to be on the basis of his cerebral dysfunction, was disclosed. He was referred for remedial instruction to a man who had worked with aphasic children and was skillful both in establishing a relationship and in circumventing special roadblocks in learning due to cerebral dysfunction. He is now progressing very well and is ready to return to public school at the seventh grade level.

Dick's educational evaluation was done privately because the school reports were uninformative. Special tutoring was recommended and Dick was protected from placement in a highly retarded academic group where there might be too much inducement for him to settle for academic dullness or mental retardation, (This, by the way, must always be given serious thought when a student is being considered for any kind of special class or institutional placement.) Two years later, Dick's school district wanted to place him in a special class for emotionally disturbed children. It was known that this class would be largely composed of severely disturbed acting-out or schizophrenic youngsters. The parents were encouraged to refuse permission to have Dick placed in this class and the psychiatrist also wrote, recommending against it. Three years after the original evaluation, Dick was operating quite competently at grade level in a medium-level group of college-bound students. He continues with his remedial work.

A bright young adult was seen recently, when our concepts of educational planning had become more sophisticated and the investigative skills of the evaluators more precise. His educational deficiencies had not been recognized by his public school, probably because he was one of a "pocket" of students from enriched, upper-middle class homes in a school district which overwhelmingly comprised culturally and educationally deprived students. Mark wanted to be one of the intellectual elite but was not at all sure that he really was. He "smeared" in the testing situation by trying to read very fast to make a good impression, thus lowering his comprehension. (His actual relaxed reading speed was not slow, as he thought, but adequate.) Mark's handwriting was execrable; at the age of twenty, he still felt it necessary to copy a letter to his psychiatrist because he could not concentrate on content, spelling, and writing at once. The educational recommendation, in this case, was that Mark must master spelling through formal or informal tutoring and learn to type before he could hope to succeed in the University. He was told by his psychiatrist that another medical or administrative discharge from the University would not be recommended unless he acquired these skills before re-entering. Mark's reaction reflected pleasure that he was intellectually competent, anger and rebelliousness at the idea that he had educational defects and was being "ordered" to remedy them, castration anxiety about the idea of cerebral dysfunction and, finally, plans to obtain tutoring and learn to type.

Most of these cases have been selected from private psychiatric practice, but this kind of work-up is now becoming available in public schools. Large numbers of older children did not have this kind of diagnosis and planning available for them. Technical information as to how the teacher should implement remedial work with a given student is still frequently lacking and school districts are all too prone to leap at over-generalized, over-standardized "solutions" rather than encouraging and subsidizing concrete, skilled, individualized diagnosis and educational planning.

NOTES
(Chapter X)

1. L. Bender, "The Brain and Child Behavior," *Archives of General Psychiatry*, 4:531, 1961.
2. Bernard S. Stell, "The Maturation of the 14 and 16 Sec. Positive Spikes," *The American Journal of Psychiatry*, 121:1, July 1964.
3. S. T. Orton, "An Impediment to Learning to Read: A Neurological Explanation of the Reading Disability," *School and Society*, Vol. XXVIII, 1928, pp. 286-290.
4. Anna Freud, *The Ego and the Mechanisms of Defense*, International Universities Press, New York, 1946 (reprinting).
5. Mary A. Sarvis, *Psychiatric Implications of Temporal Lobe Damage*, The Psychoanalytic Study of the Child, Vol. 15, International Universities Press, New York, 1960, pp. 454-481.
6. Raymond L. Clemens, "Minimal Brain Damage in Children, an interdisciplinary problem, medical, paramedical and educational," *Children* (Publ. of U.S. Dept. of H.E.W.) 8:5, Sept. 1961.

ADDITIONAL READINGS
(Chapter X)

Hellmuth, Jerome, ed. *Learning Disorders*, Vols. I, II and III. Seattle: Special Child Publications, 1965, 1966, 1968.

Hellmuth, Jerome, ed. *Educational Therapy*, Vols. I and II. Seattle: Special Child Publications, 1967, 1968.

Hellmuth, Jerome, ed. *The Special Child in Century 21*. Seattle: Special Child Publications, 1964.

Mallison, Ruth. *Education as Therapy*. Seattle: Special Child Publications, 1968.

Sarvis, M. A., "Paranoid Reactions," *Archives of General Psychiatry*, Vol. 6, February 1962, 157-162.

Solomon, P., *et al.*, ed. *Sensory Deprivation*. Cambridge: Harvard University Press, 1961.

Strauss, A. A. and L. E. Lehtinen. *Psychopathology and Education of the Brain-Injured Child*. New York: Grune and Stratton, Inc., 1947.

Strauss, A. A. and N. C. Kephart. *Psychopathology and Education of the Brain Injured Child*, Vol. II. New York: Grune and Stratton, Inc., 1955.

CHAPTER XI

Working with Groups

One sees in the literature a wide variety of theories[1] advanced as rationales for treating, counseling, guiding or educating people in groups. Many criteria for selection and matching of group members are discussed. We began to experiment with guidance groups for entirely expedient (rather than theoretical) reasons. We have found them to be an unexpectedly useful lever in many blocked or disrupted educational transactions. Yet, we have not found any criteria or any theoretical rationale which would enable us to categorize the children who might benefit from a group experience. We *have* found that criteria focused on the psychopathology or psychodynamics of individual group members were *not* useful: one cannot recommend placement in a group in terms of diagnostic categories like hyperactive children, shy children, isolated or withdrawn children, etc. Although the more we know about a child, his struggles, his past and his social matrix, the more helpful it is, this is not *necessary* for many useful group transactions, which stand on their own merits in offering children assistance with their difficulties in the educational interaction.

Only one practical generalization has come out of our experience with groups: that they will often provide an optimal approach before or in addition to individual work with lower-class, culturally persecuted, minority group children, or other groups who feel they are underdogs, particularly when there is a problem of low morale in a group of these children or in their school classroom in general. Culturally persecuted, lower-class children often like the idea of a group because they are on less of a spot with a little-known, usually white, adult. If they do not warm up to him, they can turn to another group member without loss of face. The group provides a natural medium in which the children can talk over and work through their suspicious, mistrustful attitudes, their frequently bitter feelings of ingroup and self-hatred and their beliefs that all their problems are due to discrimination against them as Negroes or other cultural under-dogs. In the group, these children can test out whether the adult will be a "good guy" (sucker) who will help them scapegoat the school, whether he will reject them, whether he will give up, or whether he can set appropriate limits as a preliminary to restructuring of the group toward more constructive problem-solving.

Except for this tentative generalization, we feel that thinking of a group as the useful next step simply depends on the guidance worker's evaluation of the child-school interaction and his (often intuitive) hunch as a trained observer who is acquainted with both children and schools.

We will give some examples to show the range of reasons for which groups have been formed. (In the next chapter, we will illustrate the *process* in working with groups.)

A GROUP IN A TRANSITIONAL ELEMENTARY SCHOOL

X School was undergoing rapid transition from Caucasian middle-class to Negro lower-class. It was a high-morale school but contained many students with serious problems. The sixth grade had undergone two traumatic losses of teachers they liked; they resented their third teacher, who was intellectually facile but impatient and strict. Five boys in this class had been "guidance cases" for years. Their problems varied but they all came from severely deprived, disturbed, chaotic and sometimes cruel lower-class homes. They all resisted learning and had varying degrees (all severe) of educational retardation. I explained to these boys that I did not have enough time to see them all individually and suggested that we meet in a group to try to understand more about how and why they got into such repeated trouble before they went on to junior high school, where their behavior would have more serious consequences. This group met regularly once a week for about six months.

GROUPS AS AN ANTIDOTE TO SOCIAL ISOLATION

Z School is located in a neighborhood where many racial groups inter-mingle and where isolation, suspiciousness and scapegoating are standard traits which characterize many families. Lower-class Negroes, the majority group in the neighborhood, seem relatively secure and present relatively few guidance problems (except in cases where gross neglect is a factor), but upward mobile Negroes, families of mixed ancestry, Spanish-American families and Poor White families tend to be uncomfortable and frequently over-protective of their children. Such an attitude on the families' part was often perceived, by school people, as criticism of the school. This obscured the real issues and raised charges and counter-charges which resulted in the child and his problem being caught in the middle.

As the guidance worker in this school, I found that early reaching out to children in this situation, at the first signs of difficulty in kindergarten and the primary grades, seemed to short-circuit the misunderstandings. Some of these children were disturbed, others were only scared and lacking in life experience.

A club which, essentially, provided the equivalent of nursery school experiences seemed to be a practical way of handling more of these typical problems than I could do on a one-to-one basis. Also, a small group (usually four to six children) seemed to be a natural bridge between the children's previous isolation and suspiciousness and the present school demand that they adjust to a large group in the classsroom and be spontaneous enough that learning could take place. (Usually, one or two aggressive youngsters were included. These aggressive children benefited from the same group atmosphere and this plan enabled the shy isolates to get to know them at first hand, under adult supervision, and thus to become less apprehensive about their behavior.)

Five such clubs have been in operation in Z School during the past two years. They have met in the teachers' lounge on my regular day at the school. The groups have been highly acceptable to the faculty. There is much mutual enrichment between guidance worker and teacher and between guidance worker and parents, based on what transpires in the club. Because few other resources are available to parents in this economically marginal neighborhood, the club usually lasts for a year, though the less disturbed youngsters may stop coming, once they are fully integrated into their classrooms. Usually the guidance worker sees that a child is now on his feet; the teacher also reports that he is now doing well academically and socially and should no longer "miss spelling" to come to the club meetings. This child, likewise, though he still smiles and waves at the guidance worker, says he no longer needs to belong to the club. There are always others to take his place.

This year, the group approach was extended to a girls' club of four eleven- and twelve-year olds, all of whom seemed to need more personalized attention than they were getting at home or from their busy teachers at school. Recently, I had a call from a mother whose child is attending Z School. Her daughter was having difficulties and was being sent home because of frequent squabbles with peers. Her neighbor's child had been in one of the clubs and was getting along much better both at school and in the neighborhood. Could her daughter join the club next fall? She'd cooperate in any way she could. So, the guidance clubs seem to be here to stay at Z School.

A GROUP THAT BACK-FIRED IN A MIDDLE-CLASS SCHOOL

For several weeks, the principal at a middle-class school told me he had been concerned because it had been necessary to punish, suspend or otherwise discipline a number of sixth grade boys who were being impertinent or downright disobedient to their teacher. None of these boys had been known to me beforehand. It was clear that the principal disliked having to handle these boys in this manner and that he found them individually responsive. Yet he had to back his teacher, too. When we discussed why these boys might be so troublesome, he indicated rather indirectly that the teacher, because of her age, was apt to be impatient with these growing boys. Few outlets were available for them, since the teacher was often not even physically well enough to take them out to games. This was one cause for their restlessness and tendency to "kick over the traces." My first suggestion was that, since the principal was the only man at this school, he himself take the class for games at fairly frequent intervals. He was a "natural" for this role and welcomed the idea, but ruefully had to admit a few weeks later, that his crowded schedule really did not allow such an approach. The boys continued to be sent to the office from the classroom and from the yard at recess time. They seemed to reinforce one another's defiant attitude. Yet, nothing they did was really serious, just mischievious.

I offered to form a group to try to alter the boys' attitudes and drain off some of their energetic needling. I discussed this with the teacher, who agreed passively to the plan—she really felt that the principal was not sufficiently severe with them.

From then on, I met regularly with a group of five boys, in the nurse's office. But somehow the group did not move. The boys had a good enough time, the group even became a means of access to two boys, where I could be helpful later on an individual basis. But basically, the boys treated me as they had treated the teacher, though more subtly so. They even tried to get me to condone (by making me a confidant) their preadolescent sexual experimentation, then evaded any discussion of the issue. The teacher, essentially, was right: they needed a man's strong hand. Once I recognized this pattern, I took the boys into the gym and let them play ball, observing their need to assert themselves and show off their growing masculinity.

It is true that, during the time I worked with the boys, they were sent to the office less frequently. Yet my impression is that the group possibly did more harm than good. The boys' basic attitude was unchanged, while their reputation as "bad boys" was solidified at school and among the parents, since they were now "bad enough to have to see the school psychiatrist" (!). I learned this later when I made a home call in the same neighborhood. Lastly, the problems of these boys in a middle class school (where anonymity cannot be taken for granted) were not severe enough to warrant the kind of action which, within the mores of this school and neighborhood, was thought of as suitable only for severe cases. The boys did survive in this somewhat impoverished class situation and could have done so without all this to do. Individual, more confidential help to two of the club members might have loosened up the negative group identity more effectively. I vowed silently that, in the future, I would take a good look at the loss of anonymity involved in starting a club and the possible stigma attached to membership, and would pay closer attention to the teacher's attitude before starting a club with her students.

GETTING TO KNOW THREE ENIGMATIC BOYS

An excellent teacher in a middle- to upper-middle class elementary school had three enigmatic fourth grade boys who defied her best efforts to incorporate them into the ongoing educational program. These were not yet children who were labelled as "problems" (by contrast with the previous group), hence there was no fixing of their reputations as problems by seeing them in a group. (This seems to be a crucial point to keep in mind in middle-class schools.) At the teacher's request, I agreed to see them for a while to try to decipher the meaning of some of their attitudes and make recommendations for classroom management.

Burke was wan, small, frail-looking. He cried in class if any attention was directed toward him. His academic work was close to nil because he was so fearful of making mistakes. I had worked with his sister, who had similar, but less severe symptoms. Both parents were extremely shy as children; they continue to be so but not to a degree which interferes with adequate functioning. The father, especially, feels that Burke will follow the same course; the mother is not so sure.

Neil looked like a "regular boy" but cried in the classroom and had temper tantrums when he made mistakes or was frustrated in any way. His academic achievement was good. I don't know his parents: they are reportedly strict and pressuring.

Ben lived "in his own world." He had a blank expression and was markedly lacking in affect except that, according to the teacher, anger smoldered in his eyes when he was pressured, although he showed no change in facial expression. His parents were shy and struggled with the same problem of expressing feelings. They were concerned and willing to consider therapy for Ben, when the timing was right. I felt Ben was brighter than his low-normal test results indicated. His thinking seemed to be slow and deep, his verbal expression confused because he was thinking on too many levels. He was involved with a great deal of fantasy but I do not believe it was unusually bizarre.

I saw these boys in ten group sessions. We played games, and, even though it was like pulling eye teeth for me, had some round table conversations. The boys progressed from almost mechanical playing of games to an attitude of a little more zest. They began to argue a good deal about turns, rules and scores (which I considered a considerable advance for these withdrawn boys). They all suffered extreme discomfort at losing but gradually this diminished and they seemed to be playing a bit more for fun. At first, when I called for them they would walk down the hall like robots; by the later group sessions they would do a little jumping, running and jostling as they came. They will be continued in a group, seen individually, worked with through their teachers, or referred for formal treatment as the situation next year indicates.

A GROUP FORMED PRIMARILY AS AN AID TO THE TEACHER

A highly experienced teacher agreed to take a second grade class which had been taught in the previous year by a beginning teacher. The class was large and contained a number of immature children. It had gotten somewhat out of hand.

The teacher's first goal, therefore, was to get the children settled down and organized into teachable groups. She made quite a bit of progress during the first two weeks but four boys did not respond to the "simmering down" program. Since I knew only one of the boys fairly well and, since time was of the essence, I proposed to see the four boys in a group as a means of planning for their more effective integration into the classroom and to assess their personal difficulties further. The plan was discussed with the principal and, with the help of the custodian, a corner was set up for us in an unused storeroom. We had the usual supplies: paper, crayons, clay, paints. The boys were told that we were trying to figure out how to help them to be successful second graders. Since this was a middle-class school, where parents were likely to wonder at any unusual approach, the parents were all telephoned and gave permission for their boys to participate in the group.

Very quickly, each boy's characteristic approach to activities and to other boys could be observed. Observation was my main goal. But one cannot just observe four youngsters without interacting with them, so there were comments geared to helping them to become aware of their own typical behavior patterns and comments directed to supporting whatever was effective in their behavior, while discouraging whatever was inappropriate.

Ronnie, who was cock of the walk at home and had an unpleasantly superior attitude, was started on a course of more realistic self-appraisal. Jack, who looked like an All-American boy, but was almost paralyzed by not knowing how such a boy was supposed to act, needed encouragement and praise when he dared to act spontaneously. Barry, who was involved in much hero-type fantasy about his sergeant father overseas (he was one of the few Negro youngsters in an upper-middle-class school), was shown how he could do good work and fit in at school. (Incidentally, he began walking to school with Jack, who lived near him, after a discussion in a group meeting of how he hated to walk to school alone. Barry added matter of factly, in this discussion, "None of the white kids will walk with me," bringing a deeply sincere response from Jack that he would— and he did.) Morrie was the only youngster known to me previously. He was an enigmatic boy from a disturbed family. I welcomed the chance to observe him with a group of his peers.

How did I use this group observation? It provided a basis at once to supplement the teacher's observations, thus facilitating her approach to the boys and their management in reading groups, etc. For instance: Ronnie was held to completing his work rather than getting away with his superior air of: "This is beneath my dignity!" Jack was encouraged to take chances even though it meant making mistakes. Barry was shown very concretely how to approach each task, so that he could experience tangible success. With Morrie, we adopted a "wait and see" attitude. In summary, my observations, passed along to the teacher, speeded up what she would have found out eventually by trial and error and gave her support at a time when she needed it.

As for the parents, who were seen after about four group sessions, my observations facilitated cooperative planning. Ronnie's mother decided to have Ronnie tutored, as his older brother had been, thus providing the needed support to Ronnie so that he could be highly successful. Jack's mother, who revealed her own lack of certainty with him, her only boy (she said she did not know what makes boys tick and always expected trouble), also agreed to tutoring with a man tutor. (Tutoring is a highly syntonic plan, culturally, in this upper-middle-class school.) Barry's mother was encouraged to work closely with the teacher to communicate to Barry that school and home were sticking together in expecting him to learn (and grow up to become a man like his father). As for Morrie, the group observation had shown him to be so deeply immersed in his complex, home-related daydreams that he was unavailable for learning, though he would go through the motions. The most useful step for Morrie was to assign him to a man trainee in the guidance department for regular relationship-oriented interviews so that we could discover more about how to work with him effectively.

The group was discontinued after six sessions.

GROUPS TO HELP WITH A LARGE-SCALE SCHOOL PROBLEM

A junior high school in a ghetto area had a student body which was largely lower-class Negro. The vigorous, outgoing, white man principal was very much involved in trying to improve his students' academic motivation and to help them to better their lot in life. He worked well with me and a male guidance worker, and was pleased by the fact that the psychology trainee whom I supervised in his field work placement was a Negro.

Naturally, then, this principal was very concerned when it looked as if about ninety of his ninth grade students (a third of the class) might not "graduate from the stage." For many lower-class students, participation in junior high school graduation ceremonies is extremely important and meaningful, as it is to their families, since it is the only graduation they may have. Many of them are destined to become school drop-outs in high school. Their families may go into debt to buy gala clothing for graduation night. Yet, one F in either scholarship or citizenship on a student's record at the fifth report card period [in about April] or a presumptive F for the whole year, in any course, keeps a student from participating in pre-graduation celebrations, such as the ninth grade picnic, and from "crossing the stage" in the official graduation ceremony. The principal wondered if seeing some of these potentially failing students in groups might be helpful.

My trainee and I agreed to try this plan. Each of us had three groups of about seven students each, selected from the ninety as the ones most likely to be retrievable. We met in classrooms in the school, since no other place was available. We had three groups composed of girls and three of boys. Attendance was not compulsory. Several times, students were made anxious by one group session and remained away from the next. Recording the group sessions on tape did not seem to upset the students. We held weekly meetings from about November until the end of the school year. Occasionally, we exchanged groups so that the members could express any mixed feelings they had toward their own group leader. We were particularly interested in whether their reactions would differ toward me (white) and the trainee (Negro). No significant difference in attitude emerged.

The content of group sessions concerned, first, "gripes" about school (particularly rigidity of routines, inflexibility of programming and lack of the "escape hatches" present in elementary schools). The boys and girls gradually moved on to discuss their own negative views of self and their suspiciousness of hyper-critical attitudes in the dominant white middle-class culture. My trainee and I helped to arrange program changes, whenever a student felt too tightly "boxed in" and a change was realistically possible. A sizeable number of "our boys and girls" were able to

avoid F's at the fateful fifth marking period and were eligible to graduate
from the stage.

NOTES

(Chapter XI)

1. See, for example, S. R. Slavson, *Analytic Group Psychotherapy with
   Children, Adolescents and Adults*, (New York: Columbia University
   Press, 1950); S. R. Slavson, "Criteria for Selection and Rejection of
   Patients for Various Types of Group Psychotherapy," *International
   Journal of Group Psychotherapy*, V:1, January, 1955; Paul Lerman,
   "Group Work with Youth in Conflict," *Social Work*, 3, October, 1958,
   pp. 71-77; and Saul Scheidlinger, "Experiential Group Treatment of
   Severely Deprived Latency-age Children, *in*, Frank Riessman, Jerome
   Cohen and Arthur Pearl (eds.) *Mental Health of the Poor*, (Free Press
   of Glencoe, and London: Collier-Macmillan Ltd., 1964), pp. 348-361.

ADDITIONAL READINGS

(Chapter XI)

Crowthers, Virginia L. "The School as a Group Setting," Social Work
   Practice, 1963. Selected Papers, *90th Annual Forum, National Conference on Social Welfare*. New York: Columbia University Press,
   1963, pp. 70-83.

Frey, Louise A. "A Social Groupwork Approach to Socially Disadvantaged
   Girls in a School," *Child Welfare* Vol. XLIV, No. 10, December 1965,
   563-569.

Merl, Laurence F., ed. *Work with Groups in the Social Setting*. New York:
   National Association of Social Workers, 1963.

Simon, Paul, "Social Group Work in the Schools," *The Bulletin of the
   National Association of School Social Workers*, Vol. 31, No. 1, September 1955, 3-12.

Vinter, Robert D., and Rosemary C. Sarie. "Malperformance in the Public
   School: A Group Work Approach," *Social Work*, Vol. 10, January 1965,
   3-13.

CHAPTER XII

The Group Process

This group was started with the simple aim of relieving a fourth grade teacher of several children whose individual behavior and interactions with others in the class seriously impeded the education of all. I undertook the project with considerable trepidation, not being at all certain that I could help make sufficient changes in the behavior of these children to justify the time involved because my schedule called for regular visits at ten schools.

Why this particular group at this particular time? I'm not sure. I was acutely aware that in most of "my" schools, the number of severe behavior problems was rapidly increasing, that working with individual children, their parents and teachers was not meeting the massive need. I felt that I *had* to find a way to "reach" more children, and I knew from experience that even irregular contacts with children who came to feel that I cared about whether they achieved in school and whether they "behaved themselves" helped the child to feel that the teacher and parents "cared" even when they were correcting or punishing. I worked with children toward this concept (that correction or punishment was not necessarily rejection) and had found that, in time, they could accept and be helped by it. But could I do this with a group? I didn't know. I did feel that I had the kind of relationship with the principal and faculty which would permit me to fail without too much "loss of face."

The group had two phases. It started with three boys and one girl in March; two of the boys moved away toward the end of the school year. Some time after school had started the following year, I added three boys from the same class, which now, however, had a teacher I did not know well. Toward the end of that school year, I added one more boy at the request of the teacher and with the approval of the principal. In the

164

course of this year, the school moved into a new building. The shifts attendant on this brought about modifications in my way of working with these children. In the old school, we had met in a large PTA room, where the abundance of space allowed me to permit more free "acting-out" behavior; in the new school, we used the Special Services room, where the instrumental music equipment presented temptations for these impulse-driven youngsters and problems of limit-setting for me. Also, in the second phase, I was not able to coordinate my efforts with the teacher's as well as in the first phase and, gradually, I began to help directly with reading, in which all the children were having great difficulty. Three of the children did not know the names of letters, not to mention knowing sounds, and they were all severely blocked in even *trying* to learn academic skills.

I will not sketch the personalities of the individuals in the group in the first phase because of the relatively short time they were together. However, I will sketch some of the action, because it was very similar to that presented in the second phase. The group met for about fifty minutes. The first fifteen minutes or so and the last ten minutes were for a "business meeting," during which we were to talk about the reason for our group and what specific efforts each member would make during the following week. All the children knew I would check with the teacher to determine how effective the "efforts" had been. I should point out that I did not bring this issue into focus until I felt quite certain that the children trusted my relationship with them; at this time they expressed no concern about my checking their progress, though often the report was decidedly unfavorable. I had assured them that I would not "scold" them (they did not know the meaning of "scold" but did understand "get on" them) and I discussed with them individually the report given to me by the teacher. This did not occur *every* week, because time did not always permit it.

Most of the period was spent in playing with toys I had brought—dart gun, balls, toy soldiers, airplanes, cars, rubber dagger, etc.—or in general scuffling and exhibition of physical feats. Hostilities of all sorts were expressed, and tempers ran high as to who was cheating, what names were called, and the like. Each child tried to be the center of attention in his own typical way: by "showing off," by playing up to me, by "tattling" on others. There was no idea of sharing. One or another of the group would be isolated by the rest in a pointed, cruel way at various times. Throughout the play part of the sessions, I remained as neutral as maintaining reasonable control permitted. I prevented open fights and, at appropriate times, took the edge off the teasing. We talked in general about ways to accept teasing and namecalling without having to fight and discussed why fighting at school was frowned upon. All were agreed that they would not like to attend a school where fighting was approved of.

During the "business" part of the meetings, the behavior which was disruptive in the classroom was clearly evident: everyone talking at the same time—scattered kind of thinking—very short attention span— jumping up to "do" something, such as playing the piano, hitting someone, etc. Fists were ready to fly at any insult or imagined insult. Requests on my part were not heard unless I became very firm about the purpose of this part of the meeting. We spent about three business meetings on choosing a name for the group. Names proposed were: "The Problems Club," "The Learning Club," "The Chairman Club," "The Club We Learn About Ourselves In," "The Club We Learn In," "Good Citizen's Club." Finally, after much name-calling, jeering, projecting blame on the teacher or other class members, and jockeying for attention, the name chosen was "The Club We Learn In."

After about eight meetings, there was a noticeable change in the children when they were with me and some mild modification of attitudes in the classroom. They were able to take correction with less hostile reaction, they could listen somewhat better, they quarreled and teased much less when with me. By now I was feeling more secure in handling situations which arose. For instance, one boy took most of the toy airplanes away in his pockets; I brought him back alone, talked to him about the fact that the toys were used in many schools, etc.—he returned most of them. Toys continued to disappear, however, and when I discussed this with the group, each member quickly accused another. I pointed out that I was accusing no one person, but we were having fewer and fewer toys to play with, so it would help to have some returned. Some were.

In the second phase, as stated above, after starting in a relatively free setting, it became necessary, in the new building, to change the kinds of activities to drawing, talking and moderately active games. During this year, I could meet with the group only every two weeks. Also during this year, I began to introduce games involving phonics. The composition of this group now was as follows:

Mary

Mary was the only girl in the group. I had known her brother and had previous contact with her family. Mary's problems centered around her inability to make progress academically, her pack-rat tendencies to accumulate papers, pencils, erasers, money, etc., without regard for true ownership, and her constant demand for attention from the teachers. She was very much the "tomboy," and could compete well with the boys in physical skills in spite of being rather small for her age. I had doubts about the advisability of including her, but took a chance that I would be able to help her identify with me rather than with the boys. Her family had been dominated by the maternal grandmother for years; this had greatly weakened the parents' position with the children. The grandmother had moved out of the home by the time I knew Mary. The family seemed close, parental attitudes on the verbal level seemed good. However, the children came to school very poorly groomed, and it appeared that they largely "shifted" for themselves, except for what care they received from Mary, the oldest girl in a large family.

Sam

Sam had a long history of severe difficulty: he soiled at school, attacked other children, made little or no academic progress. He had been placed on a half-day program and was almost intolerable on that. He was the middle child of three in the family; the other two presented no school problems. The mother worked as a typist and impressed me as a "remote" person; the father had been out of the home for many years. The grandmother, who lived near, seemed to be a warm, intelligent, motherly person. Sam was felt to be mentally very slow by the teachers he'd had. He was not an attractive boy physically, and his hostile expression did not add enchantment to his heavy features. He was as convinced as others that he was "stupid." It certainly had seemed to me that he was limited in intelligence until one day when he stayed after the others had left and began to ask questions about a current State election and about the State in general. The questions were exceptionally intelligent ones, and it became evident that Sam had absorbed a great deal of information from Social Studies. When the teacher and principal were made aware of this, and when I was able to convince Sam and his grandmother that he was not at all "stupid," his behavior and learning began to improve. In fact, the very day I told him that he'd been fooling himself and everyone else about his being dumb, he went home and told his grandmother she was going to have to help him learn to read. Whereupon, as she later told me, she turned off her favorite TV program and got started.

Mark

Mark was the youngest of four children. All of the others were doing well in school. Mark was achieving little academically, had severe temper tantrums, suffered from allergies and asthma, had few friends. The mother was active in PTA, seemed the dominant parent in my interview with the two parents. Mark was receiving good medical care at a local part-pay hospital. I suggested a child guidance clinic referral in the same institution, but the parents did not follow up on it. Mark's personality was rather colorless, he had few opinions, even his anger was not effective. He was often the helpless target of scathing comments.

Ernest

Ernest was referred by his teacher because of his intense, brooding moods in which he would "fly into" anyone or would soundlessly bang his head against the radiator or a wall. He never smiled and seemed deeply depressed. He had recently come to live with his father and stepmother, having been removed from his mother's home by the Juvenile Court. The other children remained with the mother. The stepmother appeared to be understanding and gentle; the father was interested in Ernest but prone to beat him. Ernest was the only child in this home at the time.

Keith

Keith was the oldest of five children. He was not a disturbing child in the classroom, but had done some skillful stealing in the school and seemed almost completely blocked in academic work. He had been placed for a time in a class for mentally retarded children but, on retesting, had scored too high for such a class. His stealing had a "different" flavor: when it was discovered, and he was faced with it, he readily confessed and explained exactly how he had accomplished it. (Ordinarily, there would have been a "last-ditch" denial in his socio-economic group.)

As pointed out above, the interaction among these children was, for the most part, very hostile and competitive. With the approval of the principal, I had started having milk and cookies at the end of each session, because I believe that a portion of the irritability of these children is due to malnutrition, (physical and emotional) and I hoped to send them back to the classroom somewhat calmed down from the stimulation of the relatively free group. This "treat" time gave me a chance to point out the differences between what we were trying to accomplish in our club from the purposes of the classroom. I did this in various ways, but persistently. At times, the children were very critical of the teacher, feeling she did not like them and made things hard for them. This gave me a chance to point out that, were I the teacher in charge of over thirty children, I would have to be just as "hard" on them, if they behaved the way I had seen them behave. This point is one which, I feel, must always be handled explicitly with children in order that the guidance worker does not become the "good guy" and the teacher the "bad guy" in their eyes.

"Treat time" was also a time in which the "hungry" nature of the problem was clearly in evidence. Each group member would grab as many cookies as he could and fight with his neighbor about the number —except for Keith, the stealer, who merely sat by. I allowed this to go on twice, then said that I thought I would decide how many each was to have. At first, there was some "snitching" an extra with consequent arguments. Eventually, there came to be little concern about whether one person got more than another—at least the concern was on a relatively normal child behavior level.

Now that activity was, of necessity, more curtailed and consisted primarily of drawing, talking and some games, and now that my relationship was quite firmly established, the children's fears and hopeless feelings were much more freely expressed. We talked about their experiences between meetings, when they felt they were unjustly accused of many things at school, and, on two occasions, we discussed murders which had occurred in the community. Imagination added to fact, and stories grew by accretion for whatever shock value they might have for me or for the others. The "conversations" were typically spiced with comments such as: "Yea, that bonehead Mark—he can't learn anything—he thinks a book is to play ball with!" "Oh, yea! You black African! You think you're so smart—you can't read!" "Ha! You eat meat raw off the bone

—that's why your teeth are so big." "Well, you're a yellow bushman—even your teeth are yellow." "That's better'n being a jungle black."

For some time, it was necessary for me to leave my seat to prevent raging tempers from flaring into wild fights; eventually, however, a firm statement of "Sit down, boys" was usually sufficient, as tempers were far less out of control. In the games, there was, for a long time, great glee and jeering when someone missed or didn't know something. It didn't matter that others didn't know either. Every possible method of cheating was attempted, with consequent rise of tempers. When I say that I was as neutral as possible, in terms of keeping control, I do not mean that I was inactive: there were times when I scolded them roundly, but they took it well and without much anger toward me. When belittling comments were made and names were called, I countered with some positive statement about the one being attacked and even pointed out some of the difficulties of the attacker.

The following year, I started about four weeks before the opening of school with the group of four boys who had remained in the school. The girl had moved to another school and, though I included her for these four weeks, it was not possible to keep her during the school year. The boys were delighted that she was not going to be present. The group met from about eight o'clock to nine-thirty, allowing time to go to the neighborhood store to get milk and cookies, have our "session," and have time for refreshments. The boys were all eager and able to get to school early for these group sessions. On one occasion, when all four were with me, the grocery-store proprietor said to me, "You must be a lion tamer; these are the worst boys in the neighborhood!" The boys looked chagrined. I responded to him: "That's interesting; I find them very fine boys when they are with me." This was not altogether an untruth at this time. On the way back to school, the boys clustered much more closely around me than usual and seemed quite subdued—usually there was some chasing and minor hitting.

This year I worked much more directly on reading, because they were now in the sixth grade with junior high facing them the next year. They had improved greatly in their relationship with each other, so that actual study through phonic, word, and eventually, sentence games seemed feasible. About the second term of the school year, they requested using books. I chose a science book which was actually too difficult, but it would have been unwise to try any book which they considered a "baby" book. No matter how much help each person needed (which, in some cases was almost every word), we "read" and they wanted to. Occasionally, there was some jeering comment and too much supplying of words before the poorer reader had a chance to try the word with my help but, generally speaking, this was at a minimum. In the games, also, there was a marked change in their attitude from the dog-eat-dog relationship at the beginning to an attitude of giving helpful hints so that the person could make a score. Losing became much less of a personal tragedy, as we repeatedly discussed the fact that, in a game, someone had to lose and someone had to win or there could be no game.

Sometimes we did simple experiments (the room did not lend itself to many sorts of possible experiments). One was testing the presence of starch by using iodine. We used a potato (along with other things) and it turned brown before it turned blue. One boy commented "it's turning my color!" This led to a general comparing of skin color, which led to a discussion of human skin colors and hair textures and the fact that many Negroes straighten their hair, whereas whites get permanent waves; there was some laughter when I remarked that also many whites try to get as brown as possible in the summer.*

By the end of this school year, I felt some satisfaction in the progress the boys had made, even though they were by no stretch of the imagination well-adjusted children, nor could they read well enough to handle academic work at their grade level. They could, however, listen much better to one another and to me, they had lost a great deal of their hostility to one another and to authority, they had more interest in "knowing" rather than "guessing" (previously a chronic pastime), they could lose in a game with much better grace, and they could even be helpful to each other at times with some pleasure.

Throughout all this period, I tried to keep the principal informed of my purpose and progress and got a great deal of help in keeping up with the progress and backsliding of each child in the total school setting. As often as time permitted, I discussed both his progress and his attitudes of defiance with the individual boy involved.

A JUNIOR HIGH SCHOOL GROUP—"THE LEADERSHIP CLUB"

This group was started around the needs of Sandra, a Negro ninth grader of average ability who, in a multi-problem junior high school, got

---

* This took place in the early 60's, before the community feeling changed to one of "black is beautiful" and discovered the "natural."

involved occasionally in very serious fights with her peers. She had been known to a guidance department in a nearby city and had had an apparently pleasant relationship with her guidance worker during her elementary school years. She had come to my attention in the eighth grade, when a feud with a girl friend had gotten out of hand, and Sandra was suspended for fighting. I had a conference with Sandra and her mother. There was much obvious friction between them, apparently because Sandra had been raised by another woman in another state from infancy to age 6. Suddenly, and without preparation, her mother turned up and took Sandra away with her to California. Sandra was angry with her mother but even more angry with her foster mother, who had let her go without opposition. The mother and Sandra had gone to a family agency for counseling when Sandra was in elementary school, where she was having trouble with teacher and peers. The agency contact did not continue past intake because the family moved. I referred them to the local family agency at the mother's request, because the mother presented the problem as one centering around the mother-daughter relationship. They went twice and stopped.

In the ninth grade, Sandra came to my attention again, this time because she had run for a student body office. She had a good chance of getting elected (she was popular with her classmates), when she became involved in an argument with her homemaking teacher. As with Sandra's fights, this argument got out of hand, and Sandra had to be suspended. The suspension disqualified her from running for school office. Sandra, when interviewed after the suspension, seemed to want to have a relationship with me but could not discuss her troubles on a verbal level, a problem common to many fourteen year olds. I discussed Sandra with the girl's vice principal. She indicated that Sandra was, in a way, a symbol for several other girls who also seemed anxious to enter into the mainstream of school life and had leadership potential, yet lacked the skills for "making it." These girls constituted an undercurrent of unrest in the ninth grade class and had quite a following among more marginal youngsters.

It thus seemed natural to approach Sandra with a proposal to start a club in which her problems and those of her friends in running for office and getting along in general could be discussed. Sandra seemed interested and volunteered to discuss the proposal with her friends. She thoughtfully gave me the names of several girls she planned to approach, and these names turned out to be precisely the ones the vice principal had in mind. The following week, Sandra came and told me that the girls were interested, though scared. They were willing to get together and find out what I planned to do with them. (This would also enable them to size up my personal friendliness and trustworthiness.) Sandra helped in rounding them up, and, after lunch that day, we had our first meeting.

The structure of the meetings was like a club with president, secretary, etc. As the sessions progressed, this formal structure receded in importance, was mentioned less and less, but had such secondary benefits as enabling the club to have its picture in the school yearbook, since the club was an officially sponsored activity of the school.

We met once a week about 11:00 a.m. (a time of day which is apt to be high in tension for children from poor homes, who may be hungry. The girls often brought food to the meetings for both physiological and psychological reasons.) Our meeting place was the curriculum office, which had a large oval table and was suitable and available. Having to choose a set weekly time to meet had the disadvantage of taking several girls out of one class, namely, physical education, where they were having difficulty with the teacher. This might seem to be an advantageous relief of pressure, but the teacher saw little use in my seeing these girls in a "leadership club" when they were such poor followers in her class. (Such a situation is difficult for a guidance worker, who does not want to alienate teachers because of repercussions for the girls involved and also because of the teacher's attitude toward future "guidance cases." However, the choice was unavoidable.)* Two girls in the group came out of one homemaking class, where they were having difficulty. In this case, though, the teacher felt that any attempt to help the girls improve in their attitude was worth losing a period a week from their classwork.

Aside from Sandra, five other girls became members of the group. They were all ninth graders, all Negro (the majority group in the school), ranging in tested I.Q. from 85 to 110. They represented a power group—though largely a "have-not" power group. Their behavior and academic standing in the school were characterized by frequent ups and downs. It soon became evident that stabilizing their behavior and work output would have to be accomplished before they could aspire to "official"

---

* Now, a few years later, with a changed climate in the community, this P.E. teacher has become very interested in the kind of effort this club represented. She refers to it often, and positively.

school leadership. Thus, stabilizing their erratic day-to-day functioning in school emerged as my goal.

Brief sketches of the girls will give some idea of their backgrounds. These sketches are based on partial information gleaned from casual contacts with the families of the girls (such as my sitting in on conferences between parents and the vice principal following a suspension), from previous contacts with other siblings in the same family, from the record of one girl (Jackie) who had been known to guidance at another school, etc. There was no systematic testing nor systematic work with the homes. Lack of time would have made this impossible in any case, but I also felt that this was a "natural group" of youngsters, trying to gain their place in the sun, at an age when they were beginning to move toward a more adult view of themselves.

Besides Sandra, then, there were:

Jeanette

Jeanette was a capable but often surly girl. Contact with both parents indicated that the mother was a highly religious, punitive, righteous person, who was critical of Jeanette and wanted the school to punish her severely. The father, on the other hand, whose favorite Jeanette appeared to be, encouraged Jeanette to be defiant both of school authority (in this school, the administrators happened all to be white, and there was a definite racial flavor to the father's attitude) and of her mother. Jeanette was caught squarely in a bind, and neither parent was able to offer ego-support that was useful to her in terms of school adjustment. Economically, this was a marginal family.

Julie

Julie was a very moody, sensitive girl, who was coping with an even more difficult situation. I had known her mother (in connection with the problems of a younger child) at a time when the mother had just attempted suicide. In an effort to find a stable source of income for her many children, the mother had been involved in a number of fairly stable marital and common-law relationships. None of these worked permanently, and her hopes of finding a "good man" seemed forever doomed to failure. Her bitterness over this carried over to her relationships with her children. She could never rejoice in their small successes but blamed them and the world at large for any minor difficulties.

Dolores

Dolores was the most beautifully cared for of the girls. She was very light-skinned, very attractive. Up to the ninth grade year, she was an obedient, very quiet youngster. Between the eighth and ninth grade years, she matured physically, began to use make-up in a sophisticated manner, and her aloofness turned into a deliberate wall. Nothing was known of her family life, except that it was rumored that her mother was a high-class prostitute.

Hallie

Hallie was also attractive in a rather brash way, which she had learned to conceal behind a facade of middle-class propriety. She knew just what to say, had been carefully coached by her mother in how to get along in the white world, in which the mother was a trusted domestic worker. Hallie told of being whipped at home whenever the school reported any difficulty. She seemed to take such treatment for granted.

Jackie

Last, but not least, there was Jackie, a very colorful girl, who seemed definitely more lower-class than the other five. She had been known to a guidance worker in another junior high school, where she was being considered for exemption. In that rather rigid junior high school, her near-psychotic temper tantrums, her violently obscene language when she was upset, and her generally erratic behavior with peers and adults, seemed intolerable. The guidance worker at that school transferred Jackie out of district to my school as a last-ditch effort to prevent exemption. The family later moved into the new district. The girl's guidance record indicated that her mother had been in several scrapes with the law and had scars from fights she had been in with boy friends. Jackie's older sister was more stable but had been exempted from school because of an illegitimate pregnancy. The family was on Aid to Families with Dependent Children. Jackie had made a marginal adjustment in this junior high school by dint of being placed in very stable classes with very stable teachers and by being handled as anonymously as possible. Including her in the group (she was known to the other girls but not really part of their group) was an indirect way of seeing whether she could be helped further and whether more could be learned about successful ways of working with her.

These, then, were the six members of the "Leadership Club." There is no substitute for verbatim or taped recordings of group sessions such as ours. In the absence of such records, I can merely describe the issues raised by the girls and their approach to me as an adult. The vocal members of the group were Jeanette (the real group leader), Sandra and Julie, who were more articulate girls than the others. Hallie was too well-trained to commit herself verbally but clearly agreed with this trio in their way of looking at life. Jackie was often upset by their explicitness; Dolores never said much, remaining largely aloof. Toward the end of the school year, she brought in a girl who she said also needed the group. This girl was part Spanish and part Negro. Dolores and she formed a subgroup. Dolores, who was very light-skinned and had straight hair, seemed to be indicating in this fashion that her problems like those of her friend, were different from those of the other group members. I never found a way to approach these two girls more directly.

Once the girls had taken some time with the formalities of organizing the Club, they very quickly launched into a vehement "gripe session." The first target for their hostility was the police who, they said, were forever questioning Negro kids on the streets at night, even when the children in question were not congregating or acting up but merely waiting, for instance, at a bus stop. In the next session, less vehemently, they shifted from the "cops" to their teachers. This focus was triggered by a remark made to several of them by their teacher when they had left their class to come to the club meeting, the remark being to the effect that they needed to get down to work, not be out of class for a "club." (This teacher was the P.E. teacher mentioned above who had been informed of the purposes of the club but was skeptical.) The gist of the discussion centered around the girls' feeling that all teachers were unfair and made excessive demands but that this was particularly true of Negro teachers with Negro youngsters. They liberally quoted their parents to back up their statement that everyone was prejudiced against Negroes: they did not have a chance.

At the end of this session, Jeannette asked me for a quarter, claiming she had lost her lunch money. I gave it to her with a statement that I expected it back. Half an hour later, while the vice principal and I were having lunch in the teachers' lunch room, we got the report that several girls (they all turned out to be "my" girls) had left the campus without permission. Since I knew they were due in class at that time, it became clear that they were planning to keep the "admit slips" (which I had used to get them to the group meeting) and to alter the time on them so that it would appear that they had been legitimately absent from class. The vice principal and I decided that the usual penalty—a short suspension—was in order.

I opened the next club meeting by discussing this event with the girls, in terms of their testing me and reconnoitering my position. Was I a "do-gooder" who would side with them because I felt guilty about the world's treatment of them? The answer to that was "No." Nor was I going to be played against school authorities—school rules were school rules. On the other hand, I understood their need to test me and was sorry I had fallen for it. From now on, I told them, I would collect the admit slips to keep the girls from being tempted. What interested me most, however, I went on, was that this crisis was clearly of their own making—why? But the girls were not ready to answer this question.

That whole session was taken up with a discussion of their homes and how they were forever expected to do chores around the house and mind the small children, while receiving little help in finding themselves or preparing for the future. Jeanette spoke about her older sister, who had been an excellent student and interested in going on with her education, but who had finally "given up" because of the general family apathy about her plans. Now the sister was a young married woman, restless and dissatisfied, according to Jeanette.

Julie put her situation more poignantly. "Even after you try to clean up the mess and do what she (her mother) wants, she keeps expecting the worst. The minute any of us are in trouble, she either blames it on someone or else wants to turn us over to the Juveniles. She never seems to think that a problem can be settled. Maybe she's right and there's no use in trying. My older sister got pregnant and now there's one more baby around the house." When I asked Julie about Willy, the brother I had known, she said: "Oh, he's a bad one, he's always in trouble at school, he'll end up in reform school," then added sadly, "I guess he and that baby don't have a chance."

Hallie also tuned in on feeling abused—she is the one who spoke of being given a "whupping with the belt"—but she admitted that the whippings were often needed to make her "be a good girl" and she winked suggestively to clarify her meaning. (Apparently, the whippings did not help because she "had to get married" six months later.)

Jackie had become increasingly nervous during this discussion and several times put her hands over her ears. At the end of the hour, therefore, I took her aside and asked her how she felt about this sort of talk. (I had heard that she had gotten more lively in class, was trying to do better work, but also seemed stirred up and talked too much.) Jackie launched into a tirade about her own home where her own ambivalence clearly emerged. She needed desperately to cling to her mother as the only one who could be counted on to keep her, yet her mother's angry outbursts scared her to death. The group discussion, which the other girls seemed able to handle easily enough, seemed to dig at the very roots of Jackie's personal integration. I calmed her down and suggested that I should continue to see her regularly alone and that she could rejoin the club later on if it seemed "right" then. I also promised to go see her mother to report the progress she had made at this school and as "insurance" in case problems developed in the future. She left me, calmed down and very elated. Based on my increasing knowledge of Jackie, I asked the vice principal and counselor to plan a case conference on Jackie with all her teachers, since it seemed clear that her balance was easily upset and that one-to-one counseling might heighten her anxiety. In this case conference, we discovered fairly poor functioning in one class. Several teachers reported that they had a silent agreement with Jackie that she would isolate herself in the back of the class when she became restless and anxious. The homemaking teacher reported that Jackie was trying very hard to imitate the teacher's every move, in an obvious effort to please and had become very vocally critical of certain of her classmates who did not come up to the teacher's standards of behavior—though Jackie, also, often slipped from them. In general, this was a much more favorable report on Jackie than I had expected. The consensus was to continue Jackie on her present schedule. Notes were to be put in my mail box if any significant changes were observed. This aside with Jackie is described in some detail because it was one of the important by-products of the group. Earlier attempts to work individually with Jackie had been unsuccessful. The group and the fact that, in Jackie's eyes, the other girls in it were adequate people created access to this disturbed girl.

At the next club meeting, I frankly ascribed Jackie's absence to her having become nervous at the kinds of discussion taking place. I said that she would be back when she felt ready. I asked the others about their reaction to the meetings, and they all wished for more rather than less. As Sandra put it: "And besides, you (herself) begin to see how things fit together." She began to describe a fight between her older sister and herself which had gotten out of hand and had apparently scared Sandra. What she wanted to talk about was her own part in the fight. This led to an amazingly mature discussion in the group of how they, themselves, contributed to many of their problems both at home and at school, but primarily at school. In particular, they discussed their much maligned gym class and the grades they expected to get on their report cards that day. They agreed that, if they did certain things, such as dressing for gym every day, they could expect at least a passing grade. They added that the teacher's standards were explicit and well known to them. The fact that these standards were applied rather rigidly, as I knew, did not seem to be of great concern to the girls. In the rapid-fire discussion which followed, it became clear that Julie was the only one so sensitive to another person's basic attitudes that she felt rejected by this teacher implicitly and irrevocably and could not meet the teacher's expectations. In this context, Julie began to talk about the parish in Louisiana whence her family had moved north at the end of World War II and of how her daddy had returned there, while her mother had stayed on in California. This, it turned out, was the background of all the girls' families, with the exception of Sandra, whose family had been in California for several generations.

The next session, not at all to my surprise, went on to a discussion of how the girls envisaged raising their own children. Jackie had come back to join the group and was an active participant. As anyone their age would, they were, of course, going to do it differently from their own mothers. But, to my surprise, they were not going to be very permissive. They were going to stress an education and working with the school if their children had problems; mainly, they were going to spend time with their kids, so that they could guide them better. Finally, they felt that they needed to help their kids not to use their race as an excuse, as all their parents, except Hallie's mother (who did it in reverse), were used to doing.

That day, I found a note in my box from the homemaking teacher saying that the girls were vastly more cooperative and relaxed with her.

Sandra had won a prize for making the most attractive dress of the ninth grade. Jackie continued to be a lovable nuisance. Did I know, by the way, that her family had moved way out of this school's district and that she was commuting sixty blocks daily to come to school? I followed this bit of information up and found that Jackie had given an entirely fictitious address in order to be able to graduate from this junior high school. She had apparently felt that this was necessary, as she had been referred to the office several times recently and therefore might be in danger of being transferred out; she knew that attendance at a school other than the one nearest one's residence was conditional on good behavior. While I was looking into this situation, the uncertainty of it seemed to trigger an explosion on the part of Jackie in the very class where she had been trying to be a model of behavior: she had to be suspended. I made a home call during the suspension period, found the home even more marginal than I had expected and the mother completely preoccupied with trying to exploit any minor mishap, such as a minor accident, to her financial gain. She was quite unable to be supportive of Jackie.

With the agreement of the school's vice principal, Jackie was officially permitted to finish the year in our junior high school, where she so much wanted to be. Her suspension, however, kept her from graduating from the stage or joining in any of the pre-graduation events, such as the dance and the ninth grade picnic. This school had been a "lifesaver" for Jackie, and her disappointment was poignant when she could not participate in these gala events. She came to each one, dressed within an inch of her life, and hung pathetically around on the outskirts, but at least participating vicariously.

Julie was also excluded from these events and the official graduation because she got an F grade in the physical education class. However, Jeanette, Sandra, Dolores and Hallie were eligible for full graduation honors.

The homemaking teacher reported that, on the last day of school, each of "my" girls who was in her class came up, bent over and asked to be kissed on the cheek. The teacher, who is white, said "I knew I was being tested" (for the sincerity of her feelings toward these Negro girls) "but I also knew it was much more than that." (Parenthetically, in working with culturally persecuted children, we have found that it is very important for them to get confirmation of their dignity and worth as valuable humans from people other than just the guidance worker. Unless this more widespread confirmation takes place, the children merely consider the guidance worker a "good guy," an exception to the world.)

To finish the year in style, and as a last meeting of the club, I invited the girls to my house. It had been obvious several times that they had wondered how I would act with them out in public. They had asked me to take them and their dates to a popular TV program for teenagers. I had refused on the realistic ground that I could neither transport nor adequately supervise twelve teenagers and would not do so were they my own teenage daughter's personal friends. The party at my house was the alternative.

We were to meet in front of the school on Saturday at noon. When I arrived at the rendezvous—no girls. Five minutes later, Sandra appeared in the distance, her nose in a book—a very uncharacteristic activity for Sandra. Another five minutes passed and Jeanette arrived, then Jackie came puffing up the hill. And then—nothing. Jeanette had told me that Dolores did not expect to come. Sandra volunteered that Julie's mother had called her mother as she did not wish Julie to go to my house alone. Eventually, Jeanette suggested that we drive toward Julie's house. When we got there, she had just left. We caught up with her along the way. It was obvious that all the girls were highly anxious about this trip into strange territory. We decided to drive by Hallie's house. We met her and her mother on the street, coming home from grocery shopping. When Hallie's mother saw me, she readily agreed that Hallie could come along. The girls had rock 'n roll records along and, on the way to my house, barraged me with questions about my daughter, her likes and dislikes, etc. It took only minutes, once we were home, for the ice to be broken. My daughter and her chum were the same age as the other girls, and they all had a great many experiences in common, which built a bridge. Jackie became over-excited once or twice, but the girls quietly kept her in line. During our spaghetti feed, for instance, they unobtrusively corrected her table manners. The high point of the afternoon came when the girls, all seven of them, the five Negroes and the two white girls, took a walk down the road, singing together. (This venture forth was no mean accomplishment for Negro children from a semi-ghetto in a strange, middle-class white neighborhood.)

This ending of the club is in many ways a fitting epilogue, because it showed so clearly that the club was only a beginning, a door opened, a bridge. Ideally, the real work of the club—to help these girls integrate themselves into the world at large and fulfill their potential leadership—should have been done the following year. Yet, they were to be scattered in at least four high schools. Nowhere are such clubs routine parts of school life. Maybe they will be, someday.

CHAPTER XIII

Complications at the Secondary School Level

Although the core process of task-oriented guidance is the same at the level of secondary school education as it is at the elementary level, the guidance worker's task is complicated in two important ways. These will be discussed below.

COMPLICATIONS IN STUDENTS

Adolescents go through two major developmental crises: psychosexual crises and ego identity crises. Obviously, these two kinds of crises overlap and may be seen concurrently. These developmental crises complicate the lives of adolescents and sometimes make planning for them more complex. However, the fact that they are developmental phenomena also may mean a much more hopeful outcome for a student than one might expect from the severity of his presenting difficulties.[1]

Behavior reflecting adolescent psychosexual crises is apt to be withdrawal from adults, preoccupation with peers and social status (in whatever group), lack of interest in academic work and the like. The guidance worker can interpret this to teachers as a transient, developmental behavior pattern. If the teacher is helped to keep such behavior in perspective, he can handle concrete situations with more equanimity. Compounding of the student's academic difficulties can be prevented and the student helped to solve his developmental crisis in a constructive personal, social and academic way. Eighth grade is the commonest stage on which developmental crises are played out. But the maturational range in adolescence is very great. One sees many a psychosexually immature student involved in developmental crises at tenth or eleventh grade and many a precocious developer or over-age student in a full-blown identity crisis in the ninth grade.

Identity crises have been most thoroughly discussed by Erikson.[2] The more mature adolescent asks himself unspoken questions: "Who am I?" "What am I worth?" "Will I 'make it' with friends, at work, with the opposite sex?" He may tentatively experiment with a series of identities: "Does being a delinquent fit me?" "Am I going to be a great actor?" "Am I worth nothing except as a 'brain'?" Erikson stresses the importance of recognizing this "role playing" as just that. The guidance worker can help educators to be respectful of the adolescent's tentative explorations with various identities while not becoming panicky if a student experiments tentatively with negative identities, such as adopting the mannerisms and clothing of a delinquent group or a "hippie" one. If the adult world assumes that such experimentation shows what the adolescent is "really like," the adolescent may be "confirmed" in his negative identity so that what might have been a transient exploration of a role may become fixed.[3]

COMPLICATIONS IN WORKING WITH PARENTS

As youngsters move toward an independent identity of their own, the question as to whether or not to involve their parents becomes one which needs to be squarely faced. The examples in the following two chapters indicate that, in the majority of the cases, parents were actively engaged when their support was needed, but in the case of Margaret and Jerry, the maturity of the youngsters seemed such that they could work on their own problems almost as a young adult would. In both cases, the guidance worker refrained from taking sides for or against the parents but worked with the youngsters toward a clarification of their own feelings and goals. The question becomes one of being clear with the youngster as to the guidance worker's role and options. If the youngster is ready and able to assume responsibility for himself, then parent involvement becomes a peripheral issue.

The following group of interactions illustrates problems connected in large part with students' developmental crises and ego identity problems. It will be noted that the students referred in senior high school tend to be intellectually gifted, middle-class students. We do not believe that this is a sampling error on our part. Students can almost always leave school legally by the age of sixteen and we believe that most senior high schools are not very well motivated to struggle seriously, over a long period of time, with lower-class students who may have long-term learning problems and problems of apathy, withdrawal or chronic rebelliousness.* The escape hatch for students and faculty alike is apt to be another statistic in the school dropout figures. Of course, this is a false solution both for the student and for the culture; however, at present, it seems to be the most prevalent one. It seems doubtful that a public high school which contains large numbers of such students can help them more effectively without radical changes in school attitude, alterations of curriculum, part-time work opportunities and very specific efforts to enlist the students' militancy in collaborating with interested educators in developing new models for high school education. As is often the case, there are a number of pilot projects[4] which show that this can be done, but money, people, skills and interest have not yet become available on a scale to permit wide application even of present beginning knowledge.

Ruth

Late in September, on one of my regular visiting days at a multi-problem junior high school, I saw a youngster in hysterics being brought into the vice principal's office by her almost equally upset teacher. It transpired that the child was Ruth, a seventh grade Negro girl who had just entered the school three weeks late. (Her family had kept her out of school to take her on a trip.) On this day, Ruth's first day of attendance at choral class, she had asked a student sitting next to her for information about the song the class was studying. Her Negro teacher had chided her for talking and had made a derogatory remark about parents who didn't care enough about their children to send them to school on time. At this, Ruth exploded and had called her teacher a "black nigger"—then had started to weep hysterically.

The teacher left us to return to her class and the vice principal asked me to sit in on her conference with Ruth. Ruth continued to cry hysterically, insisting that she was not going to apologize to her teacher. Her mother, who had been called on the phone, arrived to take Ruth home. The mother explained that Ruth had just started her first menstrual period that morning. This gave me an opportunity to present the problem as a developmental crisis, which I, by this time, had become convinced

---

* This situation may change rather rapidly within the present climate of ferment in education.

was the issue. Both her mother and the vice principal asked me to talk with Ruth alone, before she went home to calm down and pull herself together, in order to get cues on how to plan her return to school, when I would not be present.

By now, Ruth was much more rational and appeared intrigued by the turn of events. She spoke freely about her sense of insecurity in the new school situation. It was her first sally into the larger world from the small, tightly-knit neighborhood, known as Jingletown, where she had grown up. Having started school late had added to her anxiety and all these factors combined to produce the incident of the morning. A lucky coincidence had put me on the scene at the very beginning of the crisis. This undoubtedly prevented a ten-day suspension and helped to shift the school perception of Ruth from that of an explosive "bad actor" to that of a child in an adolescent crisis.

Ruth's cumulative records revealed her to be an essentially stable, capable girl, who was the oldest child in a cohesive, though very poor, family. Because Ruth's schedule was not yet settled at school and because I did not have a working relationship with the teacher involved in the incident, we decided to put Ruth into an art class, rather than returning her to the choral class. After a day at home, Ruth returned to school and continued there without further problems. I had no other guidance contacts with her but remained something of a friendly adult on the periphery of her school life. I noted with satisfaction that she blossomed at school, developed good dramatic talents, had the lead in a school play, and eventually, as a ninth grader, took part in advanced choral work under the very teacher with whom she had clashed. I was delighted when she asked me to attend her graduation from junior high school.

The younger children in this family have all been followed; I have kept an eye on them, held conferences with them, continued to work with the school and family, suggested special teacher placements, etc. None of these children presented a major problem but each had some kind of quirk which could have precipitated difficulty without preventive handling by the guidance department.

Pat

Pat, a Caucasian girl, had been known to the guidance worker in her elementary school but aside from being rather an odd youngster with an active fantasy life and very meager association with other children, she had been of no major concern to the school. She continued this pattern in seventh grade, where she attended a rather difficult, multi-problem junior high school, and I got to know her. Then, in the eighth grade—the grade school staff consider to be the turning-point year, when latent problems seem to gain momentum or latent assets, alternatively, may emerge—Pat went into a full-fledged developmental crisis.

She began to wear her coat at all times, her appearance deteriorated, she began to hide in corners and in the bathroom, she reported (imaginary) odd goings-on between her out-of-school music teacher and some of his pupils, she refused to go to certain classes, she had a hunted look on her face and she talked excitedly whenever she had an adult audience. This behavior gradually increased in intensity after Pat's counselor became seriously involved with her. The counselor began to believe some of Pat's fantastic tales, took an excessive personal interest in improving Pat's appearance and was rather too apt to shield Pat from the consequences of her behavior. Pat rapidly became worse. She began to stay away from school and told increasingly lurid tales to account for her absences. In reality, she spent the time sitting on a park bench.

My role as a guidance worker during this critical period was three-fold: (1) to listen to the girl's counselor and act as a consultant to her, helping her to achieve more distance and sympathetic objectivity from Pat and her plight; (2) to work with Pat, trying to gauge the intensity of her problems, helping her fight her panic, being a stable adult authority in her life and helping her focus on her capabilities as well as on the liabilities in her situation; (3) to work with the family to see how they could help or what resources they could mobilize. In a number of home calls I discovered that the father had been periodically psychotic and now was marginally adjusted in a protected job situation. The family was socially mobile downward. The financial situation was precarious. The mother investigated agencies and eventually, at a point of crisis, asked me to help her get an emergency appointment at a clinic. This was done; Pat was seen six times and the mother twice. The transaction was unsuccessful. I felt that the mother could not tolerate formal treatment for Pat or the family for fear of upsetting the precarious emotional balance in the family. It turned out that the mother could not even help to curb Pat's wandering by bringing her to school. What the family could and did do was to provide a protected haven for Pat at home to give her time to overcome her developmental crisis, which the mother attributed to the onset of puberty.

When it became clear that this was the only way in which the family could help, Pat was given a home teacher. At this time, Pat was so disheveled and withdrawn that a psychiatric hospitalization seemed imminent. She evaded the home instruction teacher by staying in bed, pretending to be asleep, refusing to get dressed, etc. I urged the teacher to be firm with Pat. Finally, one day when the mother was away from home, Pat refused to open the door and left the teacher standing on the porch for an hour. The mother returned and opened the door, the teacher marched up to Pat's bedroom and said, "Pat, if you ever do a thing like that again, that's the end of me as your teacher. I will not work with you when you behave like this and there will go your last chance of graduating from the eighth grade." Pat's bizarre behavior diminished and, gradually, she formed a good relationship with the teacher. She passed eighth grade on home instruction.

The next fall, Pat seemed to be in better emotional shape, though she said she could not return to school. I told her that we would try her in school whenever she felt ready. She was not given home instruction. After a few weeks' delay, the mother called and asked me to make a home call to arrange Pat's return to school. Because Pat was very sensitive about her odd behavior at school the year before and wanted to avoid meeting former classmates, she was placed in a different junior high school. There, she attended three periods a day, taking courses in the humanities, a field for which she had a special flair. She had a few panic reactions, which were handled firmly by the woman vice principal; they did not recur, Pat passed the three classes with good grades and completed the ninth grade.

The following fall, she became upset again. She called me excitedly about her high school placement, saying that she was too mature for tenth grade and requesting an eleventh grade placement. She had a persistent fantasy of being older than her actual chronological age. A careful tenth grade program was worked out for her and I discussed Pat's background in junior high school and her special vulnerabilities with the principal, vice principal, nurse and counselor, all of whom worked to hold this girl in school. However, Pat found something wrong with every one of her classes; her program was changed several times but Pat could not be successfully involved and finally had to be exempted for the balance of the year.

Currently, on a regular eleventh grade program, she is doing very well. She seems less isolated, more purposeful, less apt to react with panic and coercive manipulations when she is subjected to the ordinary stresses and strains of every day life in a high school. Flexible planning and support kept the doors to life and education open for this talented but unstable young lady, whose own home could not provide this model of flexibility or strength.

Unfortunately, we were not as successful with Roddy, Pat's younger brother. Roddy had been of no concern in elementary school, except that he did not work up to his good academic ability. Roddy also hit a crisis in the eighth grade but, where Pat had sought adult support, even though her relationships with adults had very pathological features, Roddy kept all adults at a distance. He would not talk with teachers or parents about any problems. He seemed to have lost all inner sense of direction and began to run away. He ran from any minor difficulty at school by hiding at home. He reacted to any minor difficulty at home by running away from home. Eventually he got involved with several other isolated, disturbed boys, of whom there were many in his neighborhood. We tried putting him into a stable, middle-class school, spelling limits out very concretely for him. This worked for a while, then he ran again. This time, he and a companion hid out for several days, then stole a large lumber truck, which they crashed, almost killing themselves in the process. Eventually Roddy's parents begged the Court to commit him to a correctional institution to avoid even greater havoc.

I have described the contrasting careers of the two oldest children in a downward mobile family beset by latent mental illness to illustrate that it is often easier, in our guidance experience, to help withdrawn panicky youngsters than to help acting-out panicky ones. Schools have more resources to cope with scared, withdrawn students, while the consequences accruing to children who act out often complicate and pyramid the original psychological problem.

Margaret

Margaret was a fourteen-year-old Caucasian girl referred by her very motherly ninth grade counselor because, in the words of one of her teachers, "When Margaret walks into the class, sadness walks in." Mrs. A, the counselor, had talked with the girl and had found out that Margaret was reacting to a family crisis. She had lived all her life in a small town in the northwest, where she had been raised by her maternal grand-parents. She described her upbringing as unusually stable; her life was happily bounded by church, school and close relatives. She had been an excellent student and, in a quiet way, a leader in her group. Her relations with her mother, who lived in the same town, had been good but not close. The mother had led a somewhat rootless existence, beset by dif-ficulties resulting from two poor marriages (Margaret was a product of the first).

Suddenly the mother remarried for the third time. She decided that this time the marriage would work and would be complete with home, child, cat and bird. Margaret was informed of this plan and brought here, where her stepfather had gotten a job. This was in September. I met Margaret just before Christmas. I was impressed with her quiet dignity, but also with her subdued appeal for help in a highly depressing situa-tion. By then her grades had fallen and she had many absences due to prolonged colds. Her mother's utopian plans for an ideal home had not worked out; there was a great deal of quarreling and bickering at home. Margaret was very homesick for the grandparents.

As I saw Margaret at irregular intervals for the remainder of the school year, it became clear that she wanted to use me as someone who would give her perspective, keep her from going off on a tangent and could help her to keep the focus on the total situation and her own goals, rather than on the mood of the moment, as a peer might have done. Our interviews were much like those one would have with an adult in a situational crisis. Margaret's counselor could not provide this perspective because she tended to get involved in more value-laden issues, such as who could make a better home for Margaret, the church-going grand-parents or the rather unstable mother.

Eventually Margaret, the counselor and I had a three-way conference in which we all agreed that our chief goal was to help Margaret maintain her own sense of stable personal integrity. This goal was supported by the fact that she had raised her grades back to a college entrance level and had made some girl friends who were quiet, intelligent, stable young-sters. She had been able to do all this in the face of a rapidly deteriorating home situation (by now, for instance, there were frequent physical fights between her mother and stepfather).

The possibility of my intervening and talking with the mother came up, of course, early in my contacts, but it was obvious that Margaret was afraid of this. She felt that her mother would make her feel very guilty for discussing home problems with me and that her conferences with me were her only safety valve for the time being. Consequently, whenever she told me of an event at home and wanted me to take sides, I refused to do so on the basis of my not having the other side of the story. This enabled me to refocus clearly with Margaret on her own role or the nature of her own involvement in the incident.

As we parted for the summer, with Margaret's future still uncertain, she commented that, whatever happened, she knew that she had not unwittingly contributed to the family difficulties. I gave her my home telephone number so that she could reach me during the summer, should she have further need for a less involved listener. I felt enriched by having known this girl. I could well understand her counselor's impulse to intervene actively on Margaret's behalf. I had had to fight this impulse myself. However, it was quite obvious that Margaret was equal to her task of focussing steadily on her personal goals and development, taking the chaotic home situation into realistic account but not being overwhelmed by it.

Eric

Eric was a Caucasian boy who was referred to the Health Department in the central Department of Special Services when he was a kindergartner. At this time, he had just been out of school for five weeks because of an operation. His teacher noted that he "is one of the more immature children just now but, as he was absent quite a while, he is just catching on to school procedures again. Short attention span—is apt to interrupt stories, etc. Likes most of the work but does not excel in any type of activity. When sister comes in, he becomes very helpless and wants her to do his work (which she is too willing to do) and wait on him." Eric's mother continued to get help from time to time with Eric's physical problems; for instance, he received home instruction during a period of illness.

Eric first came to the attention of the guidance worker when he was fourteen. His mother had asked the counselor and vice principal to have the guidance worker evaluate Eric's problem, which was an academic administrative one. This boy, in general, had done well academically but, the previous year, he had gotten a D in Latin and now, because of school policy, was refused admission to another foreign language course. Eric had made several efforts to get permission to take French because he was a college preparatory student. Permission was denied.

Eric was described as an attractive, blond, pink-cheeked fourteen year old who was shy and "spoiled" and who wept easily. When the guidance worker saw him, his eyes quickly filled with tears as he explained that he had gotten his D in Latin because "I goofed around." He said that he liked all his school subjects; his records showed that he had average grades or a bit better. He was good at swimming and enjoyed working with his father in their home workshop. Eric's mother came to school to talk with the guidance worker. She said that Eric was "no problem" at home, in the community, or with his friends. However, since being refused permission to take French, the boy had been upset, moody and depressed. The mother asked if Eric could get school credit for private tutoring in French.

The guidance worker discovered from the central office that credit for private tutoring was contrary to school policy. However, chance plays as large a part in school as in other human affairs. Eric's plight was used as an example in talking over another case with a different vice principal and the guidance worker was told that exceptions could be made to the school policy which was keeping Eric out of French "at the discretion of the principal." The guidance worker arranged a conference among all the people involved—Eric, the vice principal, the counselor and the guidance worker herself. As a result of this conference, the guidance worker recommended to the principal that Eric be given a trial in French. The principal reviewed Eric's records and then said, "Well, I always felt: why should we have the guidance workers unless we follow their recommendations? Let's try him in French and get (his teacher) to give him some special tutoring here at school so he can catch up with his class." This plan was followed and Eric, by the end of the term, was able to earn a grade of C.

Eric's problems might not be considered serious but the guidance worker felt that prompt and flexible action by school people had helped Eric to reverse a tailspin which might have had quite damaging repercussions in Eric's general academic performance and attitude toward school.

Joselyn

Joselyn was a twelve-year-old Caucasian girl in the seventh grade. She had superior ability and achieved well. She behaved very satisfactorily in school. The chain of events leading to my knowledge of her began with the fact that she made one of her teachers a confidant.

The teacher Joselyn talked to was a very warm, responsive man, who was well liked by all his students. I knew little about him other than this because he seldom had difficulties with the students and seemed to take pride in his ability to manage even the most difficult children successfully without help.

The school nurse accidentally learned that Joselyn was staying after school to talk to the teacher when he was alone in the classroom. In speaking with the teacher, the nurse learned that Joselyn also stopped constantly in his room between classes; he had responded to her plea for someone to talk to about family difficulties. The nurse suggested to the teacher that he attempt to discourage these confidences and encourage Joselyn to talk over her problems with her counselor. In spite of the nurse's attempt to be diplomatic, the teacher seemed to feel reproved. He said, however, that he would do this.

Joselyn did not like the suggestion that she talk to her counselor (a woman) and begged the teacher to continue his interest, which he did. Soon, however, the revelations that Joselyn made were of such a personal nature that the teacher became embarrassed and deeply concerned for Joselyn. He asked the nurse what to do. Hearing that Joselyn's problem concerned her relationship with her stepfather, the nurse and vice principal decided to ask me to talk to Joselyn and to have the teacher tell Joselyn that he had asked for this help.

The teacher was in class and not available to talk to me before I saw Joselyn. I examined Joselyn's elementary school record, which had no new information except a cryptic comment that under no circumstances should an attempt be made to contact the home.

Joselyn impressed me as a highly verbal, rather dramatic youngster. She was an attractive, well-dressed girl with physical development well in advance of the average for twelve. She spent most of the time discussing how she felt misunderstood by her mother and could not talk over any problems with her. She characterized her mother as "fat," unattractive to Joselyn's stepfather and "sitting all day in front of TV,"

Joselyn said that her stepfather had just returned to the family after a separation of two days but she doubted that he would stay. She said that she talked over her problems with her stepfather and became interested in talking to the teacher because of the resemblance between the two men. Joselyn is the second in a family of five children. She seemed fond of all the children, of whom she is the oldest girl. I encouraged Joselyn to tell about her earlier life in the family and she mentioned that, as a little girl, she had felt close to her mother. She thought their antagonism had been most marked during the past year. When I asked if Joselyn would like me to help work out these differences, she was emphatic that I must not contact her mother. I told her I could not promise this.

In spite of Joselyn's complaints, she did not strike me as a deeply troubled child, nor one hungrily seeking relationships. I felt that some of her statements were dramatized, since she seemed intrigued by talking to someone who deals with personal problems. She said that she wanted to become a writer and was working at that time on short stories which she hoped to develop later into a novel. I told Joselyn that I was undecided at the moment just what I might do to help her, but wondered if we might agree that she would ask to see me in the future if she felt the need to talk. Joselyn seemed pleased with this arrangement.

Later in the day, I was able to arrange a meeting with the teacher. With considerable difficulty, he revealed that the troublesome confidences Joselyn had made were remarks and questions about menstruation and sexual fantasies about a boy friend and her stepfather. Ruefully, the teacher asked how he might disengage himself from the relationship with Joselyn without hurting her feelings. We discussed how he might clarify his role as teacher with her by maintaining a more casual attitude and gradually but firmly discouraging her coming in after school. It was suggested that he think of dealing with Joselyn as he would with any other student who might have a "crush" on him. With humor, the teacher said he could do this and he laughingly said I need not bother to tell him whatever I might discover about Joselyn in the future. He thought the less he knew the easier it would be for him in his relationship to Joselyn.

I asked the vice principal to arrange a conference with Mrs. X, Joselyn's mother, at school at the time of my next scheduled school visit. The vice principal agreed that I should participate in this conference. Joselyn's counselor was alerted to the plan, to which she objected because of the notation in Joselyn's folder concerning contacts with the family. The counselor felt that if anything were "stirred up" by our seeing the mother, the vice principal and I should handle it. We agreed.

Both Mr. and Mrs. X came for the conference. Mr. X seemed quite angry. After saying a few complimentary things about Joselyn, the vice principal turned to me for an explanation of why the parents had been called. I told them we were interested in helping Joselyn to make the most of her good ability and charm, that in order to do this we wanted to talk to them as a help in evaluating some of her behavior at school. We felt that she was already well advanced into adolescence and wondered if the parents were noting typical or unusual adolescent problems in the family. Mr. X said abruptly that Joselyn was a "good kid" and there was nothing wrong. Mrs. X began to talk about Joselyn's behavior at home in general terms. I responded with comments about the usual behavior of adolescents in regard to their resistance to doing home tasks, their moodiness, and their interest in personal appearance.

Soon both parents were interestedly discussing Joselyn and Mr. X began to vie with his wife in expressing understanding of the girl. He then made several hostile remarks about his wife's treating Joselyn like a little girl in regard to clothes and said he had bought the clothes Joselyn wears to keep her from looking queer. He went on to tell how Joselyn confides in him about everything, while she knows her mother will not understand and cannot talk to her. When he said he thought such a state of affairs was deplorable, I asked if he had ever told Joselyn that he wanted her to talk over problems with her mother. Mr. X seemed to experience insight; in some confusion, he said that he had not.

Mrs. X now expressed herself more fully, revealing a sensible, maternal attitude toward Joselyn. She volunteered that Joselyn did not date, was closely supervised and that she had not worked for the past year, therefore she knew Joselyn's friends and activities well. Mrs. X also volunteered that she and Joselyn used to be close and she regretted the fact that Joselyn was pulling away just at the time when she felt they needed to be able to talk about attitudes toward boys and values leading toward adult life.

Mr. X, who had seemed lost in thought, now said it had been hard for him to talk to Joselyn about menstruation but he had done it because he thought she needed to talk about it. We agreed that this was hard, would be hard for most men to discuss, and perhaps Joselyn needed to be told that it was appropriate to talk to her mother. Mr. X then expanded upon the difficulties of being a stepfather, his love for all the children in the family (some of whom are his own) and his intense desire not to be treated by any of the children as different from a true father. He mentioned Joselyn's affection for her teacher, saying he thought this was natural and right.

The parents were told that Joselyn seemed to have a great need to talk to her teacher, who felt that Joselyn was hurt when he attempted to maintain his role of a teacher with her. Mr. X said he had not been aware that Joselyn was "overdoing" it in talking to the teacher and that he would discuss this with her. I drew a parallel in Joselyn's "overdoing it" with her father, too. He agreed and said laughingly he guessed this was partly his doing and he would take care of that too, but Mrs. X would have to be more open-minded about Joselyn's growing up if it really was going to work. Mrs. X, who seemed very pleased, said that she would try.

After a few more remarks, the conference was terminated with both parents expressing their gratitude at having been called. Mr. X's parting remark was that it was a pleasure to be treated like Joselyn's father by school people. At her elementary school, he had "blown up" because the principal kept talking about his being a stepfather and would only talk to Mrs. X.

The vice principal and I agreed that we discounted much of what Joselyn had said about family relationships after meeting the parents. The vice principal decided to tell Joselyn's teacher and counselor that there seemed to be no cause for unusual concern. I spoke to the nurse about my impressions of Joselyn's situation at home and at school. Some time later the teacher volunteered to me that Joselyn had seemed disappointed by his withdrawal from the intense relationship but had taken it well and that he personally was much relieved that the problem had been worked out.

Debby

A junior high school experienced a complete change of administrative personnel. A few months later the student body was halved and many teachers left because newly built schools were opened. The guidance worker was relatively new to this particular school when Debby, a middle-class Caucasian girl, came to her attention. Since the school was situated in a lower-middle class area having a high incidence of delinquency, it is not surprising that the faculty was chiefly concerned about children who defied authority. The vice principal, burdened with disciplinary work, was particularly sensitive about the unmet emotional needs of high-potential students.

Debby, a very obese, intellectually gifted ninth grader, was frequently absent for "illness" which was always explained and excused by her mother. She did chiefly C and B academic work. The male attendance supervisor, who had known Debby about two years, had attempted unsuccessfully for some time to refer her and her mother to a family counseling agency. In ninth grade Debby had been assigned to help her counselor with clerical work in the hope of building a closer relationship with someone in the school. Her work was highly efficient, but often interrupted by absences. The counselor and vice principal asked the guidance worker to help, saying that they believed Debby and her mother might respond more to a woman visiting the home to get Debby to come regularly to school. The counselor frankly said she could not feel positive enough toward Mrs. S to work with her. The attendance supervisor was agreeable to the plan.

When the guidance worker phoned the home to arrange an appointment, Mrs. S was distraught because Debby was missing and police were searching for her. Mrs. S. said she now agreed to the recommendation for counseling and wanted the guidance worker's help on possible community resources as soon as Debby was found. Two days later, when Debby was returned home, Mrs. S phoned to follow up this idea. She had already decided upon taking Debby to a particular psychologist for immediate diagnostic testing and merely wanted approval of this plan. She asked the guidance worker's help in arranging for Debby to be out of school "legally" until testing was completed, as she dared not let the girl out of her sight. Mrs. S readily agreed to give the guidance worker and psychologist her permission to confer about the test results.

A few days later the psychologist advised the guidance worker that Debby and Mrs. S had been referred to a psychiatric clinic. The psychologist believed that Debby had strong schizoid tendencies and that Mrs. S was more deeply disturbed than Debby, probably in like manner. Debby had not returned to school.

The guidance worker suggested to Debby's counselor that she telephone the home and tell the girl that she needed and wanted Debby back at school very much. The counselor did this but Debby did not return to school.

The consultant then telephoned Mrs. S asking about Debby's condition and her attitude about coming to school. Mrs. S replied that Debby had many fears about coming back and she did not feel able to insist that Debby go. She complained about the clinical referral, saying that the psychologist had not been able to determine why Debby ran away and neither she nor Debby wanted to "spend months trying to find out," they preferred to try to forget the whole thing. Mrs. S was willing to have the guidance worker come to talk to Debby, first assuring herself that there would be no accusations or criticism.

Mrs. S, an obese woman, met the guidance worker with a "poker face." She spent several minutes talking and "sizing up" the guidance worker, responding to the guidance worker's concern for herself and Debby, who had both gone through a distressing experience. (Debby is an only child.) With a smile Mrs. S invited the guidance worker to Debby's room.

Debby was lying on her back in bed with her eyes closed, and she did not move when Mrs. S said that "someone" had come to see her. Mrs. S motioned to a chair by the bed and left. For a little while, the guidance worker sat quietly. Noticing that Debby's eyelids quivered from time to time, the guidance worker began to talk in a low soothing tone, telling who she was, her role in Debby's school of helping young people in trouble, and her hope that she could help Debby, who must have been frightened by the things that had happened recently. Debby's eyelids fluttered. The guidance worker went on, saying perhaps Debby was afraid now of what the guidance worker might say, but she could see Debby feels very bad and she only wants to help. Debby peeped at the guidance worker. In a moment the guidance worker said people have talked and talked to Debby about coming to school, but the guidance worker can see that Debby is feeling too bad right now to come. Yet, she is missed there; her counselor is really lost without Debby's help. Still, we want only what is best for Debby. In a small choked voice Debby said she would like to come. The guidance worker said she was glad, but could understand that it might be hard to do so, maybe she could make it easier if she knew what was bothering Debby. In a tiny voice Debby said, "My grades." As Debby looked at her, the guidance worker agreed that Debby had probably gotten behind, and since school people know she is intelligent, they might think she should study harder and catch up. Maybe Debby has heard something like this about her good ability lots of times. Debby nodded, closed her eyes, and two tears slid down her cheeks. The guidance worker said she could not promise that Debby would never hear this again, but just speaking for herself, it would be enough to see Debby back in school, taking a program she could feel sure of managing—and this could be arranged. Debby wiped her eyes and raised up on one elbow. It was quickly agreed that she would return the next day and that she would drop only Spanish. Debby now became quite talkative in a relaxed way and showed her doll collection and art work, which included a beautifully illuminated chart of all the English kings and queens. Mrs. S brought in Debby's dog and mother and daughter talked in a happy, excited way about what Debby would wear to school the next day. The bedroom became full of activity, the dog romping about and Debby half out of bed after him. As Mrs. S ushered the guidance worker out, she was beaming and obviously eager to return to Debby.

Debby did return to school the next day, where her counselor made the suggested change in her program and gave her a warm welcome. The counselor really yearned to have Debby distinguish herself academically, as she had potential to do. She had been asked by the guidance worker to refrain from speaking of this, to show only her sincere pleasure that Debby was in school. As time went on it was difficult for the counselor to maintain this attitude without asking much more of Debby. She was encouraged to express her frustration to the guidance worker at intervals and was given recognition for the real effort made to continue an undemanding attitude.

The guidance worker interviewd Debby twice during the first month after her return. Debby indicated satisfaction with her academic work but preferred to dwell upon her church and Scout activities. She spoke of being presented with an expensive reducing program by her parents. After this, Debby made a point of being noticed whenever she saw the guidance worker in the halls, then bustled cheerily away. Her academic achievement continued at about the same level, though her attendance was regular. There was no discernible loss of weight during the year. Debby graduated to senior high school in June.

Chuck

Chuck is an upper middle-class Caucasian, eleventh grade boy with an I.Q. of 149 on a Stanford Binet. The school knew that he was in private psychiatric treatment. Nonetheless, the counselor was considerably unsettled when Chuck came to her asking that his academic program be reduced to four hours and consist of "light" courses (student court, library, English and swimming) because of his extreme anxiety. A school naturally becomes concerned when an intellectually gifted student presents such a request. The counselor asked me to confer informally with Chuck. (No formal referral was made of this case.)

When Chuck and I had a conference, he complained of being unable to study, do homework or stand the pressures of school. If the program he requested couldn't be arranged, he said he would have to quit school because he couldn't take it. He had a tremor, looked flushed and highly anxious. I agreed with Chuck that his program change seemed reasonable for him. Chuck's psychiatrist, when I phoned him, also concurred. He said, "We've got to do what we can. It's not too encouraging. He doesn't know if he wants to go to college or even finish high school. I approve of the four hour placement." The counselor also agreed with the plan, on the basis of his appraisal of Chuck's very real impediments to concentration and learning. Because she had known the family quite well, the counselor phoned them and discussed the plan. They agreed.

All went well for Chuck on the new program until, at Christmas time, a relative visited the family. This relative was an administrator in a large public school district on the Atlantic Seaboard. The relative became alarmed by this "inadequate" program for a bright, college-bound boy. He went to see the principal at Chuck's school and also conferred with a friend of his in the local Board of Education. He tried to have a conference with me but the principal told him that this would not be possible since he was not a member of the immediate family.

The principal called me to tell me what was going on and I checked with Chuck's psychiatrist, who reiterated his view that the lightened academic load was a correct procedure. The parents were now extremely anxious—understandably so—and I had a conference with them, re-emphasizing the psychiatrist's opinion and my observations. The parents relaxed and agreed to continue with the original plan for Chuck. Chuck had functioned well and looked much better with his altered program;

both parents and school agreed that he would have dropped out of school if he had not had the adjusted program. Chuck, in the meantime, talked with me about possible boarding schools but he said, "I get frightened because the brochures are all about the high standards, college prep, etc. I need a program like I have here or I'll quit school. Even on the swim team I get nervous; it's too much work; I get headaches, my legs ache and I hurt in my stomach."

In the spring, Chuck himself took the initiative for enrolling in the adult evening course in speed reading. The teacher of this course called me in an agitated state of mind because Chuck had blown up and become quite irrational over a small incident in class. It seemed that Chuck was trying his wings in a more demanding academic atmosphere but that this proved to be too much for him. He dropped out of the class.

Chuck has a job as a lifeguard for the summer. He continues his psychiatric treatment. The family agreed that the job would be more useful for Chuck than summer school, even though his high school graduation might be postponed. Meanwhile, he, his counselor and I have a tentative plan for him to try a full-time senior program in the fall. We will evaluate the situation at that time and take the appropriate steps.

Matthew

Matthew is an eleventh grade middle-class Caucasian student whose mother requested the help of the guidance worker in arranging a psychiatric referral for herself and her son. No formal referral to guidance had been made by the school, though they now noted that Matthew's academic work had recently been deteriorating. His mother said that he suddenly had been staying away from home overnight and had become very non-communicative with her, although, previously, their relationship had been close. Matthew's sudden academic and emotional tailspin had sent the mother into a panic.

I had a conference with the vice principal and an interview with the mother, at the place where she worked as a secretary. The mother and father had been separated for many years. This intellectual mother had to work on a job far below her potential because she had no professional training. She was a friend of several local psychiatrists and other workers in the psychosocial disciplines. She did not make it clear why she wanted to use a guidance worker as a referral source, rather than one of these friends.

Matthew emerged from the discussion as a very bright boy (his I.Q. was 143) with a "beatnik" identity. He was not interested in school. He spent all his spare time in association with a group of intelligent, off-beat students in a local University, who encouraged his beatnik identity. He played the guitar in *avant-garde* night-spots near this University and with a jazz group in a neighboring town. Matthew was "in love" with a girl who attended the University. This girl and her family were seeing a psychologist who specialized in family group interviewing. The family financial state had led me to think of the local public mental hygiene clinic as the best resource for Matthew and his mother. However, Matthew vehemently wanted to go to the therapist of his girl friend and her family. It seemed wisest to support his choice of treatment plan. His mother concurred.

Two months later, Matthew's mother stated that there had been reasonably good improvement in her relationship with Matthew. She said that she and Matthew were now able to work some things out much better. She was anxious, however, about his senior year program and wanted to be kept informed about Matthew's school plans and progress.

Terry

Terry is a handsome, sophisticated, seventeen year old Caucasian high school senior who asked to see the guidance worker to help him find a male psychiatrist. He was precise and clear in knowing what he wanted. Nothing less than a psychiatrist would do. He had formerly gone to a family service agency but stated firmly that he wanted to see a professional person with broader experience.

Terry said that his parents would be opposed to this but that he had a job and could afford to pay for treatment himself if the fees were low enough. He requested that I talk to his mother, since the adolescent clinic where I planned to refer him required signed permission from a parent.

When I phoned the mother, she was amazed at her son's request and said she couldn't understand what was troubling him: "Things like this never occur at this age but later in life, college at the earliest." She reluctantly agreed to sign a permission slip for treatment. She planned to come to the vice principal's office to sign the slip, which I had gotten from the clinic. She delayed this for several weeks, however, and Terry came to see me each week, impatiently complaining of the delay.

I telephoned the adolescent clinic and discussed the situation with them; they agreed to accept the boy for treatment before the permission slip was signed by the mother. The mother did finally formalize her consent and Terry continues to get the psychiatric help he so steadfastly requested.

Dulcie

Dulcie is a Caucasian twelfth grader who moved to this area from the Southeast last August. She lives with her older sister, a junior college teacher. The school reported her as "a very talented, vivacious, outstanding student" who was "immediately recognized by her teachers as one with exceptional ability." She had just been approved by the vice principal to take a special night class in psychology. She was on the staff of the school paper.

The counselor referred Dulcie to me because of unexpected and disquieting symptoms. She reported that Dulcie was having "sudden disturbing episodes of depression and associated neurasthenia in the past week. She doesn't know why and is very worried about it." The counselor was concerned about this unanticipated instability in a promising student.

I talked informally with Dulcie. Very shortly, she was able to tell me that her psychiatric symptoms were no more nor less than a result of being in love.

I could easily reassure the school and, once Dulcie was allowed the vapors of romantic involvement, she got along beautifully for the rest of the year and graduated with honors.

NOTES
(Chapter XIII)

1. Anna Freud, *The Ego and The Mechanisms of Defense*, International Universities Press, Inc., New York, 1946. pp. 149-189; Peter Blos, *On Adolescence*, The Free Press of Glencoe, Inc., New York, 1962.
2. Erik H. Erikson, *Growth and Crises of the "Healthy Personality,"* in Problems of Infancy and Childhood, Milton J. E. Senn, Ed., Supplement II, Trans. Fourth Conference, Josial H. Macy, Jr. Foundation, New York, 1950, pp. 46-52; and Erik H. Erikson, *Identity and the Life Cycle,*

Psychological Issues, Monograph I, Vol. 1, No. 1, International Universities Press, New York, pp. 101-164.

3. Erik H. Erikson, "Youth: Fidelity and Diversity," *Daedalus*, Vol. 91, No. 1, pp. 5-27; and Erik H. Erikson, and Kai T. Erikson, "The Confirmation of the Delinquent," *The Chicago Review*, Winter, 1957, Vol. 10, pp. 15-23.

4. Mary Conway Kohler and André Fontaine, "We Waste a Million Kids a Year," *Saturday Evening Post*, March 10, 17, and 24, 1962.

CHAPTER XIV

Complications Involving School and Community

School people, like other human beings, may get caught up in problems of conscious or unconscious competitiveness, rivalry, threats to self-esteem, authority problems and the like. Such difficulties are compounded in schools where the level of stress is high for any reason: rapid socio-economic change in neighborhood and school,[1] rapid turnover of teachers, low morale, personality difficulties between administrators, etc. The emergence of the demand for more student power, which tends to align youngsters like the ones described below with others who feel similarly "picked on," has created a new situation for which no clear pattern of intervention is yet discernible. "Student power," "Black power," "the drug scene" all present challenges to the total school establishment never openly encountered in the past. Nor are the students' efforts to become directly involved in policy-making isolated from other challenges to the educational establishment, such as the emergence of teacher power via the stepped up activities of teacher organizations including their readiness to strike; and the emergence of community power seen in the erosion of the PTA and the development of competing, anti-establishment parent and community groups who are working toward closer control of their neighborhood schools.

In a general way, one can merely state that guidance workers are in a strategic position to help keep channels of communication open, to keep the focus on the welfare and the education of youngsters at a time when power struggles may obscure such a task-oriented point of view, to use all of their skills—individually or group focused—on problem solving and on creating alliances with those forces within and without the schools dedicated to such problem-solving. The following three interactions are precursors of what we are facing today and tomorrow when difficulties among school personnel and between school and the community can compound the difficulties of a child. The guidance worker must work with and plan for the student in terms of these school attitudes; no amount of work with the student's problems in isolation will help to resolve his "bind" at school.

Generations of educators have struggled with the complications of secondary schools. Schools vary so tremendously in morale, historical ways of operating and necessary expediencies, that few generalizations are possible. We can say that there is no single pattern of psychosocial trouble-shooting which will be suitable for all secondary schools. Over-structuring of role or overly rigid preset methods for handling difficulties may be disastrous. For instance, one of the things which may be either good or bad for the secondary school student is his dispersal among six teachers. He may welcome the meeting of minds with a specialist in English or Math, or he may benefit from his anonymity; on the other hand, for some students in difficulty, this fragmentation may be catastrophic. In the latter case, it may be of great importance to get planned and coordinated handling by all the students' teachers. The guidance worker may try to do this by planning a pre-school or after-school conference in which all the relevant educators participate. Such conferences, in a high-morale school, may be extremely helpful; in an embittered or low-morale school, they may cause resentment and may consolidate the student's bad reputation.

Recognizing the tentativeness of any generalizations about secondary schools, let us discuss briefly some of the prominent difficulties. The first of these is the teacher's isolation from any psychosocial information about about his students and from any support in his efforts to include a psychosocial dimension in his educational role. The guidance worker is so peripheral to the multitude of classrooms that it is difficult for him to be helpful, except in a few specific situations. The counselors are usually inundated with their scheduling and academic duties and, at present, may lack psychosocial skills. The vice-principal is often overwhelmed with the number of minor disciplinary problems, such as students chewing gum in class, looking sullenly at a teacher, talking back, etc., in addition to the really serious situations confronting him. In high morale schools, which try to include the psychosocial dimension in their educational efforts, any added personnel are likely to be people who will work with students in difficulties—more counselors, more vice-principals—rather than people who have the primary job of supporting and informing teachers in a preventive manner. There seems to be a widespread need in secondary schools to introduce a person whose main job will be with teachers: giving and getting information, giving concrete educational support and helping teachers, especially beginning teachers, to include the psychosocial dimension in their educational efforts. As long as teachers are allowed to "swim or sink," they will approach their students in a like manner.

The most hopeful current step in resolving this impasse at the secondary level (namely, integrating psychosocial information into the educational process), lies in a widespread move to give school counselors more training in psychosocial concepts and techniques, such as skill in interviewing. This endeavor has been backed largely by the National Defense Education Act. If counselors could be helped to operate in this broadened way, they would become major trouble-shooters in the secondary school and the guidance worker could operate as their consultant. The principal and vice-principals would be freed for their proper administrative tasks and could spend more time in supporting their teachers and involving them in educational problem-solving. The following three interactions illustrate the way in which difficulties among school personnel can complicate the difficulties of a child.

Paul

Paul was a seventh grade Caucasian boy in a junior high school which was in the first stages of transition from a largely middle-class Caucasian to a largely lower-class minority-group school. The woman vice principal had been in the school for many years and had decided influence with the faculty. The new man principal was threatened by her position of prestige and influence. Paul was caught in a power struggle between them.

The vice principal, Mrs. X, had known two of Paul's siblings previously and knew his parents. Paul was the youngest of four children, an attractive boy of good average intelligence but physically somewhat immature. His mother dominated the family; his father was passive and ineffectual. Paul had a chronic reading problem which had not been budged by previous tutoring. He had not had any particular behavior problems in elementary school except that he was "mischievous" but now, in seventh grade, he was acting very rebellious, especially with women teachers. He covered his reading difficulty by clowning, became very "flip." Teachers considered him intolerable. Mrs. X was working with him and her efforts had a positive effect on Paul for a few days. However, the principal, Mr. Z, seeing Paul frequently in the office, also became involved. The power struggle was on: the boy was suspended several times and I (the guidance worker) was called in.

I saw the mother at her home. She was not particularly defensive and had reasonable insight into Paul's problems. She said that Paul had been overprotected from an early age. He was a sickly child with frequent colds and some asthmatic attacks. As a preschool boy, he had little contact with other children. The mother described the parents' relationship with each other as fairly good, although she realized that she sometimes became exasperated at her husband's passivity. The mother was willing to begin to untie Paul from her apron strings, to encourage him to join the Boys Club, etc.

With this information, I arranged a conference among Mr. Z, Mrs. X and Paul's teachers. It seemed to me that Mrs. X had been too protective of Paul, just like his mother. In order to ease the struggle for power in the situation between Mrs. X and Mr. Z, I emphasized the fact that Paul seemed to be trying to escape the domination of women (though he had responded to Mrs. X). I suggested that Paul be placed in as many classes with men teachers as possible and that Mr. Z handle him when he was sent to the office. (I had previously discussed this plan with Mrs. X to have her in accord.)

Paul experienced ups and downs at school; he was sent home on some days but long suspensions no longer occurred, once Mr. Z was explicitly "in the saddle." I suggested that Mr. Z approach Paul on the basis that boys of his age frequently had difficulty in accepting the authority of women teachers but that it was necessary for Paul to learn to handle this. Paul's academic troubles continued, though the parents did agree to get a man tutor for him. This helped the attitude of the school because they felt "something was being done" and this "something" was, in reality, not an aid the school could offer.

Given time in the changed school atmosphere, Paul began to adjust much better. In the ninth grade, he was one of the directors on the stage crew and had gained reasonable status with his peers; clowning and defiance were greatly lessened.

Annie

Annie, a Negro girl, and I (her guidance worker) were caught, at the Y Junior High School, in the deliberate attempt of the woman vice principal and certain teachers to provoke Annie into "blow ups" so that she would be exempted. Y Junior High School was under high stress as a result of very rapid socio-cultural change (from middle-class Caucasian to lower-class minority group).

I had followed Annie's progress and struggles for many years. She was an explosive girl from a disorganized family. Her mother had been alcoholic and was periodically in psychiatric hospitals so that Annie had frequent experiences in foster homes. She had reasonable success during the first two years of junior high, although there were some suspensions and some academic failures. Annie was academically an able girl and some creative writing ability had developed in elementary school.

In the ninth grade, Annie, again in a foster home, had several temper tantrums in which she "told off" the vice principal and some of the teachers in language unbecoming a lady ("vulgar and profane" in the Board Regulations—"enough to make a sailor blanch" in the vernacular). Without question, action had to be taken: the vice principal and certain teachers felt that Annie "had to go," meaning exemption. The principal did not wish this to happen because Annie's brother, who was even more disturbed and who produced nothing academically, had already been exempted. I definitely did not approve exemption, for the teachers and vice principal had provoked some of Annie's reactions. The principal backed me up and the girl was suspended.

I went to see Annie and her foster-mother before Annie returned to school—this was done in order to make a direct attack on the realistic problem, which was that Annie would certainly be exempted if she could not control her reactions. I did not try to argue with her about her feeling of justification for her acts but did point out, as I had before, that she had always had trouble accepting correction or the demands of authority. I also pointed out that no school could survive if children were permitted to defy authority in the way she had, no matter how unfairly the student felt he had been treated. I tried to help her see that there were alternatives to her outbursts, for it had already been arranged for her to be excused from class and go directly to the principal if she felt her feelings were beginning to get beyond her control. Fortunately, the foster-mother agreed that such behavior could not be tolerated in school, though in private she expressed the feeling that it was unfortunate teachers had "ordered the girl around," since Annie had never been able to stand being ordered but could easily be persuaded by requests prefaced by "Please."

I did not say so but privately agreed with the foster-mother. Still, there was no doubt in my mind that Annie was an extremely difficult girl to have in class. She was exceedingly "touchy," very ready to fight or start a fight, she denied guilt to the last stand, had been known to steal and was very difficult to "reach," being often sullen and uncommunicative. Both her foster home social worker and I had tried to obtain psychotherapy for her when she was in elementary school but without success.

Annie returned to school and the principal talked pleasantly with her but also "cold turkey." I tried to talk with the teachers, the vice principal and the counselor (who felt the same way the teachers did). However, neither the principal nor I had any real hope that the situation would work, since Annie seemed to be firmly type-cast as "a bad one." A change of program was arranged for Annie to try to eliminate some of the difficulty but there was still the probability of trouble in the halls, lunchroom and playground. We considered a change of schools but I felt that Annie would not be able to make a better adjustment in a strange situation; I believed that she would very soon find herself in the same spot. As we predicted, since certain of the faculty were determined that Annie should not be in school, it was not long before she had to be exempted for the balance of the semester. She will now go on to senior high school because of age but will be short of credits. There is a fair possibility that she will make a marginal adjustment in senior high because authority problems are much more diluted for both students and faculties at the senior high school level.

Bobby

Z Junior High School concerned me (the guidance worker) because I was used as a buffer between the vice principal and the principal in what had been a very antagonistic relationship with both role and personality conflicts between them. Also, I was unable to involve a very weak counseling staff in any meaningful work with students. They were inexperienced in interviewing and were unwilling to try to modify their educational, manipulative or moralistic approaches. Actually, I was able to use Bobby's case to lessen the antagonism between the principal and vice principal and it opened the way for me to help them gain more real appreciation for each other through later cases. The counselors and segments of the faculty still keep me in limbo, but with some teachers I have a very close and profitable relationship.

Bobby, a 13-year old Negro boy in eighth grade, came to my attention because the vice principal asked for an evaluation of his adjustment problems. After study began, it became clear to me that this request was made partly to forestall any precipitate or overly punitive action on the part of the principal in relation to Bobby and partly because a bona fide diagnosis was desired.

Bobby was a very handsome young man who dressed very neatly in a sophisticated manner and whose social poise and maturity gave the impression of a fifteen or sixteen year old, although his intellectual ability was average for his age. He had displayed a very hot temper on several occasions and recently had struck his shop teacher. Because of this "assault," Bobby's problems were being handled by the principal, although previously the vice principal had carried the disciplinary responsibility for any of Bobby's difficulties (as she did for all other children in the school).

In my first interview with Bobby, he brought up the question of racial discrimination in a pugnacious fashion. Bobby, as he discussed this, seemed to decide for himself that it was not a central factor in his difficulty. He volunteered that he had trouble controlling his temper and implied that this was the real difficulty. His only request of me was that I help him to be programmed with another shop teacher, since the principal was insisting that he work out his relationship with the same shop teacher he had struck. Bobby said he could not get along there because the teacher was "two-faced." By this, he meant that the teacher "wised off" to the boys but, when they replied in the same manner, became angry. In his anger, the teacher sometimes used physical means to discipline the boys (pushing, grabbing them by the arm or shoulder, etc.) and Bobby had retaliated because he "would not be pushed around." I told Bob that I would try to be of help to him but that I could make no commitment to carry out his wishes. Cautioning him that any violence on his part would hamper—if not completely end—my ability to help him, I agreed to meet with him the following week.

I reported back to the vice principal my impression that Bobby was not a seriously disturbed boy but one grappling with adolescent problems, who was able to discuss his difficulties on a near-adult level. The vice principal then indicated that she did not want me to discuss Bobby with the principal. She implied that Bob was programmed with teachers who, in nearly every class, handled children with sarcasm and punitive actions. (This was not stated but she said that he had a poor program and then mentioned who his teachers were. I was acquainted with them and knew their reputations with students.) I told her of Bob's desire to be reprogrammed for shop and she said she would find out if this could be done.

When I next saw Bobby, he was very agitated about having had to stand in front of the shop class and read out the conditions under which he was allowed to return to the class after his suspension. He held the shop teacher responsible for this indignity and said that he had been able to restrain himself only because he thought it would help his request for a transfer from the class. He planned, however, to protest this treatment to his counselor. I asked Bobby to let me find out more about this and talk to him again before he spoke to his counselor. (This was because I knew the counselor and felt that Bobby would worsen his position by complaining. This counselor was extremely literal and naive, deeply shocked by youngsters who asserted themselves aggressively. He had a strong desire to handle all problems by being gentle and sympathetic. When he could not do this with a child, he withdrew emotionally. I believed that Bobby would be treated in this way and would be further angered.)

I talked to the vice principal and learned that all children who have struck a teacher have to return to the same class and read aloud a set of conditions governing their return—this being a ruling made by the principal. I explained this to Bobby and pointed out that the shop teacher was "following orders" by having Bobby do this just as much as Bob was in doing it. There was a grudging admiration in Bobby's response. He said he could not "carry this any higher" than to the principal and began to talk about his own father's "toughness" in regard to discipline in the same admiring (and somewhat warmer) tone. Bob's father is an auto mechanic, which Bob also wants to become. (According to his cumulative record, which I had examined, this has been his chief interest ever since he was in second grade.) Before terminating the interview, I explained that I, too, could not supercede the principal and it looked as if Bob would have to cope with his situation as it was, insofar as he could. I offered to talk with him the following week if he thought it would help him. Bob said he wanted this "because it's good to talk to someone who is interested."

In the third interview, Bob was very tense about his relationship with the shop teacher. He was extremely unsure about whether he could continue to control his temper. I told him frankly that he could not afford to lose control and explained exactly what a review board action would mean to him. (In Bob's city, teacher assault could easily be a strong reason for taking a student's case to the centrally located review board which has power to recommend to the Board of Education that a student be permanently expelled from the school system.) Following this statement, Bob relaxed and discussed the problems he had with both girls and boys because they assumed that he was older than his actual age and how he had to resort to all sorts of subterfuge to maintain leadership and personal dignity. At the end of the session, he said he would like me to give him some tests next time and tell him what his abilities were best suited for, in terms of future preparation for an occupation.

I discussed Bob with the vice principal again and happened to state rather enthusiastically how much I liked him, as well as my fear that he would never adjust to his shop teacher. The vice principal suggested that I send a memo to the principal about this problem. I did so immediately but heard nothing from the principal.

The next week, Bob was not particularly interested in discussing school problems. I administered the performance section of the Wechsler Intelligence Scale for Children.

One week later, the principal stopped me in the hall and thanked me for the memo. He said he had talked to Bob's shop teacher and believed the teacher's attitude was better. I told the principal that Bob had been impressed by having his problem handled by the "top man." The principal said rather painfully that it might have helped Bob but he had not been helpful to others. (I have almost no relationship with this formal, remote, upper-class Bostonian man and I was very surprised at his statement. I simply said that he seemed not to take full credit for what he had done for Bob and I suspected he was minimizing the help he had been to others, too.)

Bob took the verbal section of the WISC on my next visit to the school and we discussed the unreality of his impression that he was "only good with his hands." We also discussed his behavior while taking the performance section earlier, in terms of his perfectionistic demands upon himself and his rage when he was frustrated or disappointed with his performance. He agreed that setting "kinder" goals would be a good idea.

The following week, the vice principal told me that Bob's father had been to school the day before, demanding to talk to one of Bob's teachers and that the secretary had arranged for them to meet. The principal was not at the school so the vice principal had participated. Bob was also present. Bob and his father had been quite offensive verbally toward this man teacher. The visit had taken place because the teacher had been sarcastic with Bob, then had sent Bob to the office for "talking back" and, when Bob was slow to comply, had pushed him from the classroom, throwing his sweater into the hall after him. The next day, when I was at the school, Bob was not there. His family had no phone and the vice principal asked me to stop by the house and talk it over. Bob had not been suspended.

I made a home call and found Bob's mother packing to move; she had kept Bob at home to help her. She asked me to talk to her and we sat down amid the clutter. At this point, the case shifted from a school focused one to a relationship with the mother which continued after the move was completed and involved Bob's younger brother in elementary school.

For a short time after the move, Bob continued in Z Junior High School but the mother moved him to his neighborhood junior high school as soon as she was assured that the family would be accepted in this more middle-class and more heavily Caucasian neighborhood. My relationship with the mother, as far as Bob was concerned, was focused on interpreting Bob's adolescent adjustment problems, helping the mother to manage the relationship between Bob and his very adolescent father (whom I also met), and supporting the mother who often felt overwhelmed and discouraged, though she possessed great warmth and emotional strength.

This case is not rare with respect to the way in which administrative rivalries complicate the management of a student and his problems. I spoke to Bob's counselor once—he was not much interested in discussing Bob and seemed to view my interest in the boy as something of an intrusion. (He had not submitted a referral sheet because the vice principal had involved me in the case without discussing Bob's need for my services with the counselor.) The counselor's manner was quite self-satisfied as he told me of the many interviews he had held with Bob, speaking in a pontifical manner. (Bob had told me: "I never get anywhere talking with Mr. Doe, I don't know why he keeps calling me in.") This case also is an example of the subject-matter, non-student orientation of the teachers in this school. I had talked to them before and I did not discuss Bob with any of them because I knew that I would only be treated to a lecture on the respect due teachers, the discipline code and my lack of appreciation for "reality."

COVERT HYPOCRISY IN SCHOOLS

The case of Hans, a middle-class Caucasian boy, illustrates a needling boy who took his teacher at literal face value (in order to needle) and was reacted to by the school with punitiveness which involved hypocrisy. School people may be well-meaning (as in the case of Gloria X and her sister, chapter seven), malevolent (as in the case of Annie, chapter fourteen) or moralistic, as in the case of Hans, which follows. Parker* has discussed the problem, which occurs in our present culture, because adults, in general, have become uncomfortable about being directive or authoritative, confusing this with authoritarianism. Adults in this stage of development, who pride themselves on handling children "democratically," often resort to hidden or covert manipulation, telling the child he can use his own judgment or do what he likes but then—when the child's judgment or behavior does not suit them—acting hurt, sulking, becoming punitive or reproaching the child for his immaturity. In our chapter on the Guidance Process (Chapter II), we gave several examples of hidden attitudes, for instance that of moving a child to a new class "because it is smaller," when the actual reason for the move was that the child's previous teacher detested him. Hans provoked and then got caught in such a bind.

---

* Beulah Parker, "Hidden Hypocrisy," unpublished paper, Berkeley, Calif.

Hans

Hans came to my attention as an eighth grader, while attending a stable, middle-class junior high school, because he had turned an English assignment into a highly caustic spoof on some of the school staff. The assignment had been: "Write a page on any subject of your choosing, being careful to use appropriate punctuation." Hans had done just that, yet he received an F for the paper because of its inappropriate content. The situation was further complicated by the fact that the young, inexperienced English teacher did not want Hans back in his class. Therefore, the issue became one for the boy's counselor and the vice principal to handle. Hans involved both of them in highly legalistic arguments around the fact that he had explicitly satisfied the assignment—which, indeed, he had; his English and punctuation were excellent. He would not concede that the disrespectful nature of his paper was open to criticism. The case was referred to me.

I reviewed the information available in the school record and it became apparent that this very intelligent boy had never been well integrated into a school group, had always acted superior and sarcastic with classmates and teachers. To some extent this reflected the family situation, which was also highly isolated and isolating. Hans' father was described as a brilliant man who had failed to reach his potential and now seemed bitter, lonely and, at times, mean. Hans' mother was said to be afraid of her husband—an impression I confirmed. Hans seemed to be stewing in the juice of his own self-imposed isolation and the reactive group antagonism.

With the onset of adolescence, his problems apparently became intensified. His mother came to see me reluctantly, but found relief in sharing her anxiety about Hans. She was concerned because of his lack of friends, his fascination with chemical experiments (all of an explosive kind), his preoccupation with Dracula-type shows. While she had opposed a referral to guidance in the abstract when it had been suggested to her by Hans' counselor, she agreed to it once there had been face-to-face contact.

From that time on, I saw Hans fairly regularly during the remainder of the year. Our discussions were essentially those of two lawyers discussing technicalities: "Was he within his rights if . . .," etc. Gradually, I was able to involve him in viewing the technical issues in the broader framework of human relations and his own future goals. He continued to be manipulated by the school staff and he continued to manipulate them, trying over and over to "sneak" inappropriate material into his assignments. However, he slowly began to see a parallel between the situation at school, where his use of sharp wits and maneuvering got in the way of true learning, and the maneuvers and sarcasm at home, where these methods were used to sidestep the basic issue of his father's serious emotional difficulties.

Hans finally brought in a pamphlet directed to the families of the mentally ill, saying that he believed this was his problem. He began to talk at length about his father and about his own fears, nightmares and compulsions to play with fire. At about this time, he was caught fooling with the master switchbox at school and was suspended. I had another conference with his mother, who could see that Hans was testing whether or not we would deal more openly and honestly with his problems. She agreed to talk to her husband about Hans' difficulties but called back later to say that she simply could not do so, she could not face the repercussions. I commended her for her honesty in letting me know, adding that once Hans knew where he stood his anxiety might lessen.

The whole situation was then fully discussed with Hans, the emphasis being on our mobilizing honesty and directness in him and among those who were working with him. With his knowledge, I arranged a staff conference involving all his teachers, his counselor and the vice principal, to support everyone in a more open, less anxious approach to Hans. They were all encouraged to let Hans know if they felt suspicious about his activities or motives. For instance, his new English teacher now openly asked to see the first drafts of his share in writing a class play, to avoid hurt feelings, unpleasant surprises and punitive consequences for Hans. His Latin teacher gave him an A on a Latin notebook in which he did an excellent job of showing Latin roots in English words, even though he also dwelled on the Latin Emperors' bloodthirsty activities.

As summer approached, Hans became very anxious again and insisted that he was going to spend the summer reading gory stories and watching murder shows. He could think of no activities with other kids. I finally stated flatly that I thought stewing in his own juice was dynamite for him and, that since he disliked the idea of camp, summer school seemed the only alternative. I presented this suggestion to his mother in his presence. To my surprise, she jumped at the suggestion and was not deterred by Hans' objections. The two classes selected were Ancient History and a science seminar for gifted youngsters, both classes being taught by intellectually gifted adults.

In spite of his verbal protest, Hans attended regularly and did well. He met several classmates of his own ability and interests. Friendships began, which carried over this year. While he is still a rather sarcastic, cold youngster, he has had no difficulties this year and is well integrated into his very bright peer group, with whom he is going on to high school. He has become quite proficient in chess and was the student leader of the chess club, under the aegis of the Latin teacher who volunteered to let these students come into her room and play chess at lunchtime. As far as I know, the difficult family situation remains unchanged.

TRUANCY

Adolescents who are chronic truants or come into other conflict with the law have, and present, special problems. They, too, are involved with developmental crises and ego-identity problems but their involvement with probation and the courts (though it can work either for or against them or do both) does complicate their situation. The first two of the following interactions mention a truancy referee and an informal truancy hearing before him. In the city where these youngsters live, there is an arrangement between the attendance workers from the public school Department of Individual Guidance and Attendance and the Probation Department, by means of which one probation officer is designated as a Truancy Referee. When he and the attendance worker on a case feel that it might be helpful or a useful preventive step, this Truancy Referee can hold an informal hearing with the child, parents and attendance worker. Such a hearing often precludes the necessity for a later, formal hearing before the Juvenile Court Judge and consequent legal action. The first two interactions are written by an attendance worker.

The third interaction, written by a guidance worker, describes the complication for a boy and the increased difficulties for his guidance worker because the boy is involved with the law. His regular probation officer worked long, hard and constructively with him but probation department investigators who did not know him put him in danger twice of commitment to State correctional institutions and his future is quite uncertain because of the hazards of administrative machinery and possible disposition of his case by people who do not appreciate how much progress he has made.

Anthony

Anthony was one of several children of Spanish background who transferred from parochial to public school in the ninth grade. The public school was attended predominantly by Negro youngsters whose aggressive, truculent behavior put Anthony and his friends into a state of "culture shock." The less structured, "wilder" situation confused Anthony. He did a good deal of quiet testing of limits. Soon, he began to stay out of school, spending his time in the "shack" in his back yard. His friends in the neighborhood joined him there. They formed a club— "The Mafia"— and collected weapons, both formal and informal. Anthony would explain to his mother, after these days of truancy, that he had not felt well. She accepted this and sent notes to school saying he was ill.

The school was concerned about Anthony and let me—their attendance worker—know about his suspiciously frequent absences. Anthony had definite leadership quality and the mothers of the "Mafia" members became increasingly concerned as their boys also became truant from school. Neither the parents nor the school were then aware of the formation of the "Mafia" and, as these were boys who had not given trouble of any kind to anyone previously, the parents were much mystified. Another boy in the "Mafia" gave the existence of the club away to me. Actually, it turned out that the "Mafia" was organized for "self defense" against an imaginary club of Negro boys called the "Road Runners." One incident of a Negro boy chasing a boy of Spanish background had been exaggerated in the minds of Anthony and his friends into a whole hostile, potentially assaultive club against which they should prepare to defend themselves.

I talked with Anthony and he developed a good face-to-face relationship with me. He was the youngest child in a family where the parents, particularly the father, were older than usual for a boy of Anthony's age. Conferences with me did not improve Anthony's attendance, though the boy seemed to like me and talked rather freely. It seemed, as is common with boys of Spanish cultural background, that Anthony was not going to be influenced or directed by a woman and that the father's authority in the home should be strengthened.

Anthony was therefore referred, with the concurrence of the Truancy Referee, to the Probation Department for an informal hearing. In this hearing, the Referee talked very firmly with Anthony. He pointed out the seriousness of the situation, its effect on Anthony's school work, Anthony's harmful influence upon the neighborhood boys and the possibility of subsequent legal action through the Juvenile Court if this behavior continued. The fact that this probation officer could also speak Spanish to the father exerted a marked effect.

Although it had been obvious that the father did not ordinarily concern himself with the children, he now—with the support of the Truancy Referee—took a firm stand with both the mother and the boy. Anthony returned to school and stayed there, the six other members of the "Mafia" followed suit and there have been no further problems with any of them.

Sue

Sue is a tall, slender, attractive Caucasian girl, thirteen years old, who recently has been making a fairly good adjustment at school with some academic success. It has taken some years of persistent follow-up by the attendance worker and the involvement of several agencies to achieve this.

Sue's parents are middle-aged, formerly middle-class, socially mobile downward. This is the second marriage for both of them. The mother's two daughters by her first marriage have been in the home until recently. Both of them dropped out of school in the tenth grade. The mother is apathetic, has ulcers and is a listlessly poor housekeeper. She seems to have no friends but enjoys her older girls' company. At the slightest excuse, these girls have always stayed home from school and spent the day chatting with their mother. The father is somewhat morose and drinks a good deal. Sue's birth was not wanted and her father has paid little attention to her except to be very indulgent with her from time to time for no externally perceptible reason.

Sue has better than average intelligence but has gotten further and further behind her class because of her frequent and prolonged absences all through elementary school. Her mother always excused these absences as illness. When she came to school, Sue got along with other children and participated in small groups on the playground but had no close friend except Anne—with whom she sometimes stayed away from school.

In class, Sue was always quiet. She was at grade level academically only in reading.

In Sue's public school department, it is the policy for the school nurse to handle elementary school absenteeism, avoiding premature labelling of a child as truant. However, attendance workers are available on call and I was asked to follow Sue when she was in the fifth grade. Sue's mother by now occasionally confessed that she simply could not make Sue get up and get dressed in the morning. There were hectic scenes between the mother and the girl, but Sue did not get to school. In home calls, I tried to evaluate the whole family pattern, which made staying home from school and chatting with one another so attractive. It seemed that the family's isolation from other contacts and mobility downward intensified their involvement with each other. This involvement had pathological features and increased the family isolation but was much more comfortable than the demanding outside world.

The school and I planned various ways in which Sue's interest in school might be stimulated. Special projects were planned for her to take part in, she was made monitor for the nurse, etc., but none of these measures was successful in preventing Sue's persistent truancy. Psychological testing emphasized that, although Sue suffered from some constriction and feelings of inadequacy, she was also getting major satisfaction out of manipulating her family and other situations.

Sue's paternal aunt was a school teacher in another city. This aunt became very concerned about the family and urged family counseling. On my next home visit, the mother discussed this recommendation with me; she appeared to accept the need for some help of this kind but never actually could bring herself to do anything about it. Home visits continued to be ineffectual in helping Sue's mother to set limits and enforce regular school attendance.

Finally, in order to give the mother support in her handling of Sue and to try to help Sue accept the fact that school attendance was not only important, but a legal requirement, Sue was referred to the Probation Department. The truancy referee conducted an informal hearing, discussing school problems with Sue and family problems separately with the mother. Sue agreed to go back to school; the mother decided that she and Sue would go to a family counseling service for help. Sue, with the mother's consent, was placed on informal probation. Sue returned to school, the mother made and kept a counseling appointment and some progress seemed to have been made.

I remained very dubious about durable improvement, however, since intractable attendance problems of this kind tend to have a very tenacious, sticky quality and Sue had become a skillful manipulator.

Sure enough, suddenly Sue again became "ill." We learned that her oldest half-sister was illegitimately pregnant and that arrangements were being made for her marriage. In the midst of this family upheaval, Sue had her first menstrual period. Several weeks ensued in which Sue seemed to be really in a panic. She refused to go to school, to the counseling service, or to see her probation officer. I saw her frequently at home and finally got her to return to school. As she emerged from this period of panic, Sue seemed to be in an increasingly open power struggle with her mother. The mother had dropped her counseling sessions.

Sue moved on to junior high school, where she made a good social adjustment but did little academic work. After a few months she began again to be absent frequently. Many home calls and talks with the mother again brought the mother's reluctant admission that Sue was openly refusing to go to school, that she was staying away from home nights if she chose and that she was flagrantly defying her father as well as her mother.

At this point the Probation Department filed a petition to bring Sue into Juvenile Court for "being beyond the control of her parents" and for truancy. The Court considered not only Sue's problems but those of the family. Both parents agreed to family counseling and are making a real attempt to adjust their difficulties. Sue had met in the Court both an agency which understands some of her problems and an authority which cannot be manipulated. She is now attending school and is beginning to have some academic success. I consider Sue's outcome as dubious with respect to school and with respect to her future life adjustment. She is probably moving toward exemption from school, dropping out when she is sixteen or being placed in a custodial residential setting. It seems likely that her own children will be raised in the same pattern to have similar problems and that a new generation of attendance workers, however active their approaches, will go through the same plodding steps to a similarly unproductive end. There is a chance, however, that if Sue can progress academically enough to get some feeling of pleasure from school, she will take a step forward in constructive adjustment.

It may be that children from these ingrown homes with the strong regressive pull of the home need special school placements which, like the "Sunshine Classes" for physically handicapped children, would provide a protective, informal environment. In such classes, the school might succeed in altering the pathological environment of home and gain some leverage with children like Sue, whose severe truancy gave the school little chance to work with her.

Thurman

Thurman is the middle of five children in a lower-class Negro family. The family became notorious when the father's arrest on charges of forgery made headline news. This family was one of the first Negro families in a previously all-white neighborhood and school. Latent hostility flared into the open following the father's arrest. (The father used the money obtained from forgeries to clothe his children in style.) The oldest boy, in the face of the public disgrace, refused to graduate from the stage. All the children reacted. Thurman, then nine, had to be suspended for using vulgar language. Edward, the youngest boy in school, reacted even more violently (partly because he was a more disturbed boy). He had to be suspended from school for gross disobedience and eventually was placed in a foster home and attended a different school. (Edward failed to adjust there, was eventually returned home, spent most of his time at home in bed or hiding from the attendance supervisor. He was eventually committed to a correctional institution as incorrigible.)

As a sequel to this acute crisis in the family and the father's being sentenced to prison, the mother took to her bed with the youngest child, a baby girl, and refused to cook or in any other way to care for her family. The social worker for Aid to Families with Dependent Children and the guidance worker who was working with Edward and Thurman arranged to take the whole family on a picnic as a realistic gesture to indicate that people *did* care about the family's plight. (Five years later, the mother described this to me with tears in her eyes as having done just that.) This picnic seemed to break the spell for the two oldest children; they returned to school and subsequently had uneventful school careers.

Thurman's future course, unfortunately, was not so benign. He reached junior high school three years later. His school situation was complicated because he was a virtual non-reader, a fact he tenaciously denied. (Thurman told me, many years later, that at first he had been too scared at school to pay attention to reading. Just as he was ready to get started, the family disgrace and turmoil made him close up; he was afraid to expose himself for fear he would be made fun of. By the time these attitudes had changed, the age-appropriate time for learning to read was long past and Thurman had to struggle with a severe reading problem.) Even in his slow-moving sections, there was much work Thurman could not do, yet he would create a scene with the teacher over some imagined slight, rather than admit his inability to do the work. There was constant turmoil. Eventually, we placed him in a small group for maladjusted pupils with a highly gifted teacher; here it began to be possible to work with his basic attitudes.

It was a long hard road. Thurman watched everything going on in the class with eagle eyes. Every time the teacher praised a youngster, Thurman became disruptive. He had to be sent home many times for the balance of the day, to calm down. (In this class, formal suspensions were reserved for infractions of major school rules, such as fighting, smoking, etc. Truculence, restlessness, etc., were handled, just as a headache might be, by removal for the balance of the day.)

Gradually, Thurman moved from being a disruptive outsider to wanting to be the teacher's pet. He was helpful in keeping the room clean, worked very hard on his reading, began to have some insight into his habit of taking it for granted that everyone was discriminating against him because he was Negro. I began to see him fairly regularly in individual sessions in an attempt to lessen his huge demands for attention. He was primarily anxious to find out who was "telling on him" and tried incessantly to size up my relationship to his teacher, so that he could protect himself more adequately and could be on the offensive rather than the defensive. He was very shrewd in sensing everyone's personal Achilles' heel. I felt that my attempts at reaching him were premature. Thurman was aware of the fact that his teacher was fond of the thorough-bred cocker spaniels she raised and he made threats against the dogs whenever he felt ignored. He also made life miserable for some youngsters who had been added to the class later than he. There were many minor incidents and a number of warnings to Thurman that we were not sure we could go on with him. Eventually, he exploded into angry rage in the library, used obscene language and tore a book up.

Thurman was suspended. During the suspension, the principal of the school and I made a home visit to discuss the possible need for a temporary school exemption. Thurman's mother launched into a tirade against the school and its unwillingness to help kids. Thurman listened to this for a few minutes, then politely but firmly interrupted his mother. Speaking to the principal, he explained that he had had plenty of time to think and that he wanted to stay in school. He realized, he said, that he had been giving his teacher a bad time and that, if given another chance, he needed to change his attitude. He thought he could do so.

The principal and I were impressed with his poise and arranged for him to see his teacher; we made the planning for Thurman's future conditional on his discussion with her. He came to school that afternoon. The teacher was able to review with him his excessive demands for attention, his pattern of feeling discriminated against and the manner in which incidents tended to arise and to be blamed by Thurman on others. Both felt that the air was cleared. Thurman was readmitted.

He was also on probation for shooting a BB gun in the city and for loitering. The teacher and I had an excellent working relationship with Thurman's Probation Officer, who had shown an explicit interest in keeping the boy in school and appreciated the skilled work of the teacher. Since Thurman's mother had referred to this probation officer as someone she trusted, we asked him to step up his home calls to drain off some of the mother's anxiety. He agreed to this and did so.

The change in Thurman was dramatic. He became the unofficial older brother to all the other youngsters in the adjustment class. His behavior in his shop and gym classes improved so much that he was made a teacher's assistant in both classes. His gym teacher, who had despised Thurman earlier, asked to have him for a Junior Coach and commented on his leadership ability. His shop work went on exhibit. Only occasionally were there complaints about his pushing kids around in the halls, when no one was looking. None of these reports could be sustantiated.

Thurman and I talked several times, primarily to discuss his present progress and planning for the future. We reviewed his assets and liabilities, specifically his reading problem, in relation to his desire to become a cabinet maker. This was a realistic goal for Thurman since he was highly skilled in working with wood. Thurman wanted me to arrange a program for him in which he could take his academic work with mentally retarded students, since he felt that he could learn academically in that situation but could now operate successfully in regular classes in shop, gym and art, where he had no difficulty. I had to explain that this perfectly sensible plan (which had been worked out for a former classmate of Thurman's in the adjustment class) was probably out of the question for him because his I.Q. would prove to be too high. I promised to arrange testing for him in the future.

Summer provided another chance for growth. Thurman asked me to arrange for him to go to summer school, where he could work on his reading. Summer school policy ordinarily excludes children with known, severe behavior problems, but, on my request, an exception was made in Thurman's case and he was admitted. That fall, the summer school principal went out of his way to let me know that Thurman had been a model student. He earned a D for his work in reading and an A in citizenship. Yet there were disquieting signs too. He had been picked up at a swimming pool and taken to Juvenile Hall because he peeked into the girls' bathroom and made obscene remarks to a Caucasian girl. The investigating Juvenile Officer (who was not Thurman's regular Probation Officer) was thinking in terms of commitment to a State correctional institution. He reported that Thurman was in solitary confinement because he refused to take orders from a Caucasian counselor at Juvenile Hall. Luckily, I was able to document some of Thurman's progress and the boy's own commitment to continue his struggles to "make it." I could also point out that the insubordinate attitude toward white authorities had been much more prominent in Thurman's past, that he was now almost over paranoid attitudes and feelings of being discriminated against in school and that it was undoubtedly his incarceration which was causing the flareup in these attitudes. Thirdly, I warned the Investigating Officer that Thurman's mother would undoubtedly be paranoid and explosive initially but that, if he could sit through this, she would also show her strengths and commitment to helping her children as best she could. After visiting Thurman's mother and confirming this prediction, the Investigating Officer changed his mind and recommended that Thurman be continued on probation with his previous probation officer.

Thurman started his ninth grade year in junior high school as the old-timer and big brother in the adjustment class. He was soon tested by an experienced psychologist and earned an I.Q. score in the nineties. She summarized her impression of the boy as follows: "Thurman is trying to fly with the angels. He is poised, sincere, intent on 'making it' in school. Projective tests show that, deep down inside, there is much turmoil, particularly in relation to his own family. This he is trying to deny. It is hard to tell which side will win. One cannot help but admire this boy's efforts." I quote this statement because it confirmed exactly my own opinion and that of the adjustment class teacher.

For several months, things went well. Then the trouble at home with Thurman's brother Edward, came to a head. The police were looking for Edward. Thurman became upset. In rapid succession, always without eye-witnesses, Thurman was accused of being involved in two attacks on vulnerable, scared Caucasian youngsters. At first he denied all involve-ment, then admitted knowledge of the incidents. (This happened at a time when some Caucasian parents were voicing reluctance to send their children to this school because of rumored beatings, extortions, etc. The school was trying to counteract this impression by increased vigilance and more severe punishment of offenders.) When Thurman was accused of a third such incident (later verified), he was given a ten-day suspension.

After a few days, Thurman and his mother came to school. This time, Thurman was hostile and quite sure he had been wrongly accused. He made no effort to stop his mother's explosive outburst and her often quite incoherent diatribe against the school. Later, I found out that Edward had just been committed to a State correctional authority. The traumatic impact of the father's imprisonment seemed to be reactivated by Edward's fate and Thurman reacted in the old paranoid way. He was exempted from school for the balance of the year.

A few weeks later, Thurman came to school and made friendly ap-proaches to his teacher and me. He talked about returning to school, wanted help with high school planning, wanted to go to a high school where (since I do not work in a high school) his former guidance worker, who had known him in elementary school and served the district high school, could follow him. He also asked me to arrange again for summer school so he could work on his reading. He was to call me back to make final arrangements for this (meanwhile, I had set it up with the school and he had been admitted). The last day of school, I received a routine notice informing me that he was in Juvenile Hall. I talked with the Investigating Officer, again a stranger to Thurman, and discovered that the boy had been booked for violation of probation. He had shot a BB gun at a dog and then sworn at the dog's owner when she berated him.

It seemed inevitable that the Officer would recommend Thurman's commitment to the State correctional authority, in view of what he saw as a very poor family situation and poor school adjustment. I will again do my best to emphasize Thurman's progress, strengths and very real skills.

What would be the best planning for this boy? It is doubtful that he could succeed in a large high school without an adjustment class and his home situation is highly chaotic. Placement in a punitive or high-security correctional institution will almost certainly ruin Thurman's chances of becoming a productive and self-respecting adult; his paranoid attitudes would be confirmed and his direction would undoubtedly change to that of an anti-social career. The ideal plan for Thurman would be a small institution where he could get (1) intensive remedial reading; (2) major vocational training in his beloved woodwork and cabinet making; (3) staff attitudes and behavior which actively and systematically counteracted and tried to reverse any consolidation of Thurman's paranoid attitudes.

One cannot help agreeing that Thurman is partly right in his feeling that one is at a disadvantage when one is Negro, poor and from a disturbed family. His misbehavior in the community has always been of a minor kind; the two times he has seriously been considered for commitment to State correctional facilities were both offenses for which such drastic action almost certainly would not be in the offing for a middle-class Caucasian boy. Thurman has made marked progress: his suspiciousness, mistrust and feeling of being picked on were steadily giving way, he had achieved a good deal of poise, he had realistic grounds for improved self-esteem. The school and community have been able to help him some but, perhaps, not enough. The kind of school program which could be offered was, at best, a patchwork of "lesser evils," not a truly optimal program. Being on probation, while sometimes a support, was also an added hazard for Thurman. The future of this poignant, creative and potentially productive citizen is uncertain.

NOTES
(Chapter XIV)

1. Bernard Lander, *Toward an Understanding of Juvenile Delinquency: A Study of 8464 Cases of Juvenile Delinquency in Baltimore*, Columbia Studies in History, Economics and Public Law, No. 578 (New York: Columbia University Press, 1954).

ADDITIONAL READINGS
(Chapter XIV)

Meyer, Henry J., Edgar F. Borgatta, Wyatt C. Jones. *Girls at Vocational High. An Experiment in Social Work Intervention.* New York: Russell Sage Foundation, 1965.

Schafer, Walter E., and Kenneth Polk. "Delinquency and the Schools," *Task Force Report: Juvenile Delinquency and Youth Crime. Report on Juvenile Justice and Consultants' Papers.* Task Force on Juvenile Delinquency. The President's Commission on Law Enforcement and Administration of Justice. Washington, D.C.: U. S. Government Printing Office, 1967, pp. 222-277.

Wheeler, Stanton and Leonard S. Cottrell, Jr. *Juvenile Delinquency, its Prevention and Control.* New York: Russell Sage Foundation, 1966.

Epilogue

Public education is primarily a group process and has limited facilities, in the average classroom, for dealing with children who deviate too markedly from the group in any way (too troubled, too resistive, too gifted, too rebellious, too intellectually under-nourished, etc.). Guidance workers and other specialized personnel are brought into a public school to correct for the standardization inherent in the group classroom approach. The guidance worker is the champion of the individual with his unique vulnerabilities and his unique potentialities.

Since Sputnik, American education has been moving in the direction of more and more rigid standardization. Children who could not meet academic expectations or conform have increasingly been "handled" by excluding them from school. There were—and are—articulate proponents for institutionalizing this process. They argue for early separation of the academically able and docile from the rebellious, the apathetic, the disturbed, the under-achiever and the late developer. Public education seemed for a while to be in serious danger of losing its right to the designation of "public," becoming, instead, a publicly *supported* educational system for the development of an intellectual élite.

Fortunately, an important counter-trend is gaining rapid momentum in the wake of the civil rights movement and the renewed concern for educating the poor. In the foreseeable future, a somewhat chaotic situation may well exist, as educators cope with new formulations of old problems and decide how to utilize the funds which are rapidly becoming available. Undoubtedly, after a period of trial and error, a more pluralistic pattern of education will emerge.

The guidance worker's role—not yet crystalized in the culture—may become even less clear for a time, as an increasing number of people concern themselves with the psychosocial dimension in school and community. New staffing patterns may well emerge. It seems probable, however, that indifference to psychosocial services will soon be a matter of the past.

The future danger for the psychosocial worker in the public school is apt to be on a more highly sophisticated and subtle level. There is a trend in the selection and development of administrators to favor an articulate, personable, intellectually knowledgeable (and usually sincere) person who sees the guidance worker as one who can facilitate his administrative manipulations. This trend is analogous to that seen in industrial psychology, to the use of psychological research in the interest of more effective advertising, etc. Administrative manipulations are necessary, of course, and do not, in themselves, imply misuse of the guidance worker. Yet, unless the guidance worker is keenly aware of his own professional identity and responsibility, he may find his efforts being used merely as a sophisticated rationale for maneuvers which are not justifiable in terms of his own professional ethics or devotion to public education. Such measures are often used to avoid the blood, sweat and tears involved in individualized planning for a child and accommodating the educational system to meet his needs; they are particularly attractive when the population explosion threatens to burst school houses at their seams.

The task-oriented guidance worker must, in the present stage of development of American education, redouble his efforts to help plan for the individualization of students and facilitate the student's productive integration into the ongoing educational process. He must also combat trends toward too much standardization, ossification, and premature structural solutions, inflexibly applied.

Many projects have demonstrated that all kinds of students can be involved in a fruitful educational process. The guidance worker gives these constructive experiments and daily efforts in American education his enthusiastic endorsement and collaboration.

Index

passive dependency, 45
participant observer, 42
Pat, 186
pathogenic aspects, 40
"patient," 3
pattern of child development, 27
Paul, 207
peer relationship, 22
perceptual disturbances, 140
personal problems of teachers, 20
personalities of teachers, 21
personality conflicts, 210
personality organization, adult, 40
Peter, 108; characterological patterns chronic, 110; compulsivity, 109; fearfulness, 109; food fads, 109; neurotic symptoms, acute, 110; sleepwalker, 109; symptoms crystallize, 110
Petrucchio, 103; "black sheep," 104; "culture straddle," 104; save face, 105
Piaget, Jean, 44, 47
planning, overly generalized structural, 70
point of access, 26
policy-making system-wide problem solving, 53
population at risk, 71
poverty, 28
predictable hazards, 68
predictions, accurate, 40
pregnant school-age girls, 71
pre-natal care, 71
prevention vital to special education, 150
primary behavior disorders, 29
primary teachers, 21
principal authoritarian, discipline-oriented person, 12; implicitly condones misbehavior, 12; interaction with, 17; partnership with, 18; vice principal power struggle, 207
priorities, 21
private school, 34
probation, informal, 221
probation officer's authority, 68; counseling, 68
problem shared, 43
problem solving, 42; joint, 42

problems in peer relationships, 124
professional identification, individual, 57; model, 4
prognosis, 29
"programmers," 4
programs, 4
projective data, 40
projects, demonstration and consultation, 58
promotions, 34
Prompt Intervention, 30
psychiatric, 7; disturbances, 29; emergency service, 63; hospitalization, 188; reference points, 29
psychiatric consultant, 49; assists in diagnosis, 55; continuous relationship with guidance department, 56; direct services rare, 55; early use of, 51; lacks knowledge of others' job, 54; magical problem solver, 52; member of school guidance department, 56; not an educational specialist, 54; outside, 55; participation in faculty activities, 55; reputation, 52; supportive role, 55; talks to groups, 56; task operational and interactional, 56; too threatening, 54
psychiatric consultation to high administrative echelons, 52; to public school guidance departments, 49
psychiatric consultant's role integrative not discordant, 54
psychiatry, anti, 28
psychoanalysts, 3
psychodynamic changes in personality, 41; variables, 39
psychogenic etiology, 149
Psychological Consultation in the Schools, 46
psychological generalities, teachers not assisted by, 20; identification with each other's roles, 54; trouble shooting, individual, 80
psychological testing, 1; movement, 2, 4
psychology, 1
psychopathology, severity of as a criterion for treatment, 63